Education and Civic Culture in Post-Communist Countries

Edited by

Stephen Webber
Lecturer
Centre for Russian and East European Studies
University of Birmingham

and

Ilkka Liikanen
Researcher
Karelian Institute
University of Joensuu
Finland

palgrave

in association with
School of Slavonic and East European Studies
University College London

First published 2001 by
PALGRAVE
Houndmills, Basingstoke, Hampshire RG21 6XS and
175 Fifth Avenue, New York, N. Y. 10010
Companies and representatives throughout the world

PALGRAVE is the new global academic imprint of
St. Martin's Press LLC Scholarly and Reference Division and
Palgrave Publishers Ltd (formerly Macmillan Press Ltd).

ISBN 0–333–96384–9

This book is printed on paper suitable for recycling and
made from fully managed and sustained forest sources.

A catalogue record for this book is available
from the British Library.

Library of Congress Cataloging-in-Publication Data
Education and civic culture in post-communist countries /
edited by Stephen Webber and Ilkka Liikanen.
        p. cm. — (Studies in Russia and East Europe)
        Includes bibliographical references and index.
        ISBN 0–333–96384–9
        1. Educational sociology—Russia (Federation)—Congresses.
        2. Educational sociology—Europe, Eastern—Congresses.
        3. Post-communism—Russia (Federation)—Congresses.
        4. Post-communism—Europe, Eastern—Congresses. I. Webber,
        Stephen L., 1967– II. Liikanen, Ilkka. III. Series.
        LC191.8.R8 E39 2001
        306.43'0947—dc21
                                                        2001021720

10   9   8   7   6   5   4   3   2   1
10   09   08   07   06   05   04   03   02   01

Printed in Great Britain by Antony Rowe Ltd, Chippenham, Wiltshire

Contents

Part II   Nationality Reframed

Part III   Identity Matters

Part IV   Towards a Brighter Future?

List of Tables

List of Figures

Acknowledgements

This volume is a product of co-operation between two research networks: the Study Group on Education in Russia, the Independent States and Eastern Europe; and the Forum for the Study of Civic Culture in Russia and the Baltic Sea Region. The editors wish to acknowledge the efforts of the members of these networks in planning, organising and participating in the international conference on 'Education and Civic Culture in Post-Communist Societies', held at the School of Slavonic and East European Studies (SSEES), 13–15 November 1998. We would also like to thank the director of SSEES, Professor Michael Branch, both for hosting the conference, and for his role as editor-in-chief of the series in which this volume is published.

Henrik Stenius, Director of the Finnish Institute, provided support in the planning and organisation of the conference, while the Academy of Finland and the Soros Open Society Foundation gave substantial financial assistance to a number of overseas participants.

The editors are extremely grateful to Jeremy Smith and David Randall for their valuable help and advice in producing this volume, and to Paul Holtom and Tuula Nylander, who provided much-needed assistance in preparing the manuscript.

STEPHEN WEBBER and ILKKA LIIKANEN
Birmingham and Joensuu

Notes on the Contributors

Risto Alapuro is Professor of Sociology at the University of Helsinki, Finland. His studies include *State and Revolution in Finland* (1988). He is currently working on social networks and joint action in Russia and Estonia.

David Čaněk is a postgraduate student at Charles University, Prague, Czech Republic. He is the author of a book on the representation of ethnic minorities in contemporary Czech history textbooks (*Narod, Narodnost, mensiny a rasismus*, 1996), a shorter version of which appeared in the German-language journal *Bohemia* in 1998. At present he is completing his doctoral research on the situation of ethnic minorities in Czech and Slovak schools (1945–99), sponsored by the Open Society Institute, Budapest.

Darejan Javakhishvili is a clinical psychologist, and a member of the Foundation for the Development of Human Resources (Georgia), in which she is the head of the section on child and adolescent rehabilitation. She has written a wide range of publications on issues concerning the psychosocial rehabilitation of refugees, coping with traumatic experience, and overcoming perceptions of an enemy image. She is working currently on a manual of psychosocial rehabilitation.

Kaija Heikkinen is a researcher at the Karelian Institute, University of Joensuu, Finland. Her field is ethnology and she is currently working on ethnic, in particular Finno-Ugrian, and feminist movements and networking in Russia. She is the co-editor of the publication *Grazhdanskoe obshchestvo na evropeiskom severe* [*Civil Society in the European North*] (1996).

Ilkka Liikanen is a researcher in historical sociology at the Karelian Institute, University of Joensuu, Finland. He is the author and co-editor of studies on nation-building and political mobilisation in Finland. His publications in English include Heikki Eskelinen, Ilkka Liikanen and Jukka Oksa (eds), *Curtains of Iron and Gold. Reconstructing Borders and Scales of Interaction* (1999). He is currently working on a comparative study of civic culture and nationality in north-west Russia and Estonia.

James Muckle is a former Senior Lecturer in Education, and Special Lecturer in Russian Studies, at the University of Nottingham, England. His publications in the field of nineteenth-century Russian literature include translations, articles and a monograph. He is the author of two books on the Soviet school, and numerous shorter studies of education in Russia and the USSR.

Margarita Pavlova is Research Fellow at Latrobe University in Melbourne, Australia, and Scientific Director of 'Technology & Enterprise Education in Russia'. She is author of many articles and books on technology education, and co-author of *Obrazovatel'naia oblast' Tekhnologiia: Teoreticheskie podkhody i metodicheskie rekomendatsii* [*The Educational Area Technology: Theoretical Approaches and Teaching Methods*]. Currently her research is focused on a comparative study of the concepts of technology and technology education in Australia, Great Britain, USA and Russia.

James Pitt is Visiting Fellow at the Department of Educational Studies at the University of York, England. He is a consultant to British and international curriculum development projects in the areas of technology education, and education for sustainability. He is co-author of *Obrazovatel'naia oblast' Tekhnologiia: Teoreticheskie podkhody i metodicheskie rekomendatsii* [*The Educational Area Technology: Theoretical Approaches and Teaching Methods*], and is currently researching and writing on how to teach school students how to design.

Liubov Pivneva is Doctor of Political Science, and a Professor in the Department of Sociology and Politics at Skovoroda Kharkov Teacher-Training University, Ukraine. She is the author of *Higher Education in the USA: Social and Political Aspects* (1992). She is currently working on the problems of political culture and education.

Natalie Sarjveladze is a psychologist with the Foundation for the Development of Human Resources (Georgia). Her publications include a chapter on a conflict management programme for refugee children, included in a manual on methods of psychosocial rehabilitation. She is currently researching the role of folk diplomacy meetings in the psychosocial rehabilitation of Internally Displaced Persons.

Gerlind Schmidt is a research fellow at the German Institute for International Educational Research, Frankfurt am Main, Germany. She has contributed to a range of research projects in the field of comparative education, focusing on Eastern European countries, with, more recently, an emphasis on Russia and the CIS. She is the co-editor of *Education and National Identity in Russia* (1999) (in German), which includes translations of documents such as the Federal Law 'On national cultural autonomy'.

Jeremy Smith is Lecturer in Twentieth-century Russian History at the Centre for Russian and East European Studies, University of Birmingham, England. He is the author of *The Bolsheviks and the National Question, 1917–1923* (1999), and is currently writing a general history of nationalities questions in the USSR.

Svetlana Stephenson is a Research Fellow in European Social Policy at the University of Luton, England. She is the author of numerous publications on social inequality and social exclusion in Russia. She is currently working on a book on homelessness in Russia.

Pentti Stranius is a researcher at the Karelian Institute, University of Joensuu, Finland. He is currently working on the history of Russian and Soviet intelligentsia.

Anna Temkina is a lecturer in sociology and gender study at the European University, St Petersburg, Russia. She is the author of *Russia in Transition: The Case of New Collective Actors and New Collective Actions* (1997). Her publications also include articles on gender issues in contemporary Russia.

Eva Thun is Senior Lecturer in Language Teaching Methodology and Women's Studies at the Teacher Training College, Eotvos Lorand University, Budapest, Hungary. Her publications include articles on gender issues in education and on feminism in Hungary. She is currently working on a research project exploring gender representation and communication in education within the framework of an OTKA (Hungarian National Research Fund for Social Studies Research) research grant.

Janet G. Vaillant is an Associate of the Davis Center for Russian Studies, Harvard University, USA. She is a frequent participant in international projects on curricular reform in Russia and the author of articles on contemporary Russian schools. Her publications also include a history textbook, with John Richards, for US schools, *From Russia to USSR and Beyond* (second edition 1993). She is currently doing project work and research on civic education in Russia.

Stephen Webber is Lecturer in International Security at the Centre for Russian and East European Studies, University of Birmingham, England. He is the author of *School, Reform and Society in the New Russia* (1999) and a number of other publications on the Russian education system. He is now researching aspects of society–military relations in Russia.

Elena Zdravomyslova is a senior research fellow at the Centre for Independent Social Research, St Petersburg, and the Institute of Sociology, Russian Academy of Sciences. She is also a lecturer in sociology and gender studies at the European University, St Petersburg. She is the author of a number of publications on social movements and gender issues in contemporary Russia. Her publications in English include K. Heikkinen and E. Zdravomyslova (eds), *Civil Society in the European North. Concept and Context* (1996).

1
Introduction

Stephen Webber and Ilkka Liikanen

In the study of post-communist societies – among researchers in the West, at least – the concept of civic culture has grown in prominence in recent years. This can be seen as an indication of the significance placed on searching for signs of the development of 'civil society' in these countries, but perhaps even more so as a reflection of the criticism levelled at approaches that have measured the development of post-communist societies against simplified Western models of 'civil society.'

Such criticism has led researchers to reconsider the classic operationalisations of civic culture introduced by Gabriel Almond and Sidney Verba in the 1960s (see Almond and Verba 1963), and to embark on new directions in the study of democracy and political culture in post-communist contexts. It is possible to discern two major modifications in approach that elaborate further or go beyond the civil society debate. First, instead of analysing civil society as such, through the analysis of formal organisations or by conducting opinion polls on democratic and totalitarian attitudes, civic activity and civic culture are increasingly examined in relation to the state. Politics is seen as a mediating field between state and society, and national variations of its forms are studied against the background of national history, earlier experience of nation-building and the traditions of social and political mobilisation. Second, instead of searching for signs of Western modes of organisation, there is a growing number of studies examining the particular preconditions for collective action in post-communist societies. These studies often focus on the level of people's everyday social interaction, which, it is suggested, is a major factor in defining their identity and their capacity to act collectively.

The notion that education plays a key role in these approaches formed the rationale both for the preparation of this volume and the organisation of the conference that preceded it. The aim was to emphasise the complexity of the multi-dimensional picture of the civic culture/education interface, and thus move away from an emphasis on systemic analysis, and assumptions that education policies devised at the state level are necessarily implemented

1

as they were intended. Even under the communist systems, the nature of the education received by students was the product of bargaining and attempts to dominate the societal debate on education. Within the confines of limited political, media and individual freedom, we may discern a process of negotiation in the sphere of education whose importance has been undervalued and understudied.

Indeed, the subject of education has, in general, tended to be afforded relatively little attention by Western specialists on post-communist countries (note the infrequency with which issues relating to education appear in the indexes of publications on these countries, for instance), with the focus instead lying on the outcomes of political struggles and marketisation policies, armed conflicts and the more obvious social problems such as crime and mass destitution. Alongside such matters, though, it is important to recognise the potential influence that struggles for recognition and domination seen in the sphere of education are likely to have on the future character of these societies.

This neglect has been compensated for to some extent by the veritable explosion in the numbers of collaborative international projects on educational issues that have been set up by, for example, the European Union and other organisations and funds in Europe and North America. In research on post-communist transformations, however, education is still only seldom afforded the attention it deserves, as a factor that does not just hinder, but that may also promote the emergence and development of a new type of civic culture.

It is most important to recognise, for example, the role of education in influencing patterns of social relations within these countries. Such developments as the introduction of private education, and the imposition of restrictions on a child's access to non fee-paying, state-funded education, may be seen as the product of a new kind of social conflict. In the context of a post-communist transformation, these issues acquire an additional degree of complexity, as any discussion of such notions as equality and individual choice are heavily tainted with perceptions of the legacy of the communist system.

On the political level, the need to make a break with the past was markedly expressed in the early 1990s in the education policies pursued in some ex-communist countries. Reform efforts appeared to be based as much on a remedial approach, designed to 'remove' or even 'destroy' the legacies of the communist system, as on the need to introduce new ideas and render the education system ready to deal with the demands of the post-communist period. Later in the 1990s, this trend appeared to be moderated, as what was perhaps the underlying factor behind the pursuit of remedial policies, a fear of a return to the old political system, has receded.

It is still of concern, however, that educational issues often appear to receive little coverage or recognition within a good number of post-communist societies. In the context of what can be described as a 'shallow' societal debate on education, the limited participation of the public, politicians, business leaders and others in a meaningful discussion on educational issues can lead to the neglect of education even to the point where the future of certain parts of the education system are placed in jeopardy. A breakdown in the functioning of societal safety nets, which served during the communist period to limit cases of social exclusion and child delinquency, for instance, has led to the escalation of social problems among children and adolescents in many post-communist countries. With regard to the education policies that are introduced, the absence of a more intensive and meaningful public debate can lead to what we might term a 'false consensus' on reform aims, with the result that the deeper meaning (and potential social consequences) of certain policies are insufficiently understood. This reflects, perhaps, a broader pattern in which the question of what kind of civil society and civic culture these societies are aiming to develop has yet to be answered sufficiently, or even discussed fully.

The significance of such issues, and thus the study of the interrelationship between education and civic culture, was underlined repeatedly at the international conference on 'Education and Civic Culture in Post-Communist Societies' that was held at the School of Slavonic and East European Studies in November 1998, following which the contributions to this volume were developed. Among the questions raised at the conference were:

- What can trends in the development of post-communist education systems tell us about broader patterns of social, political and economic change in post-communist societies? Are these reforms (which can often be seen to be leading to a diminished role for the state) advancing the formation of a Western style of 'civil society', or are these societies moving beyond the models of modernity?
- To what extent are the experiences of citizens of post-communist societies similar or different? Has the presence of what was supposed to be a common (i.e. communist) basis for the education systems of these countries meant that they have faced similar problems, and sought similar solutions to them, during the transformation period? Or have national historical contexts, and contemporary economic and political ambitions and capacities, led them to differing conclusions with regard to the 'right' path for reform?
- To what extent is discussion of certain contemporary trends in Western education systems (for example, a growing emphasis on citizenship education, lifelong learning provision, the acquisition of technological skills and the importance of fostering notions of tolerance and equality) seen as relevant for various post-communist countries?
- To what extent are certain processes that have been identified as significant in research on social change and educational development in

Western European and North American societies (for example, individua-
lisation, the 'risk society', an apparent decline in respect for authority and
institutions, concern over education 'standards' and a heightened
emphasis on issues of identity, including tolerance of others) relevant to
discussions of education and civic culture in post-communist societies?

The opening chapter of Part I, 'Reviving Civic Culture', addresses the
relationship between education and civic culture from three different angles.
Risto Alapuro examines the social networks of St Petersburg teachers, offering an insightful review of recent discussion among social scientists on
the subject of civil society, and mapping new directions for the study of the
transformation process in Russia and Eastern Europe. Alapuro examines
the preconditions for – and obstacles to – collective action on the level of
people's everyday social interaction, and argues that, certain difficulties
notwithstanding, there are several ways in which the social identity of
individuals can be linked to processes of organisation and action, both in
the sense of open challenge and the ability to disrupt.

Ilkka Liikanen (Chapter 3) studies the role of the educated elite in the
social and political mobilisation launched by *perestroika* and *glasnost'*. His
case study on the Karelian Republic displays how cultural capital was used
constantly during the mobilisation period to challenge the power structure
and those possessing 'political capital'. Liikanen concludes that this rivalry
between those possessing 'cultural capital' and 'political capital' did not end
with the collapse of communism, and that these concepts can serve as a
useful tool in the analysis of the present transformation period.

Pentti Stranius (Chapter 4) studies the role of the Russian intelligentsia
during and after the collapse of the Soviet Union. The first part of his chapter
examines the status and functions of the intelligentsia during the Soviet
period, and he suggests an interpretation of the relationship between the
fight for cultural freedom and the existence of elements of civil society
within Soviet society. The second part of the chapter examines the self
images and conceptualisations of society typical to artists and educated
professionals of present-day north-west Russia, and provides an analysis of
discussions on 'the breakdown of culture' and the 'death of the Russian
intelligentsia'.

Part II 'Nationality Reframed', studies questions of nationality and ethnicity in post-communist education and education policies. The chapters
focus on basic problems of how to organise the teaching *of* ethnic groups,
and how to plan teaching *about* ethnic groups. Sensitivity to problems of
everyday practices challenges the often inconsistent Western interpretations, that too readily identify Russian nationalism simply as a sign of the
rise of archaic, pre-modern forces in society, while at the same time apprais-
ing minority nationalism as one of the driving forces of emancipation in
post-communist circumstances.

In his chapter, Jeremy Smith (Chapter 5) draws a multilayered picture of the long-term development of Soviet policies on national schools. Smith notes that even if Western impressions of the decline of the national schools in the Union Republics are likely to have been exaggerated, it became clear during the *glasnost'* era that national schools were not altogether successful in their task of implementing the policy aim of producing bilingual children. This, however, did not always prove to be related to a policy of deliberate Russification. On the contrary, as a whole the national schools played a major role in preserving the national languages and preventing the spread of the Russian language.

David Čaněk (Chapter 6) studies the position of the German, Polish, Slovak and Romany minorities in the Czech education system during the postwar period. The focus is on the specific educational politics of the state, as well as on the educational accomplishments of the minorities. While the changes that have taken place after 1989 have meant that the minority problem has been recognised in a new light, certain minority groupings, especially the Roma and immigrants from Slovakia, have faced substantial new difficulties.

In Gerlind Schmidt's chapter (7), the foundations of national education in multi-ethnic Russia are analysed. Schmidt distinguishes three diverse settings with different problems: the national republics of the Russian Federation, multi-ethnic regions with non-Russian indigenous inhabitants, and multi-ethnic urban centres. Special emphasis is given to the development of national education in Moscow. In this multi-ethnic megapolis, which is also the capital of the Russian Federation, new problems of tolerance and ethnic diversity have emerged, which cannot be solved by the means of traditional minority politics.

Kaija Heikkinen's examination (Chapter 8) of the ways in which ethnic groups in north-west Russia continue to work for the recognition – and survival – of their identity and cultural heritage provides a bridge between the clearly interrelated themes of the preceding section, and Part III, 'Identity Matters'. This brings together a selection of chapters that demonstrate the centrality of such issues as ethnicity, religion and gender identity to the overall processes of societal change in post-communist countries. Heikkinen's fieldwork focused on the use of school museums as a vehicle for preserving ethnic history. After decades of neglect by the authorities with regard to the identity of ethnic minorities, such museums are educating children from the ethnic group in question, and the local population as a whole, to understand and respect their past.

Research into such notions as the 'hidden curriculum', which have engaged the interest of many researchers of Western education systems in recent years, was highly restricted in communist systems – at least with regard to discussion of socialist approaches to education. It is significant, therefore, that Eva Thun (Chapter 9) notes the importance of the concept of the hidden curriculum to studies of gender representation in Hungarian school textbooks. Indeed, if societal debates on education in these countries are to move from a 'shallow' to a more 'open' (informed) level, and engage the public more fully and actively, an awareness of such issues is vital. With regard to the question of gender, Thun demonstrates that attempts to leave the communist past behind are not necessarily accompanied by change in more deeply rooted social and cultural traditions (in fact, these may even be strengthened). The negative effects of the officially proclaimed liberation of women during the communist period, for example, seem to have led to a backlash against notions of true equality in post-communist Hungary, a situation that, Thun contends, is reflected in the materials used to educate the young.

The chapter by Anna Temkina (Chapter 10) offers an account of how social movements have affected the agenda of discussion among social scientists, and to some degree even the curricula of higher-education establishments. Temkina shows how the development of gender and women's studies in Russia has been closely connected to the rise of the women's movement, and how today the different trends in gender and women's studies are often still connected to discussions and disputes within and between various organisational patterns in the movement.

In Elena Zdravomyslova's chapter on what she terms the 'hypocritical sexuality' of the late Soviet period (Chapter 11), we are shown how the legacy of debates on sexuality, and the physical and psychological restraints imposed on sexuality during the Soviet period, are still seen to exert a heavy influence on Russian society today. The contrast between the sexual liberation that Russia is experiencing, along with the clear demand for increased provision in sex education expressed by the public, and the reaction of more conservative bodies and organisations (such as the Orthodox Church, nationalist groupings and traditionalist pedagogues) is striking.

The issue of religious education has proved a contentious one in the development of post-communist education systems, with religious organisations often keen to assume a place in the formal process of social and personal education provided in state-run and private establishments. As James Muckle notes in his chapter on competing approaches to spiritual and religious education in post-Soviet Russia (Chapter 12), there is an ongoing debate as to whether religious education should be officially permitted in state schools, while notions of religious tolerance and freedom are hotly contested issues that hold the interest of religious bodies, politicians and the public alike.

In the final part, 'Towards a Brighter Future?' the various social and structural challenges facing children and youth, and those who work with them, are discussed. There has been an increasing amount of discussion in many post-communist countries of the possibility of the emergence of a 'lost generation', with public concern (fuelled by media reports that range from the informed to the hysterical) expressed with regard to the possible long-term effects of the problems experienced by children and adolescents. There is no doubt that such concerns are justified: the values vacuum that has accompanied the transition period has led to the risk of generational rifts, while the breakdown in welfare systems has left many children vulnerable to the vicissitudes of the 'free' market. Svetlana Stephenson explores the situation of homeless children in Russia, drawing on the evidence of a research study that she and her colleagues conducted. Using their results, it is possible to identify a certain exaggeration in the claims of the media and the perceptions of the public with regard to the actual numbers of children on the streets in Moscow. Stephenson's detailed analysis also shows that the causes of the growing vulnerability of children and youth lay not so much in the collapse of the once extensive system of social control over the young, but in the impoverishment and marginalisation of significant sections of the population.

Darejan Javakhishvili and Natalie Sarjveladze (Chapter 14) provide an account of their work with (child and adolescent) Internally Displaced Persons in Georgia, and demonstrate the extent to which trauma, fear and hatred, generated among children and adolescents who have witnessed ethnic conflict, can be successfully dealt with through programmes of psychosocial rehabilitation. Their work in fostering dialogue, reconciliation and understanding among young Georgian and Ossetian children is to be applauded; and it is to be hoped that such programmes will help this new generation to learn from, and avoid repeating, the mistakes of the past decades. It is notable that the programme was supported by a foreign funding body (from Norway), a sign that such conflicts and their aftermath, while out of the public eye for the most part in the West, are, fortunately, not entirely forgotten.

Turning to questions of formal education, Stephen Webber (Chapter 15) examines the issue of the culture of the Russian school and teaching profession, a subject that has been relatively little studied to date, but which offers a valuable insight into the capacity of the school and the teachers to engage in an ongoing, evolutionary change effort. Webber offers an optimistic conclusion that the schools are showing signs of adapting their culture to suit the demands of the reform agenda, and that a process of institutionalisation of reform has begun to take place within the school system. He notes, however, that such internal progress is likely to be thwarted unless the external context of the school–society relationship improves, and the schools receive the material and moral support they need from their society.

The achievements that can be gained through successful and sustained reform efforts, and the problems that such efforts can encounter, are shown tellingly by James Pitt and Margarita Pavlova, in their account (Chapter 16) of promoting change in the technology curriculum of Russian schools. While it is understandable that those in charge of the school reforms in Russia emphasised the need to effect radical revisions in the social science and humanities disciplines, there was an attendant risk that technical and science subjects may not receive the attention they deserve. As Pitt and Pavlova note, the innovations that they have advocated in Technology teaching have the potential not only to contribute to the much-needed revival of Russian industry – a point that is not, it seems, wholly appreciated by the business community in that country – but also to the general process of inculcating civic values among the young.

In Liubov Pivneva's chapter (17), the relationship between education policy and processes of nation-building are highlighted. Pivneva demonstrates the ethnic, political and social tensions that have arisen in the Ukrainian higher-education system since 1991, as it has struggled with the needs of internal reform, while at the same time responding to, and trying to influence, changes taking place in Ukrainian society as a whole.

The book concludes with a review by Janet Vaillant of progress in the field of civic education in Russia (Chapter 18). While the issue of citizenship education has only relatively recently begun to receive emphasis in many Western education systems, it is now increasingly seen as a vital element of a young person's experience at school. In contrast to this comparatively short history, post-communist systems can draw on the (rather negative) experience of political education imposed and monitored by the communist authorities in the past. In reaction to this heritage, the question of citizenship education, and of the broader subject of personal and social education, has been high on the agenda of priorities of educationalists in post-communist countries. While, as Vaillant shows, differing political traditions and notions of civic identity often need to be recognised and overcome in interaction between educationalists from the West and post-communist countries when they collaborate on such issues, teachers in these systems have already come a remarkably long way in establishing new and often very innovative approaches to teaching this subject. Indeed, the value of well-run and effective projects such as that described by Vaillant is that such co-operation can be very much a two-way process (in contrast to certain less enlightened Western-run projects seen in recent years), in which both sides stand to benefit from learning about one another's experiences.

Perhaps the most telling feature of the collection of essays presented in this volume is the emphasis given to questions of identity, to the recognition of the views of individuals and groups at the grass roots. This is a significant factor in countries which, during the communist period at least, were more used to the suppression of (at worst) or disinterest in and disregard for (as a rule) the views of the population. Across the post-communist countries, a complex, sometimes contradictory, at times even explosive set of dynamics is involved in the interplay between the pursuit of educational reform, and processes of nation-building and the development of civic culture. Policies promoted at the national, regional and municipal levels are intermingled with, and challenged by, the efforts of professional groups, ethnic minorities, religious organisations and individual citizens, all trying to gain recognition for their identities and values in a situation of considerable flux and confusion. Analysis of issues relating to education, both in the sense of formal and organised processes of instruction and study, and in the broader sense of how people are learning to adapt to life in post-communist societies, can tell us much about the ways these identities, and these countries, are developing.

Reference

Almond, G. and Verba, S. (1963). *The Civic Culture: Political Attitudes and Democracy in Five Nations*. Princeton: Princeton University Press.

Part I
Reviving Civic Culture

2
Reflections on Social Networks and Collective Action in Russia

Risto Alapuro

A turn to 'micro' analysis

The initial enthusiasm about democratisation in post-Soviet Russia has subsided among Western and Russian scholars alike. Optimistic Western accounts of socio-political movements and the emergence or re-emergence of 'civil society' (for example: Kukathas *et al*. 1991; Lewis 1992; Sedaitis and Butterfield 1991) have made room for disillusionment as pressure groups and political parties have proved weak or transient. 'Civil society' has increasingly disappeared from Russian social scientists' vocabulary as well. *Grazhdanskoe obshchestvo*, a borrowed concept devoid of a Russian history behind it, has proved more an inspiring symbol and an object of identification than an appropriate concept in analysing the Russian reality (Volkov 1996: 90–1).

In reaction, a number of Western scholars have turned to studying people's everyday experience. The argument is that interpersonal practices should give information about the preconditions for solidarity and joint action, or the lack of them, because strategies of challenge and survival are elaborated above all at the level of daily interaction. Katherine Verdery (Verdery 1996: 15, 209) advocates an 'anthropology' or 'ethnography' of the state in studying the transition from socialism. It 'should treat states not as things but as sets of social processes and relations', study them 'at close range from within [their] daily routines and practices'. (See also Hann 1992 and 1995; Kideckel 1995; Hann and Dunn 1996; Burawoy and Verdery 1999).[1]

How useful is this approach in the examination of people's relationship to the state in Russia, and especially in the study of their capacity to put pressure on the state? In reflecting on these issues I will refer to a set of data on social networks and to research based on it. The data was collected in 1993 among 40 secondary school teachers in St Petersburg. They kept standardised diaries during a period of 15 days and registered all personal contacts they considered significant. They then completed the information by enumerating those significant persons whom they had not met or contacted during the research period; a who-knows-whom matrix was thus constructed for all network members. Finally, a short biographical interview was conducted.[2] Similar data was gathered in Helsinki. Some observations from Helsinki are contrasted below with those from St Petersburg in order to clarify peculiarities of the Russian results.

Collective action and obstacles to it

The study of collective action, and of organisation as one of its components, is firmly anchored in the analysis of interpersonal relations. Charles Tilly, the central proponent of the resource-mobilisation model of collective action, has stressed them over many years in somewhat varying forms (for example, Tilly 1978: 7, 62–4; 1996: 6–8; 1998: 454–7). Here I follow the formulation in his classic account of two decades ago. According to it (Tilly 1978: 7, 63), a group's capacity to act is shaped by interests, mobilisation, and opportunity, but 'most directly' it is affected by the organisation understood as a combination of *categories* (for example, industrial workers, intellectuals, Orthodox believers) and *networks* of people linked to each other by an interpersonal bond. The idea of organisation says that the more organised a group is, or a set of individuals comprising *both* a category and a network are, the more extensive are its common identities (based on a shared category or shared categories) and its internal networks. Organised groups are necessary for people to be able to act independently of, or in opposition to, the state authority in a sustained way.

From this perspective, the most fundamental question in Russia is what kind of potential is there for the formation of organised contenders, that is, of sets of individuals comprising both a category and a unifying network that apply 'pooled resources to influence the government' (Tilly 1978: 52)? It is obvious that the preceding Soviet period prevented people from organising themselves in this sense. Often the key problem is seen in a certain kind of homogeneity of the social structure. Claus Offe, for example, argues that in the 'forcibly homogenised societies of state socialism' no 'sufficiently formed protagonists, associations and issues', necessary for competitive democracy, could consolidate themselves (Offe 1996: 37). In these countries no labour market existed and the bulk of the adult population consisted of so-called working people (*trudiashchiesia*) who had similar incomes and uniformly regulated housing, living and educational standards. An 'atomised'[3] social structure of 'repressed difference' prevailed, and there was no such differentiation in the division of labour, cultural identity and status interest that is requisite for democratic politics. This kind of politics can find an appropriate content of issues and divisions only if interest coalitions and mediating bodies emerge from the system of the social division of labour, and this process can take place only in a somewhat developed free-market society.

That is, Offe depicts a contrast between atomised social structure, not conducive to organisation and collective action in the East, on the one hand, and the articulated civil society based on the division of labour in the West, on the other. Teachers in advanced capitalist societies illustrate Offe's point. A well-established line of analysis maintains that the relative bargaining strength of members of the middle class, such as teachers, fundamentally depends on their possession of educational qualifications. Teaching is a *professional* occupation. Those belonging to it offer on the market 'specialised symbolic skills', the marketability of which is normally protected by an enforcement of 'closure' of occupational entry (Giddens 1973: 186). Normally the closure implies a professional interest organisation based both on a shared category and an internal network as the main precondition for joint action.

Personalisation of social ties

Let us take a look at St Petersburg teachers and their networks in order to see what distinguishes them from their colleagues in Helsinki. What kind of relationship prevails in St Petersburg between the classification based on the division of labour (which defines the teacher's occupation) and the actual classification(s) made by teachers themselves in their daily encounters with other people? To what extent do the teachers' networks follow the boundaries of their profession, or of their social stratum more generally, and in what ways is a common identity attached to the common profession? This examination helps us to assess the extent to which the Russian teachers in this study can be considered to be representatives of a professional occupation capable of forming interest organisations. The data also shed light on an occupation that plays a key role in the socialisation of the new generation. The importance and the difficulties of this task have become pronounced in the 1990s, when the state and the nation are being defined and redefined in Russia. Therefore any peculiarities of the occupation are interesting in their own right as well.

An example is a 31-year-old, Leningrad-born teacher of Chemistry, Nina V.[4] Her father is a maintenance man and her mother an office worker. Her ties with the kin are very close, and her network forms a milieu or a circle. The configuration of the mutual connections between her contacts indicate that her kin, her husband's kin, and her old friends are intermingled and that many ties link this cluster to the professional milieu. The fact that Nina V. has preserved a large number of ties with her kin, and that the kin is located within a dense larger cluster, implies that she maintains links with working-class people. Such connections, which are common in St Petersburg, strikingly differentiate the Russian teachers from their colleagues in Helsinki, where such networks are overwhelmingly limited to a middle-class social milieu.

A central mechanism, on which the strong presence of kin and (old) friends from working-class and low white-collar occupations is hinged, is provided by the constraints of *housing*. They have major ramifications in Nina V.'s life. First, Nina V. lives in her parents' apartment, a *khrushchevka*[5] of two rooms, with her husband, their child and her parents. This arrangement is necessitated by the severe housing shortage characteristic of St Petersburg and more generally of urban life in the Soviet Union and Russia. A considerable number of other St Petersburg teachers in this study share this situation with Nina V. The generational dependence constitutes a tangible mechanism of social power.

The links of Nina V.'s colleagues with her closest circle are also reinforced by the housing conditions. She has found a workplace in the vicinity of her home, just as many other teachers who have participated in previous research studies in St Petersburg have done (see Lonkila 1998). Because of the housing shortage, her apartment and its location are more or less a given, and she has thus adapted her other decisions to this fact. Therefore, like many of her colleagues, she has sought a workplace as a function of where she lives (notably to avoid making long and complicated connections in getting to the school), not the other way around.

This process shows a structural constraint which does not exist for the teachers studied in Helsinki, but which has shaped and continues to shape Nina V.'s social itinerary. While in Helsinki and other Western cities the market-regulated neighbourhood segregation provides an important source of class structuration (cf. Giddens 1973: 108–10), its does not function in Nina V.'s case. Her situation is inconceivable in Helsinki, where, in contrast, the teachers have chosen their apartments on the basis of the location of their school or, more commonly, because of considerations that have little to do with the exact location of the workplace.

This individual example shows mechanisms that are far from being exceptional among the Russian teachers studied. The above aspects in Nina V.'s situation are indicative of the constraints and incentives functioning in the social space around the teachers in St Petersburg. Many of them live in a spatially-reduced circle of the home and the school. This is an indication of the pervasive *personalisation* of the social ties which is rare or non-existent among the Helsinki teachers. Such patterns of Nina V.'s everyday life as housing and work depend on personal acquaintance or on kin, which exert power in matters presumably public in character. This is not true in Helsinki where non-personal, market-regulated mechanisms account for the choice of apartment and normally the choice of the workplace as well, and where there are no mechanisms conducive to the proximity of the workplace to the apartment.

A glimpse into the interpersonal relations of one St Petersburg teacher illustrates the observation that the teaching occupation, or a 'middle-class milieu', does *not* appear as the main structuring principle in network formation. The *category* of teacher has no predominant role in network formation, shown in this case by the fact that colleagues constitute no distinct cluster of acquaintances, separate from other, socially variable relations, and that other middle-class occupations cover only a part of the non-kin ties. The teacher's identity apparently does not manifest itself as a *professional* identity in the sense that it does in Helsinki, where networks are more homogeneous socially, and where purely or predominantly professional relations with colleagues are common, not to mention the presence of a professional interest organisation in many respondents' networks.

This picture fits well with Offe's portrayal of the atomised social structure of repressed difference. In the sea of uniform 'working people', where class structuration and, more specifically, the occupational structuration are defective, it is very difficult, it seems, to form strong occupation-based networks and a common professional identity, that is, to organise as a professional group.

Work-based sociability

However, this picture does not adequately reflect the nature of the absence of organisation among St Petersburg teachers. Although organisation may be lacking, the situation does not involve atomisation. A clue is provided by the personalised character of social relations. It becomes very clear in Markku Lonkila's (1998) detailed analysis of the meaning of the work for these teachers, in which he concluded that interpersonal relations break the horizontal group formation in a way that makes the occupational category of teacher seem a source of shared identity only to a limited extent (see also Alapuro and Lonkila, 2000). This is true despite the fact that a considerable number of colleagues and other social relations mediated through the workplace are present in the teachers' networks.

First, they recorded considerably more pupils and their parents among their social ties than did the Helsinki teachers. Both the diaries and the interviews testify to particularly strong affective bonds between teachers and their pupils, exemplified by expressions like *vtoraia mat'* (the second mother) as a nickname for the class supervisor. The Soviet-era importance of the idea of moral upbringing (*vospitanie*) certainly manifested itself in the self-conception of many St Petersburg teachers.

Second, Lonkila found that both the decision to become a teacher and the course of careers were often affected by instrumental considerations to attain 'personal goals or to avoid structural constraints such as housing shortage or internal migration' (Lonkila 1998: 708), rather than by expectations concerning the occupation itself. Even more important is that the occupation and the workplace constituted for the teachers a source of varied social relations in which professional and personal spheres of life were mixed. The position at work was frequently used for mutually beneficial arrangements, including *blat* exchanges (that is, the use of connections; see Ledeneva 1998). A great proportion of the teachers' informal exchanges in general were effected through ties related to the work milieu. Hence the personalised character of the relations: the other teachers in the networks 'were not only colleagues but...teachers of our respondents' children, their exchange partners and...those living in the vicinity' (Lonkila 1998: 706). Work was largely important 'as a social milieu providing an arena for socialising, child care and access to informal resources mediated through work' (Lonkila 1998: 710). The findings reinforce, in Lonkila's view, the impression of a certain weakness in the teaching profession. The point is that contrary to Offe's and many others' image of the atomised social structure, the lack of a 'sufficiently formed protagonist' based on the division of labour and cultural identity is fully compatible with the existence of close work-based sociability in which the colleagues play a central role.

This compatibility can be exemplified by an extreme case. Igor B. is a 35-year-old teacher of Physics, born in Leningrad. His father is a university professor, and his mother and older brother are teachers, as is his spouse. The intergenerational professional continuity is accompanied by an almost corporatist network. Among the 51 adult persons Igor B. has listed, 20 are teachers of various kinds, including family members, several colleagues and friends–colleagues. Many people have related intellectual occupations. The network graph displays a milieu with many interconnecting ties between subclusters: the core family links together kin, friends, and colleagues.

Yet even in this case of a strong professional continuity, working-class people or lower-level nonmanual employees can be found in the network. A couple working in the militia and a cook are characterised as close persons. The former are relatives of his wife, while the cook works in the school. And even in this case the professional sphere is mixed with other spheres in the workplace sociability which gives a personalised flavour to work-based or work-mediated relations. There are other cases resembling that of Igor B., with a strong socio-professional continuity and a predominantly intellectual network.

Bases for networks

A crucial question, then, is how this kind of personalised, work-based sociability is related to an eventual professional organisation in the post-Soviet Russia. Will the category of occupation be modified to become a similar base for a (professional) identity and to play a similar role in the coupling of categories and networks as in the West – if there will be a market for the teachers' 'symbolic skills' (cf. Jones 1991)? Not necessarily. The occupation may more or less permanently play a different role from that in the advanced West both in the constitution of networks and in the identity formation linked to the occupation.

In looking first at network formation, it is useful to remember that occupation in a narrow sense is only one of those structures which may serve as the basis for networks. The point is well made by Simona Cerutti (Cerutti 1990; see also Cerutti 1996) in her study of artisanal occupations in seventeenth-century Turin. She found that only at a certain historical moment was the labour-based 'technical' division converted into a framework for action. In trying to understand why this happened she took notice of the place the occupation had in the definition of the artisans' identity and in their coalition formation, as well as of their access to other than directly work-related resources. That is, she paid attention to the kind of aspects mentioned above. But she also examined varying representations the artisans made of themselves, the vocabulary they used in describing themselves or in speaking of their work, and she was interested in the city as a scene or stage of the artisans' activities or even as an actor which was an essential part of their activities. These latter ideas are worth pursuing in the further examination of the place of the occupation in the St Petersburg teachers' lives, and in their comparison with their counterparts in Helsinki.

Cerutti's work also makes it very clear that the matter of which categorisation prevails is ultimately a matter of power. This is a central aspect of Pierre Bourdieu's examination of the relationship between 'objective structures' and the systems of classification related to them. This analysis may be seen as one way of making the network-category linkage. The relationship is a question of struggle and domination. '[S]ystems of classification constitute a *stake in the struggles* that oppose individuals and groups in the routine interactions of daily life as well as in the solitary and collective contests that take place in the fields of politics and cultural production' (Wacquant 1992: 11, 14, emphasis in original). The social taxonomies, such as occupation, which organise the representation of groups are 'at every moment produced by, and at stake in, the power relations between classes' (Bourdieu and Boltanski 1981: 149).

Cerutti's and Bourdieu's works well illuminate the fact that the representations of structurally similar groups, such as the occupational group of teachers, may be variable. A common occupation can serve as a basis for different networks and categorisations and for different relations between them, and the combinations are not necessarily conducive to organisation. Moreover, these analyses ultimately question the self-evident role of the occupation itself as a basis for networks and shared categories. This is an important insight in analysing Russia. And in fact, this is what a Russian sociologist of work, Leonid Gordon, argues. According to Gordon, the Soviet workplace structuration suggests organisation and mobilisation based not on occupations but on the *labour collectives*, which in the Soviet period provided the framework for the workplace co-operation and participation and access to various benefits:

In the early stages of a post-totalitarian evolution, any favourable conditions for the initial development of mass political activity are confined to
those cells of society where the social links were preserved.... In Russia,
these include... labour collectives; [they] truly were (and still largely are)
society's basic social cell.

(Gordon 1997: 344)

For Gordon, the labour collectives constitute the only available basis that
can structure a challenge by the majority of people in an otherwise little-
organised society. In stressing the importance of the workplace, he considers
that economic, political, and cultural aspects could be fused in such a way
that Russian organisations would be rendered 'multifunctional' and therefore different from the specialised Western interest organisations (Gordon
1991a and 1991b; see Alapuro 1993: 207–10). 'Multifunctionality' in network formation entails a categorisation that undermines the formation of a
common *professional* identity. Therefore it is reminiscent of what Lonkila
calls, in a different context, 'multiplex sociability' in the St Petersburg
teachers' lives: in dealing with their occupation one has to describe 'the
functioning of their intergenerational family ties, exchange relations and
physical proximity of home and work' as well (Lonkila 1998: 710).

Gordon may be right or wrong – pessimistic views of the political effectiveness of the labour collectives have been voiced as well (for example,
Clarke and Fairbrother 1994) – but his suggestion merits attention because
it once again highlights the multi-dimensionality and even the ambiguity of
an occupation-based or, more generally, work-based identity. The fact that
the lack of a work-based protagonist is accompanied by a dense work-based
sociability implies that the organisation and collective-action perspective
does not fully account for the people's repertoire to act *vis-à-vis* the state in
Russia.

Identity formation

This issue raises the question of the limits of the adequacy of the organisation and collective-action model in Russian conditions – after all, the reflections made above indicate the propensity, or lack of it, among the teachers in
St Petersburg (and perhaps among Russians somewhat more generally) to
organise and to act collectively.

An aspect of this question can be approached by looking at the identity
formation side in the coupling of networks and categories. Viewed in the
category-network perspective, teachers in St Petersburg presumably face
severe difficulties in creating or maintaining a collective identity implied
in this model. In the above discussion it was assumed that there is a linkage
between a particular identity and the participation in organised action: the
more a group is organised, the more extensive are its common identity

(based on a shared category or shared categories) and its internal networks (Tilly 1978: 63). The idea has been developed and refined by Doug McAdam and Ronnelle Paulsen in their use of the notion of 'identity salience': 'identities are conceptualised as being organised into a hierarchy of salience defined by the probability of the various identities being invoked in a given situation or over many situations' (McAdam and Paulsen: 1993: 646; the definition itself comes from Stryker 1981: 23–4). McAdam and Paulsen suggest that movement participation is encouraged if the potential recruit has prior organisational or individual ties, and if these ties, first, reinforce the identification with a particular salient identity and, second, 'help to establish a strong linkage between that identity and the movement in question' (McAdam and Paulsen 1993: 663).

As plausible as this proposition may seem, it nevertheless postulates a 'particular salient identity' and links it to prior ties in a manner that appears strange in the Russian context. It presumes a hierarchical set of identities that are available in different ways in different situations, and then an actualisation of one of them. It is as if there existed a repertoire of identities to be invoked – as if a set of salient identities were available, waiting for a coupling to take place between one of them and an organisation or a movement.

The image seems to capture well a situation in which an individual may 'come out' with his or her identity to find allies and to identify with them, and to create or to join a movement – like an American gay or lesbian, for example, can do, in making a private identity both public and common. But this is not what gays or lesbians did in the Soviet Union or what they probably do even in the post-communist Russia. In studying them David Tuller found that theirs was a 'pride that revelled in the concealment of a private life rather than its disclosure; a pride that cherished the secret by sharing it with the chosen few rather than the masses' (Tuller 1996: 30). The Russian gay or lesbian identity was highly salient, but it was not available to be linked to a movement or organisation; these people 'had little inclination to create a bond with those they didn't know, and would never trust' (Tuller 1996: 21–2).

The example may be extreme but the description seems familiar in the light of what was said above regarding the personalised character of the teachers' social ties. It refers to the prevalence of identities not instrumental in the construction of organisations and organised movements. The importance of such identities is stressed by Oleg Kharkhordin (1996: 350) who argues that 'Soviet dissimulation' remains a stable legacy from the past:

> The Bolshevik revolution did not explode the distinction between public and private and then reestablish it in a different form. Rather, it swept it away and replaced it, in the long run, with a division between the 'social,' which consists of transparent 'public' *and* 'personal' [*lichnyi*] lives, and an

unseen, unrecognised private [*chastnyi*] which does not exceed the most intimate. The dissimulation covering this intimate sphere became the most profound practice of Soviet society.

(Kharkhordin 1996: 360)

This kind of situation seriously limits the availability of salient identities to encourage movement participation. The private (*chastnyi*) sphere can provide an identity to be linked to a movement only with great difficulty, even if the identity itself may be highly salient. More feasible is that, perhaps, the social in the sense of public and personal (*lichnyi*) finds a role, in a modified form, in an eventual organisation and action; in fact, this is what Gordon seems to suggest.

Dimensions of challenge

In the Russian conditions, organisation and collective action appear secondary to a non-contentious relation to the state (and to other powerholders). The nature of social ties rather points to different 'survival strategies', defensive mobilisation as an extension of the group's everyday routines that is induced by a threat from outside (Tilly 1978: 73, 75), attempts to keep the state at arm's length, maybe 'tactics' as the 'art of the weak' practised in conditions imposed by others (Certeau 1990: 60–1), and the like.

In agreement with this orientation, St Petersburg teachers have more personalised ties anchored in the workplace than their colleagues in Helsinki, and they are more tied to the functional core of the school institution, the pupils, through an ideology of moral upbringing which stresses the particular school community as the basis of loyalty. At the same time, they are less tied than the Helsinki teachers to the profession inside the school or to the common profession shared by colleagues in many other schools. This kind of social organisation appears to constrain the propensity to exert pressure on the state, because it tends to be inward-oriented: the integration within the community may be strong but the linkages with extra-community networks are relatively weak (see Woolcock 1998: 171–2).

A conclusion of the significance of these tendencies, and of the entire preceding discussion, could simply be that civil society is weak in Russia: there are strong and multiplex, and at least in part, defensive intra-community ties, but linkages across civil society remain comparatively weak. A more nuanced view is possible, however. At least three different modes appear feasible, the role of which depends on the character of the governmental control and on the degree of the governmental effectiveness (that is, the capacity of the state to implement policies).

Two modes are familiar from the previous discussion, namely the organisation and collective action as ways to put sustained pressure on the state, and a defensive orientation with a particular workplace as the basis of solidarity. Both are discernible in the recent action of the teachers who, by Russian standards, have been an exceptionally active group.[6]

A Union of Workers in Education and Science exists (*Rossiiskii Profsoiuz Rabotnikov Obrazovaniia i Nauki*), with a Union for School Education (*Profsoiuz Rabotnikov Shkol'nogo Obrazovaniia*) as one of its sections. However, even though this organisation has played a role in teachers' interest struggle, it still aims largely at provisioning social and cultural facilities as was the case during the Soviet period. The orientation – understandable in the light of the scarcity prevailing – apparently continues to reinforce the workplace-level integration.

A related story emerges from the main form of teachers' collective action in the 1990s, the strikes. As a rule they have been demonstrations and other sporadic outbreaks, organised by strike committees, rather than instances of sustained long-term pressure on the state through a refusal to work (Sutherland 1999: 120–30). A widely-used justification for the reluctance to resort to (long-term) strikes is that they would do more harm to the pupils than benefit the teachers. A strike does not necessarily lead to a stoppage of the school work. It may happen, for example, that only teachers who happen to be exempt from teaching take part in the strike or that striking is 'delegated' to designated teachers.[7] It is as if teachers were defending a community whose core is the pupil rather than waging a professional interest struggle.

In these two examples the organised pressure on governmental agents and the community orientation seem fused. In other words, a new dimension has appeared in the Russian repertoire in the form of the organised interest activities, but it is imbued by the earlier sociability and coping strategy. The latter aspect may seem a remnant from the Soviet period, an aptitude that, with time, will progressively give way to the interest struggle peculiar to the new, democratising Russia. Yet more pertinent is to characterise the fusion of the old and the new as an adequate response to a *new* situation, in which the state has, it is true, somewhat democratised itself, but has also lost much of its effectiveness, for example, its capacity to meet such commitments as tax collection and the control of inflation and, more generally, the maintenance of a decent standard of living for the majority of the population. The new element, the organised interest struggle, is a response to the new character of governmental control but, at the same time, governmental ineffectiveness provides a reason for inward-oriented survival strategies to persist. Traditional ways of co-operation are preserved not as a remnant of the past but as a way to actively adapt oneself to the present conditions. What may appear 'as "restorations" of patterns familiar from socialism', may be responses to new conditions, 'produced by them rather than remnants of an older mentality', as Michael Burawoy and Katherine Verdery put it (Burawoy and Verdery 1999: 1–2).

If this reflection is valid, a democratic development and an increase in the effectiveness of the state would reinforce the integration through organised interest struggle, and, correspondingly, a further increase in the ineffective-ness would accentuate the importance of the mutual trust networks (see Tilly 1999). Yet even in an ideal case of democratisation, it is reasonable to hypothesise that the community orientation would continue to mark Russian civil society, perhaps indeed in a way reminiscent of Gordon's idea of 'multifunctionality'. It is in this spirit that Chris Hann opposes 'civil society debates [which] hitherto have been too narrowly circumscribed by modern Western models of liberal individualism' and its 'impoverished understanding of social relationships' to 'the exploration of civil society [which] requires that careful attention be paid to a range of informal interpersonal practices' (Hann 1996: 3). In advocating the latter approach he stresses the role of 'culturally specific patterns of generating trust in human communities', or 'trust and solidarity between individuals' (Hann 1996: 5, 6).

There remains a third alternative. In it the trust networks also play a role. In the eventual return of an authoritarian system, whatever form it might take, people's trust-bearing networks could serve not only as the basis for getting along, but also as a vehicle of evasion of governmental detection and even, in extreme cases, as a source of active defence against the state. In the latter case no interest organisation would ensue but rather a *disruptive* protest, described by Richard A. Cloward and Frances Fox Piven:

> Power... is interactional; it is embedded in patterns of social relationship. People without valued things or traits can sometimes make others do what they want because those others depend upon them, and the more so in a society of intricately interdependent relations. It follows that people... exercise power on those occasions when they mobilise to withhold the contributions they make to institutional life.
>
> (Cloward and Piven 1984: 588–9)

If an authoritarian system were to be reintroduced, the ability to disrupt, grounded on interdependent relations between the state authorities and the population, may prove more useful than interest-based organisation.

The ways outlined above of challenge or co-operation should not be seen as mutually exclusive, but rather as different aspects of action. Arguably these modes of articulation with the state – especially the interest-based integration and the coping but perhaps even the (disruptive) protest – are peculiarly intertwined in the Russian repertoire. Finally, they should not be seen only as reactions to the character of the state, but also as part of a process of interaction with the state, both moulding it and being moulded by it.

Notes

1   Curiously enough, an opposite tendency has gained strength among Russian social scientists. Large-scale reflections of the peculiarity of the Russian culture and macro

speculations of the special character of different civilisations have multiplied themselves (see Temkina and Grigor'ev 1997).

2 The study was carried out both in St Petersburg and Helsinki; in the latter city the number of teachers involved in the study was 38. The data were collected or their collection organised by Markku Lonkila and Anna-Maija Castrén in the Finnish research project 'Social Networks and Particularities of the Finnish Culture', financed by the Academy of Finland. The study is a part of a larger project initiated and led by Maurizio Gribaudi at the École des Hautes Études en Sciences Sociales in Paris. On the project and the procedures in the collection of the data see Gribaudi 1998.

3 In quotation marks. Offe cites here George Schöpflin 1991.

4 Obviously the names are pseudonyms.

5 A '*khrushchevka*' is a popular term for a type of apartment building that was built in large numbers during Khrushchev's period in office, to ease the housing problem. It is of a small size: a kitchen, bathroom and two rooms.

6 See *Rossiiskii Statisticheskii Ezhegodnik* 1995, 64.

7 Interview with Raisa Shestakova, lecturer at Herzen's teacher training institute, St Petersburg, 21 January, 1999.

References

Alapuro, R. (1993). 'Civil Society in Russia?' in J. Iivonen (ed.) *The Future of the Nation State in Europe*. Aldershot: Edward Elgar, pp. 194–218.

Alapuro, R. and Lonkila, M. (2000). 'Networks, Identity and (In)Action: A Comparison Between Russian and Finnish Teachers'. *European Societies*, vol. 2, no. 1, pp. 65–90.

Bourdieu, P. and Boltanski, L. (1981). 'The Educational System and the Economy: Titles and Jobs' in C. Lemert (ed.) *French Sociology: Rupture and Renewal Since 1968*. New York: Columbia University Press, pp. 141–51.

Burawoy, M. and Verdery, K. (1999). 'Introduction' in M. Burawoy and K. Verdery (eds) *Uncertain Transition: Ethnographies of Change in the Postsocialist World*. Lanham MD: Rowman and Littlefield, pp. 1–17.

Burawoy, M. and Verdery, K. (eds) (1999). *Uncertain Transition: Ethnographies of Change in the Postsocialist World*. Lanham MD: Rowman and Littlefield.

Certeau, M. de (1990). *L'Invention du quotidien. I. Arts de faire*. Paris: Gallimard.

Cerutti, S. (1990). *La Ville et les métiers. Naissance d'un langage corporatif (Turin, 17e-18e siècle)*. Paris: Éditions de l'École des Hautes Études en Sciences Sociales.

Cerutti, S. (1996). 'Processus et expérience: individus, groupes et identités à Turin, au XVIIe siècle' in J. Revel (ed.) *Jeux d'échelles. La micro-analyse à l'expérience*. Paris: Gallimard & Le Seuil, pp. 161–86.

Clarke, S. and Fairbrother, P. (1994). 'Post-Communism and the Emergence of Industrial Relations in the Workplace'. in R. Hyman and A. Ferner (eds) *New Frontiers in European Industrial Relations*. Oxford: Basil Blackwell, pp. 368–97.

Cloward, R. and Fox Piven, F. (1984). 'Disruption and Organization: A Rejoinder' *Theory and Society*, vol. 13, no. 4, pp. 587–99.

Giddens, A. (1973). *The Class Structure of the Advanced Societies*. London: Hutchinson.

Gordon, L. (1991a). 'Protiv gosudarstvennogo sotsializma: novye vozmozhnosti rabochego dvizheniia' *Politicheskie issledovaniia*, no. 1, pp. 67–79.

Gordon, L. (1991b). 'Rabochee dvizhenie v poslesotsialisticheskoi perspektive' *Sotsiologicheskie issledovaniia*, no. 11, pp. 3–17.

Gordon, L. (1997). 'The Labour Movement in a Transitional Society: A Force for or Against Reform in Russia' *International Review of Sociology*, vol. 7, no. 2, pp. 337–58.

Gribaudi, M. (ed.) (1998). *Espaces, temporalités, stratifications. Exercices sur les réseaux sociaux*. Paris: Éditions de l'École des Hautes Études en Sciences Sociales.

Hann, C. (1992). 'Civil Society at the Grassroots: A Reactionary View' in P. Lewis (ed.) *Democracy and Civil Society in Eastern Europe*. New York: St Martin's Press – now Palgrave, pp. 152–65.

Hann, C. (1995). 'Philosophers' Models on the Carpathian Lowlands.' in J. Hall (ed.) *Civil Society: Theory, History, Comparison*. London: Polity Press, pp.158–82.

Hann, C. (1996). 'Introduction: Political Society and Civil Anthropology' in C. Hann and E. Dunn (eds) *Civil Society: Challenging Western Models*. London: Routledge, pp. 1–26.

Hann, C. and Dunn, E. (eds) (1996). *Civil Society: Challenging Western Models*. London: Routledge.

Jones, A. (1991). 'Teachers in the Soviet Union.' in A. Jones (ed.) *Professions and the State: Expertise and Autonomy in the Soviet Union and Eastern Europe*. Philadelphia: Temple University Press, pp. 152–66.

Kharkhordin, O. (1996). 'Reveal and Dissimulate: A Genealogy of Private Life in Soviet Russia' in J. Weintraub and K. Kumar (eds) *Public and Private in Thought and Practice: Perspectives on a Grand Dichotomy*. Chicago: University of Chicago Press, pp. 333–63.

Kideckel, D. (ed.) (1995). *East European Communities: The Struggle for Balance in Turbulent Times*. Boulder CO: Westview Press.

Kukathas, C., Lovell, D. and Maley, W. (eds) (1991). *The Transition from Socialism: State and Civil Society in the USSR*. Melbourne: Longman Cheshire.

Ledeneva, A. (1998). *Russia's Economy of Favours. Blat, Networking and Informal Exchange*. Cambridge: Cambridge University Press.

Lewis, P. (ed.) (1992). *Democracy and Civil Society in Eastern Europe*. New York: St Martin's Press – now Palgrave.

Lonkila, M. (1998). 'The Social Meaning of Work: Aspects of the Teaching Profession in Post-Soviet Russia' *Europe–Asia Studies*, vol. 50, no. 4, pp. 699–712.

McAdam, D. and Paulsen, R. (1993). 'Specifying the Relationship between Social Ties And Activism' *American Journal of Sociology*, vol. 99, no. 3, pp. 640–67.

Offe, C. (1996). *Varieties of Transition: The East European and East German Experience*. Cambridge: Polity Press.

Rossiiskii Statisticheskii Ezhegodnik (1995). Moskva: Goskomstat Rossii.

Schöpflin, G. (1991). 'Post-Communism: Constructing New Democracies in Central Europe' *International Affairs*, vol. 67, no. 2, pp. 235–50.

Sedaitis, J. and Butterfield, J. (eds) (1991). *Perestroika from Below: Social Movements in the Soviet Union*. Boulder CO: Westview Press.

Stryker, S. (1981). 'Symbolic Interactionism: Themes and Variations' in M. Rosenberg and R.H. Turner (eds) *Social Psychology: Sociological Perspectives*. New York: Basic, pp. 3–29.

Sutherland, J. (1999). *Schooling in the New Russia: Innovation and Change, 1984–95*. London: Macmillan – now Palgrave.

Temkina, A. and Grigor'ev, V. (1997). 'Russland als Transformationsgesellschaft: Konzepte und Diskussionen (1990–1996)' *Sozialwissenschaft in Russland 2*.

Tilly, C. (1978). *From Mobilization to Revolution*. Reading MA: Addison-Wesley.

Tilly, C. (1996). 'Citizenship, Identity and Social History' In C. Tilly (ed.) *Citizenship, Identity and Social History* (International Review of Social History, Supplement 3), pp. 1–17.

Tilly, C. (1998). 'Social Movements and (All Sorts of) Other Political Interactions – Local, National, and International – Including Identities' *Theory and Society*, vol. 27, no. 2, pp. 453–80.

Tilly, C. (1999) *Processes and Mechanisms of Democratization*. Manuscript.

Tuller, D. (1996). 'Gay Pride, Russian Style' Paper presented at the conference Private Life in Russia: Medieval Times to Present, Ann Arbor, Michigan, October 4–5.

Verdery, K. (1996). *What Was Socialism, and What Comes Next?* Princeton, NJ: Princeton University Press.

Volkov, V. (1996). '*Obshchestvennost*': An Indigenous Concept of Civil Society?' in K. Heikkinen and E. Zdravomyslova (eds) *Civil Society in the European North: Concept and Context*. St Petersburg: Centre for Independent Social Research, pp. 90–5.

Wacquant, L. (1992). 'Toward a Social Praxeology: The Structure and Logic of Bourdieu's Sociology' in L. Wacquant, and P. Bourdieu (eds) *An Invitation to Reflexive Sociology*. Chicago: University of Chicago Press, pp. 1–59.

Woolcock, M. (1998). 'Social Capital and Economic Development: Toward a Theoretical Synthesis and Policy Framework' *Theory and Society*, vol. 27, no. 2, pp. 151–208.

3
Educational and Political Capital and the Breakthrough of Voluntary Association in Russian Karelia

Ilkka Liikanen

In October 1989, just two weeks before the collapse of the Berlin wall, the French sociologist Pierre Bourdieu visited East Berlin. In his lecture to East German students he further elaborated some of the main themes of his famous book *The Distinction*. Bourdieu asked himself whether the theoretical model presented in the book could also be applied in the DDR, and on what conditions. His brief reconsiderations open an interesting perspective on late-communist societies, and especially on the role that education and educational capital played in them.

Referring to his basic analysis of cultural and economic capital and life-styles, Bourdieu proposed that the main difference between, for instance, France and the DDR, lay in the fact that in the DDR economic capital was officially, and largely even in practice, removed from the field of making distinctions. Consequently, the relative weight of cultural capital had become more decisive in the socialist system. Still, it was clear that access to goods and services was not dependent solely on differences in cultural and educational capital, even if the official meritocratic ideology asserted the opposite. Evidently, other bases for making distinctions existed, and some other type of capital remained which was unequally apportioned, and which caused differences in consumption, lifestyles and status. This special type of capital, characteristic to communist countries, Bourdieu called *political capital*.

According to Bourdieu it was political capital obtained in the party and state apparatus that gave those who possessed it private access to goods and services that were, in principle, available to the public. As other forms of capital were more or less thoroughly controlled, political capital became the most important requirement for making distinctions. In this situation the political nomenclature had very few challengers in the battle over controlling the field of power, other than those possessing cultural and educational capital. Bourdieu even supposed that the main reason for the recent conflicts and changes in communist countries lay in the competition between the possessors of political capital and those possessing educational capital (even if the scholars, intellectuals and technocrats themselves often came from the political nomenclature). For Bourdieu it was evident that those possessing educational capital were the most impatient and most prepared to rebel against the privileges of those possessing political capital. Furthermore, they were best able to turn the principles of equality or meritocracy against the nomenclature, and thus challenge the bases of its demand for legitimation. This tendency was clearly apparent in the way the intelligentsia preached 'real socialism', which would replace the caricature that the *apparatchiki*, the men and women of the state and party apparatus, had created.

Bourdieu ended his Berlin lectures by asking whether the intelligentsia was able to form a lasting alliance with the ruled, that is, whether it was able to align itself with the uneducated workers who perhaps appreciated the everyday tokens of capitalism more (the refrigerator, the washing machine, the Volkswagen), or with the middle-class functionaries whose jobs at that moment were under threat, and who were hardly inclined to turn down the instant material satisfaction that capitalism, in spite of all the risks, seemed to offer (Bourdieu 1998: 25–9).

Today, almost a decade after the fall of the Berlin wall, we know some of the answers to these questions. Thus, we are perhaps better equipped to estimate how well the concepts of Bourdieu recognised the fundamental features of the political and social change in late-communist societies. In this chapter I will consider the relevance of the concepts of *educational capital* and *political capital* to an analysis of the events that occurred inside Soviet society during the late 1980s and early 1990s. Based on a case study of social and political mobilisation in Soviet Karelia, I will try to analyse, in particular, whether the conflicts inside the Soviet system can be understood as conflicts between the possessors of political and educational capital and, if this is the case, how and on what conditions did the elite succeed in aligning itself with the masses?

In Western public discussion, the fall of communism and the development towards civil society in the Soviet Union is often depicted as the work of self-sacrificing intellectuals who wanted to break the ideological monopoly of the Communist Party and fought to enlarge the sphere of free public discussion. Obviously, Bourdieu's concepts lead us to study this heroic history on more prosaic terms. They allow us to examine on everyday level 1) the position of the educated elite in the Soviet system, and 2) the role that conflict of interests between the different elite groups played in the mobilisation of the opposition movement.

The concrete object of my study is the emergence of the so-called Popular Front movement in Soviet Karelia. In the first part of the chapter I will analyse its social background, forms of organisation and the role that intellectuals played in its rise and fall. My analysis is built mainly on newspaper material and interviews with movement activists carried out in Petrozavodsk and St Petersburg. In the second part I will try to summarise the specific features of the Karelian case by comparing the development of the Popular Front movement to the Estonian Popular Front. At the end of the chapter I will briefly come back to Bourdieu's question of the possibilities of an alliance between the educated elite and the people.

Tradition and change in Russian Karelia

In many studies concerning the republics of the former Soviet Union, the nationalistic intelligentsia has been attributed a major role in the breakdown of the old power structure (for example, Carrére 1994). And indeed, the challenge to official Soviet ideology was quite often formulated on the basis of earlier ethnic and cultural traditions. Furthermore, in many cases the campaigns for promoting native language and culture played a significant part in launching broader social and political mobilisation (Bremmer and Taras 1993). In other words, knowledge of earlier ethnic traditions was especially valuable as educational capital in challenging the old nomenclature, and support for ethnic campaigns was very often a critical component in building a link between the elite and the people and in mobilising popular support for the opposition movement. In this sense, cultural and linguistic traditions, as a special form of educational capital, had great significance for the rise of the opposition movement in the republics of the former Soviet Union and, ultimately, for the forms of present-day political culture in them.

What kind of preconditions did the earlier ethnic and cultural traditions create for the rise of new civic and political culture in the autonomous republic of Karelia? The area of the present day Karelian Republic has always been an ethnic, religious and political frontier zone. Since prehistoric times it was inhabited by a Finno-Ugrian Karelian population in the west and a Russian population in the east. For centuries it formed the religious watershed between western and eastern Christianity, as the Karelians, unlike the Finns, adopted the Orthodox religion. During the first wave of European state-making it became the battleground between the Russian and Swedish empires, and latterly since the late nineteenth century, Finnish nation-building and Russian revolutionary turmoil have set their deep marks on the nationality question in Karelia (Laine 1994: 13–25).

During the early Soviet period the building of socialism in the so-called Karelian Workers' Commune (est. 1920) and the Karelian Autonomous Socialist Republic (est. 1923) had a clear national colour. However, it was neither the titular people, the Karelians, nor the largest population group, the Russians, but the Finnish Reds, who had emigrated from Finland after the abortive revolution of 1918, who set the tone for the construction of the new socialist culture. Alongside Russian, Finnish was used as the 'national language' in administration and education, and in this sense the Bolshevik nationality politics, which during the 1920s were often advantageous to the indigenous peoples, favoured the immigrant Finns in Karelia more than the native Karelians (Kangaspuro 1998: 153–6; Smith 1997: 281–307).

In the late 1930s, the waves of the Great Terror engulfed the Finnish Reds (and many of their Karelian and Russian collaborators), now classified as 'counter-revolutionary nationalists' (Kangaspuro 1998: 142–53; Rentola 1994: 31–3, 44–50, 60–4). Stalinist politics once and for all made Russian the main language of education, administration and the party apparatus. In 1937, the elimination of the Finnish elite was complemented by the Finnish language being stripped of its status, and by promoting the creation of a Karelian literary language, which was to be adopted for a short period as the second official national language of education and administration (Antti-koski 1998: 214–15).

In 1940, after the so-called Winter War against Finland, a new Karelian–Finnish Soviet Socialist Republic was established, and Finnish was again adopted as an official national language. It did not, however, achieve the same position as before, nor did the Karelian dialects. The Finno-Ugrian languages and dialects lost their position in administration and education and, during the following decades, the circumstances varied from brutal Russification to a demonstrative nurturing of Finnish literature and culture, which could hardly conceal the fact that the younger generations of Finns and Karelians faced inevitable assimilation into the Russian majority. By the 1980s, the rapid and firm assimilation and massive settlement of new immigrants had made the Finno-Ugrian population a small minority (in 1989 it stood at 13.1 per cent), which, at least in the towns, largely shared the Soviet identity of the Russian majority (Klementiev 1991: 59–60; Laine 1996: 77–92).

By the time that the *perestroika* reforms opened up new possibilities to organise and openly express alternative identities, the Karelians and the Finns in Soviet Karelia possessed few resources for national or ethnic revitalisation. The Finnish language cultural elite had lost its central political possession and lacked living contacts with the assimilating Karelian population. For the Russian majority, the omnipresent Soviet identity was much closer than the titular – territorially based – 'Karelian' identity. And still, in spite of the assimilation of the minorities and the seemingly stable adoption of the common Soviet identity, *glasnost'* seduced the intelligentsia to take up earlier ethnic and national traditions, and led to the establishment of contentious movements among both the Finno-Ugrian minority and the Russian majority.

Educational capital and the breakthrough of voluntary association in Soviet Karelia

From the very beginning, the educated elite played a significant role in social and political mobilisation in Soviet Karelia. Especially during the first phase of the new voluntary association, it is obvious that members of the intelligentsia used the non-governmental clubs and societies to strengthen the relative weight of educational capital. The Karelian scholar Anatolii Tsygankov has presented a basic periodisation of the new civic activities that arose in the Karelian Republic since the beginning of *perestroika*. Tsygankov distinguishes three phases in the development of new civic culture during Soviet time:

1 the rise of cultural clubs that broadened the arena of public discussion to political issues (1987–88)
2 the heyday of ethnic movements and the Popular Front of Karelia, which were the first organisations openly to challenge the hegemony of the Communist Party (1988–89)
3 the birth of rival political parties, which marked the collapse of the old one-party system (1990–91) (Tsygankov 1995: 86–94).

Each of these periods was marked by the active role played by the intelligentsia. The first political clubs questioned the legitimation of power by raising the slogan of 'real socialism' – thus acting in much the same way that Bourdieu described in his analysis as an activity typical for intellectuals. The two most famous clubs in the capital town of the republic Petrozavodsk, at least, represented this feature clearly. The History and Literature Club established a library of political literature and organised discussions about how real socialism would look according to the texts of the classics of Marxism. The same circle of intellectuals and students was active in the so-called Memorial movement, which started to study the crimes of the Stalinist period, and thus fostered an alternative view of history which was set against the official ideology. Another society called Socialist Pluralism questioned the legitimation of the political elite more by way of irony and carnivalisation but, for all its artistic anarchism, it can be considered to be an example of setting educational capital against political capital obtained by service in the party apparatus (Tsygankov 1991: 115–42).

The ethnically and territorially based movements that characterise the second phase were sparked much in the same way by scholars and journalists, who set the 'real history' of the Karelians and Finns against the official ideology, and elaborated programmes to strengthen the autonomous status of the republic. The Karelian Popular Front was able to mobilise popular support even among the Russian language majority. Among the organisers of the movement, Finns were well represented, but the main body was formed by younger generation Russian professionals unsatisfied with the way the economic system and the administrative apparatus worked. The movement had no clear ideological profile other than that of setting out a federalist opposition against Moscow and the communist party, and when political parties were allowed to form it soon split into various minor party groupings (Tsygankov 1991: 15–61).

In his analyses of post-Soviet political culture in the Republic of Karelia, Tsygankov has described the present stage as the 'age of exhausted exhilaration'. He concludes that up to 1990, many people had the conviction that they were able to affect the renewal of society. They were, however, to face disappointment. The arena for free discussion and diverse opinions that the movements and clubs constituted in the heyday of *perestroika* was destroyed by the logic of political conflict, which demanded ideological homogeneity. The Popular Front, which represented the 'foremost example of the participation of the masses in the political life of the republic', fragmented because of ideological disagreements and political contradictions. Here Tsygankov specifically stresses the role of the ethnic movements in the breakdown of the opposition movement and civic activity in general. According to Tsygankov, the 'extremist' ethnic movements bear great responsibility for the split in, and collapse of, political activity, which is now weaker than in 1989–90 and still declining (Tsygankov 1995: 90–4).

Such views are very common among the intelligentsia in the Karelian Republic and, to a great degree, characterises how those involved in these activities tend to set a focus on the first phases of the movement, which most clearly represented the conflict between the possessors of educational capital and political capital. For the former activists, the basic identification is with the ideal of the enlightened citizen who acts and expresses himself or herself freely in the public sphere. The turn towards ethnic movements and populist politics easily appear as a counter force to this civilised community of intellectuals (Stranius 1996: 151–61).

However, if we examine the whole field of civic organisation, rather than focusing just on the politically active elite, and see it as part of everyday social interaction, some features of the process appear in a very different light. According to an analysis of the local Finnish-language newspaper *Neuvosto-Karjala* (later *Karjalan Sanomat*) the rise of the few openly political discussion clubs was from the very beginning foreshadowed and accompanied by a broader wave of cultural societies, discussion clubs, youth organisations and sport clubs. From 1985 to 1989, over 100 new voluntary associations were mentioned in the newspaper. Even though most of these organisations did not openly challenge the prevailing system in the sense that the political clubs mentioned by Tsygankov did, they too enlarged the area of public discussion and autonomous civic activity and, in this sense, implemented new forms of civic culture. This activity has not been declining since the early 1990s but, on the contrary, has broadened every year since the collapse of the Soviet Union. In this sense, the exhaustion of the educated elite is not necessarily shared by the people, even though grass-root activity evidently lacks the hegemonic drive it had during the last years of Soviet power (Liikanen 1996: 155–9).

Maybe the situation can be seen more as an example of the difficulties Bourdieu predicted for an alliance between those possessing educational capital and the bulk of the population. This question is closely linked to the significance of the national and ethnic organisations as a mobilising force, which, according to the evidence in the Finnish-language press, was greater than generally acknowledged. From 1989 to 1994, 28 different ethnic associations were mentioned in *Karjalan Sanomat*, and their meetings were often the largest mass gatherings of the period (Heikkinen 1996: 65–70). Tsygankov, too, emphasises their importance, but he seems to view their role mainly as an indication of the intensification of a populist battle for political power, and the decline of rational public debate and civic participation (Tsygankov 1995: 90–1). To consider their political significance, it is perhaps necessary to look beyond the conflicts between educational and political capital inside the communist system, and examine another aspect of the mobilisation process: the constitution of a new political arena.

Popular Front movements and boundaries of the political arena

In this section an attempt is made to illustrate the peculiar conditions of the relationship between the educated elite and the population in Karelia, by employing a comparison with the development of the Popular Front of Estonia. From the present-day perspective, this type of comparison is no longer simply a question of somewhat similar movements in somewhat similar north-western border areas of the Soviet Union. The movements have already achieved a rather different place in history, and their development has been defined from rather different reference points.

In Estonia the Popular Front has become part of the history of the struggle for independence. In standard Estonian historiography its rise is seldom pictured as a social or political phenomenon, but rather as a new 'national awakening', mainly as a cultural movement fighting for the reconstruction of Estonian identity (Taagepera 1993). The story of the Popular Front of Karelia is not a 'history of the winners' to the same extent as this, and it has not became part of the new *civic religion* of the state. As far as it is remembered, the standpoint of the examination has primarily been the history of the collapse of the Soviet system. On one hand, the Front represents an increase in civic activity which was made possible by *perestroika*. On the other, it has been seen as an expression of the failure of the communist reformers and the opposition in their attempt to rally strong civic activity in support of their policies. In both processes, questions of nationality and self-identification were central, but often remain outside the history of the Popular Front (Tsygankov 1991: 55–61).

The Estonian scholar Andrus Park has presented an interesting analysis of the turning points in the collapse of the Soviet system in Estonia. Park's periodisation is one of the few interpretations in which the development of the Popular Front of Estonia is not seen primarily as part of the national awakening, but as part of the social upheaval related to the crumbling of the

Soviet system. In his analysis Park distinguishes three main phases in the collapse of the Soviet system:

1 the revolution from above
2 the emergence of opposition mass movements
3 the transition to pluralist quasi-parliamentarism.

This periodisation offers an interesting starting point for considering the role of the educated elite and the preconditions for the birth of a political bloc capable of attracting large scale popular support (Park 1995: 326–39).

The revolution from above and the rebellion of the intelligentsia

According to Park, the first phase covers the years 1985–87, and was marked by 'the revolution from above' in 1985 (through which he hints that the first sparks came from Moscow), the rebellion of the intelligentsia in 1986 (through which he defines the social background of the first initiatives for action) and finally the reinvention of national symbols in 1987 (the Memorial Day demonstrations, which for Park mark the onset of popular mobilisation) (Park 1995: 326–27; see also Hosking 1992: 180–201).

Park's notion of the 'revolution from above' as the initial phase is easy to accept, even with regard to the Karelian Republic. The idea that the impetus came from Moscow and not from the local opposition forces, dissidents or nationalists is obviously valid as far as civic activity in Karelia is concerned. The first non-governmental voluntary associations established in Karelia in the mid-1980s, the discussion clubs, temperance and sports societies were, in most cases, inaugurated by the local and district party and Komsomol organisations. The initiative often came from a younger generation of party functionaries who were committed to Gorbachev's reform politics. At least in some cases it was also the conscious objective of the reformers to create horizontal organisational structures external to the party machinery at the local level. At this stage association activity, however, sought only in a limited way to strengthen civic organisation outside party control. Ultimately, the idea was for associations and clubs to recognise the political leadership role of the party (interview with Stanislaw Pilnikov, former Komsomol secretary and Karelian representative in the last Supreme Soviet, Pitkäranta July 1995).

With regard to Andrus Park's notion of the 'rebellion of the intelligentsia', it is obvious that we can hardly speak of a similar phenomenon in Karelia in 1986. Still, various cultural and discussion clubs were established at that time, and even if these clubs did not take an active stand against the dominant system, they did extend the possibilities of free discussion and expressing opinions. In this sense they sparked a process of constructing a new arena of political discussion and action. In Karelia the actual year of the 'rebellion of the intelligentsia' would more plausibly be 1988, when the first openly political clubs were established: the History and Literature Club and Socialist Pluralism in Petrozavodsk, and Democratic Initiative in Kostomuk-sha. Still, the most momentous expression of the 'rebellion of the intelligent-sia' was undoubtedly the founding of the Popular Front of Karelia in November 1988. Though the Front strove from the outset for broader mass mobilisation, the participants in the meeting establishing the Front were predominantly members of the intelligentsia – for example, scholars, jour-nalists, artists, actors. Perhaps the strata were even narrower than in the case of Estonia, as the administrative and economic elite did not participate to the same extent. It is important to note that the Karelian Front did not employ openly national slogans, but rather represented a federational image, with claims to economic independence (Tsygankov 1995: 87–8).

The Estonian re-invention of the national symbols in the 'Memorial Day riots' of 1988 is understandably not apparent in 'multicultural' Karelia. As it was, glorious dates and figures from the past simply did not exist in Karelia, at least not in the same sense that the history of Estonian independence could offer. However, to some extent parallel notions were involved in the activities of the so-called Memorial groups, which became public precisely in 1988. In a similar way they awakened memories of the Stalinist past which were set in opposition to the prevailing ideology. Among the national minor-ities the ethnic organisations openly promoted alternative cultural and civic identity. Furthermore, they re-introduced a repertoire of free collective action that had been strictly controlled by the government. Although the Finno-Ugrian populace represented only little more than 10 per cent of the total population, the meetings of the Ingrian and Karelian organisations were among the first non-governmental mass demonstrations in the Kare-lian Republic. In a sense they embodied the endeavour to build a link between the elite and the population – and at the same time to set the limits of it (Klementiev 1996: 142–5).

Opposition mass movement and the re-orientation of the ruling elite 1988–90

This second phase of mobilisation in Estonia did not have a direct counter-part in Karelia. The mere notion of an actual mass mobilisation in the case of Karelia is problematic. Efforts in this direction were made, however. In particular, the Popular Front of Karelia sought from the very outset to culti-vate a mass organisation, first as an internal opposition to the Soviet system, and later as an open challenger to the hegemony of the CPSU. Still, the Front achieved only limited success in mass organisation (at its height it had about a thousand members) (Tsygankov 1991). When compared with Estonia, an easy explanation can be found in the fact that the Karelian Front lacked similar resources: the strong national sentiments shared by the majority of the Estonian population. In a more sophisticated way we may state that the opposition movement in Karelia did not possess the same cultural and organisational capital (alternative collective self-identification and memories of how to act collectively) that the Estonians had acquired during the period of independence (Ruutsoo 1996: 101–8).

However, in spite of the more divided ethnic base, the Popular Front in Karelia still managed to achieve considerable influence in reconstructing the polity. As a political force, the Front won its greatest success in the Supreme Soviet elections of 1989, when it successfully challenged and defeated the candidates of the party apparatus in the capital city of the republic, Petrozavodsk (Tsygankov 1998: 6–60). Politically, it had no clear ideological profile, but was more important in destroying the idea that the Communist Party enjoyed the undivided popular support of the people.

At least as significant a factor as the partial mass mobilisation is the fact that the ruling elite, that is, those who possessed political capital, did not fragment in Karelia and ally itself with the mass organisations to the same degree as it did in Estonia. Although the Karelian leadership adhered to the reform politics of Moscow, it only did so reluctantly, and adopted a clearly negative attitude towards the political mass actions represented by the Popular Front. This became obvious, for instance, in the restrictions which were placed on Popular Front meetings, and in the pressure exerted on its leaders (interview with Sulo Nokelainen, former member of the leading group of the Karelian Popular Front, May 1996). Among the Karelian political elite there was no willingness to stimulate a general mobilisation through demonstrations and popular organisation. Neither the banners of the national minority movements nor Russian nationalistic slogans could offer the old party elite an acceptable programme to ally with a mass movement and the 'people'. In this sense, it can be concluded that neither of the two main requisites for successful collective action were fulfilled in the Karelian Republic: in the crucial phase, the mass movement remained modest in size, and the ruling elite, those possessing political capital, did not split into rival groupings and never allied with the mass movement on a large scale. As a result, no strong hegemonic bloc was formed.

Pluralistic quasi-parliamentarianism

According to Park's periodisation, the third phase of the collapse of Soviet power in Estonia was characterised by conditions of quasi-parliamentarianism. In Estonia this phase occurred in the years 1990–91. Park maintains that it was typified by relatively free competition in elections and the (formally unobstructed) opportunity for the opposition to participate. In practice, political competition was, however, limited by the influence of the institutions and practices of the Soviet era, which were still strong. Park notes that this phase lasted until the unsuccessful coup in Moscow in 1991, when the power of the Communist party was 'symbolically destroyed' (Park 1995: 238–9).

In the case of Karelia, this description of the third phase seems to fit the heyday of the Popular Front particularly well. The Front achieved its most visible role during the election campaigns of 1989 and 1990, when it functioned as a challenge and alternative to the official party candidates. Following the collapse of the Soviet system it was, however, unable to institutionalise itself as a popular political movement. As in Estonia, the Front split into competing parties and national groups, but in Karelia none of them succeeded in gaining broad political influence. The first party groupings were often modelled after Western organisations such as the Social Democrats or the Greens, but these images could not achieve substantial popular support (Tsygankov 1995: 88–90).

It can be concluded that the Popular Front of Karelia played an important role as an organised political opposition, but only in a particular phase, that of the quasi-parliamentarianism circumstances of the 1989 and 1990 elections. In the longer run it failed to establish itself as a new kind of political force which could have mobilised popular mass support and thus expanded the scope of the political system in the direction of civil society. In many ways it reflected more the re-orientation of the intelligentsia, who had the opportunity and the capability of acting within the framework of the old political arena – and the emerging 'public sphere'. The bulk of the people had the option to support them or not, but had little to do with the formation of the images offered them. The Popular Front challenged the power structure in the name of the people. In terms of nationality politics the Front, however, was not a national movement, not even an ethnic one. It was most of all a movement in defence of the autonomous federal status of the republic. This was, however, not a strong enough goal for active popular identification, but in the longer run it led to part of the opposition joining forces with those holding power, and became a central factor affecting the construction of identities after the breakdown of the Soviet Union.

Educational and political capital and the Popular Front

As seen, in Soviet Karelia, too, the ideologisation of power, the challenging of the legitimation of power in the name of the people, played a role in popular mobilisation. The institution of the principle of voluntary association among the different nationality groupings was inherently tied to the constitution of a new political arena. Ethnic movements were the first to spark an ideological battle over political hegemony and contest the right to represent the people. In this sense the propagation of national and ethnic solidarity not only demonstrated the building of an 'imagined community', but was also a factor in preparing the ground for mass organisation, and for broadening the scope of the political system outside the circles of the old elite.

Still, during the Soviet period this process did not proceed very far. The rapid politicisation of organisations of the educated elite, and the great political influence some of these associations had during the *perestroika* years, did not create lasting ground for broader popular support. In fact, it may be that it is only after the collapse of the Soviet Union that we can speak of the maturation of a new type of civic culture in the Karelian Republic.

Today civic action is developing on the level of more invisible grass-root associations connected with the everyday life of the citizens, their livelihood and recreational activities. Contrary to the notion of 'exhausted exhilar-ation', this type of organisation is not fading, but is instead, judging from the number of clubs and societies, continuously growing. In an important sense these organisations represent a new type of construction of social practices from below, which may in the long run prove to be more profound than the images offered by the oppositional intelligentsia during the break-down of the Soviet Union. The question remains whether this new identity construction can become a part of a new polity formation and the creation of hegemonic blocs from below.

In any case, it seems clear that the organisations of the educated elite that played a significant part in breaking down the Soviet system are not an adequate indication of present-day development in civic culture. Their rise reflected more the processes of segmentation and competition inside the old political system, and among the possessors of educational and political capital. Their great achievements were won under the conditions of the pluralistic quasi-parliamentarism. They offered an alternative identification to the official Soviet definitions, but did so mainly through images borrowed from the West. They lacked a solid backing from voluntary association and self-identification from below. In this sense, the exhaustion of the organisa-tions of the radical intelligentsia is not necessarily a sign of general political stagnation. On the contrary, it may be that it is the birth of a broader political culture that is pushing the heroes of the transformation period into the margin. Maybe the concept of political capital should not be limited only to the conditions of the communist rule, as Bourdieu did, but should be seen as a counterpart to educational capital and the emerging economic capital also in the circumstances of the transformation period. This new political capital is, however, not obtained inside a closed party or state apparatus, but by attracting popular support on a new kind of political arena established between the state and the organisations of civil society. Maybe this type of challenge to the rule of both educational and economic capital is, in fact, vital for sustainable democracy.

References

Anttikoski, E. (1998). 'Strategii karel'skogo iazykovogo planirovaniia v 1920–e i 1930–e gody' in T. Vihavainen and I. Takala (eds), *V sem'e edinoi: Natsional'naia politika partii bolshevikov i ee osushchestvlenie na Severo-Zapade Rossii v 1920–1950–e gody*. Petroza-vodsk: Izdatel'stvo Petrozavodskogo Universiteta, Kikimora Publications Series B, Aleksanteri-instituutti, pp. 207–22.

Bourdieu, P. (1998). *Järjen käytännöllisyys. Toiminnan teorian lähtökohtia.* Tampere: Vastapaino.
Bremmer, I. and Taras, R. (1993). *Nations and Politics in the Soviet Successor States.* Cambridge: Cambridge University Press.
Carrére, d'Encausse, H. (1994). *The End of Soviet Empire: The Triumph of the Nations.* London: Basic Books.
Heikkinen, K. (1996). 'Religion, Gender and Ethnic Organisation' in K. Heikkinen and E. Zdravomyslova (eds) *Civil Society in the European North. Concept and Context.* St Petersburg: Centre for Independent Social Research, pp. 146–9.
Hosking, G. (1992). 'Popular Movements in Estonia' in G. Hosking, J. Aves and P. Duncan (eds) *The Road to Post-Communism. Independent Political Movements in the Soviet Union 1985–1991.* London: Pinter Publishers, pp. 180–201.
Kangaspuro, M. (1995). ' "Ison vihan" tausta Karjalassa. Vuoden 1933 puoluepuhdistus ei etene Karjalassa toivotulla tavalla' in A. Laine (ed.), *Kansallisuus ja valtio. Karjala ja Komi nuoren Neuvostoliiton tasavaltoina 1920– ja 1930–luvuilla.* Joensuun yliopisto, Karjalan tutkimuslaitos, Monisteita No 5/1995, pp. 133–50.
Kangaspuro, M. (1998). 'Finskaia epokha Sovetskoi Karelii' in T. Vihavainen and I. Takala (eds), *V sem'e edinoi: Natsional'naia politika partii bolshevikov i ee osushchestvlenie na Severo-Zapade Rossii v 1920–1950–e gody.* Petrozavodsk: Izdatel'stvo Petrozavodskogo Universiteta, Kikimora Publications Series B, Aleksanteri-instituutti, pp. 123–60.
Klementiev, E. (1991). *Karely. Karjalazet. Etnograficheskii ocherk.* Kareliia, Petrozavodsk.
Klementiev, E. (1996). 'Formation of a Civil Society and National Movement in the Republic of Karelia' in K. Heikkinen and E. Zdravomyslova (eds) *Civil Society in the European North. Concept and Context.* St Petersburg: Centre for Independent Social Research, pp. 142–5.
Laine, A. (1994). 'Karelia Between Two Socio-cultural Systems' in H. Eskelinen, J. Oksa and D. Austin (eds) *Russian Karelia in Search of a New Role.* Joensuu: University of Joensuu, Karelian Institute, pp. 13–25.
Laine, A. (1996). 'Suomalaiset Karjalassa – kaksi nousua ja syvenevä assimilaatio' in I. Liikanen and P. Stranius (eds) *Matkalla kansalaisyhteiskuntaan? Liikettä ja liikkeitä Luoteis-Venäjällä.* Joensuun yliopisto, Karjalan tutkimuslaitoksen julkaisuja No 115, pp. 77–91.
Liikanen, I. (1996). 'The Politics of Civic Organisation. The Karelian Republic in a Comparative Perspective' in K. Heikkinen and E. Zdravomyslova (eds) *Civil Society in the European North. Concept and Context.* St Petersburg: Centre for Independent Social Research, pp. 155–9.
Park, A. (1995). 'Turning-points of Post-Communist Transition: Lessons from the Case of Estonia' *Proceedings of the Estonian Academy of Sciences 44/3,* Tallinn: Estonian Academy Publishers, pp. 323–32.
Rentola, K. (1994). *Kenen joukoissa seisot? Suomalainen kommunismi ja sota 1937–1945.* Juva: WSOY.
Ruutsoo, R. (1996). 'Formation of Civil Society Types and Organisational Capital of the Baltic Nations in the Framework of the Russian Empire' in K. Heikkinen and E. Zdravomyslova (eds) *Civil Society in the European North. Concept and Context.* St Petersburg: Centre for Independent Social Research, pp. 101–8.
Smith, J. (1997). 'Education of Minorities – the Early Soviet Experience', in *Slavonic and East European Review,* vol. 75, no. 2, pp. 281–307.
Stranius, P. (1996). 'The Role and Drama of the Russian Intelligentsia' in K. Heikkinen and E. Zdravomyslova (eds), *Civil Society in the European North. Concept and Context.* St Petersburg: Centre for Independent Social Research, pp. 150–5.

Taagepera, R. (1993). *Estonia. Return to Independence.* Boulder CO: Westview Press.
Tsygankov, A. (1991). *K grazhdanskomu obshchestvu.* Petrozavodsk: Kareliia.
Tsygankov, A. (1995). 'Nuutuneen riemun aika', *Carelia* 4, pp. 86–94.
Tsygankov, A. (1998). *Prishestvie izbiratelia. Iz istorii vybornikh kampanii v Karelii 1989–1996.* Petrozavodsk: Kareliia.

4
The Intelligentsia and the 'Breakdown of Culture' in Post-Soviet Russia

Pentti Stranius

I am a foster-child of the Soviet system. Its faults and merits have become a part of me . . . In the economic situation in which the intelligentsia is living in Russia, I think that the most important 'Soviet merit' was that the old system 'prepared' us to despise money.

(Aleksandr, film director, St Petersburg, January 1996)

Following the collapse of the Soviet Union the 'breakdown of culture' has been much discussed in Russia. In common usage the concept refers to the disintegration of the economic and cultural unity of the country, the spread of pulp culture in literature and cinema, and ultimately to the 'death' of the Soviet intelligentsia (see Gessen 1997; Kagarlitskii 1992; Levada 1994; Levinson 1994; Lisovskii *et al.* 1993; Siniavskii 1997).

Sometimes the 'collapse of culture' and the 'death of intelligentsia' are seen as a natural result of a long historical pattern. It is said that the total repression of the Soviet period had such a debilitating effect on the intelligentsia that it had no power left to fight when freedom came. According to this mode of thinking, the total absence of traditions of civic culture during the Soviet period predestined the failure of attempts to build a modern civil society after the collapse of the communist system (see Shkaratan and Gurenko 1990: 153–62).

This pessimistic view can be contested both historically and in regard to the activities and attitudes of intellectuals in present-day Russia. As many Russian researchers have observed, some possibilities for developing civil society existed even inside the totalitarian system, especially in the sphere of culture. In the first part of this chapter I will consider the degree to which the history of the New Economic Policy (NEP) in the 1920s, the so-called 'thaw' under Khrushchev, and *perestroika* under Gorbachev demonstrated the existence of elements of active civic culture inside the one-party system. It is evident that during these periods the atmosphere of freedom played an important role, not only in the consciousness of the elite intelligentsia, but in a much wider range of cultural life. How was this reflected in the structure of society, and did it create civic traditions that survived in the conditions of totalitarian state control? For example, is it possible to verify the common notion that it was particularly the generation of the 'thaw' (the Russian '60s'), that saw the opportunity in the *perestroika* period to influence history for a second time, and thus play a decisive role in the collapse of totalitarianism? (Stranius 1998: 7–24; Voronkov 1996: 143–9).

The intelligentsia in Russia has always acted as a special buffer between the establishment and the masses. The lack of a petty bourgeoisie has meant that the intelligentsia has, in a sense, played the role of the middle class. Accordingly, culture has in Russia been a more important sphere for the development of civil society than in Western Europe. In this sense the role of the Russian intelligentsia has been decisive. Did this role end with the collapse of Soviet Union? Does discussion of the 'breakdown of culture' imply a change in the position and self-understanding of the Russian intelligentsia?

The second part of this chapter discusses this problem through an analysis of the contemporary attitudes of Russian intellectuals. The basic material for the research has been collected through in-depth interviews conducted in three cities: in St Petersburg, and in Petrozavodsk and Pitkäranta in the Karelian republic. The interviews illustrate different voices from the old and new Russia: researchers, teachers, doctors, engineers, writers, film directors and journalists. Many seemed even to be experiencing a personal crisis in their lives and had a need to discuss their problems with outsiders. In this chapter both the voice of the so-called 'creative intelligentsia' and that of the 'proletaricised' teachers will be heard.

The tragedy of the Soviet intelligentsia

Wars, terror and, in the end, economic stagnation marked the lives of the inhabitants of the Soviet Union. In addition to these evils, the Soviet system punished the intelligentsia in even more sophisticated ways. The intelligentsia had three interludes, three possibilities in which to breathe and realise its potential by slightly opening the door to the freedom of speech and creative work. But each time the door was slammed shut in its face (see Stranius 1997: 54–7).

During the period of NEP in the 1920s the development of some elements of civil society inside the one-party system can be observed. Of course, even during NEP, 'private enterprise' was still an extremely atypical phenomenon in Russian towns, and a market economy and 'petty bourgeoisie' existed only in the margins of the dictatorship of the ruling proletariat. Still, we can note an atmosphere of partial freedom in cultural life, in the Russian avant-garde and popular culture of the very early 1920s. It is even said that the intelligentsia acted as the most important 'agent of modernisation of the society' (Levada 1994: 208–14). In terms of modernistic culture, Maiakovskii, Esenin, Gorkii, Eisenshtein, Vertov and the whole Russian avant-garde shook the world as much as the '10 days' in October 1917. For a certain period of time it seemed that a society of freedom, brotherhood and equality had been born, and that those who possessed 'cultural capital' (see Bourdieu 1998: 25–9) were playing a major role in this revolutionary process.

In spite of the enthusiasm and ideological inspiration that innovative approaches to art, literature and cinema represented, the modernists and their organisations were left in the margin and finally were crushed. The authors themselves could hardly understand how they had helped to create the image of the new hero: the harsh, determined Bolshevik in a leather jacket. In the early 1930s this hero stepped forth from the screen and from the pages of books, and took vengeance on his creators through open terror and censorship in the name of socialist realism (see Iurina 1987). The official artists' unions took the place of the rival modernist clubs and societies of the 1920s, and *Sotsrealizm*, the aesthetics of censorship, contributed to the decomposition of civic activity of the new Soviet intelligentsia.

As Soviet life showed, 'instruction' represented a very powerful force in society. By the end of the 1950s, the first generation to have grown up wholly in the Soviet system had matured. The intellectuals – as the 'first teachers', and even their descendants as well – were themselves engaged in the organisation of the instruction system but, at the same time, the first objects of it. The re-education of disobedient intellectuals was achieved through constant attacks on alien elements ('enemies of the people'), self-criticism, and ultimately the camps (the GULAG-system). The first stage in re-education was to institute internal censorship among the intelligentsia, which led to the so-called militia-inside behaviour. There was a militiaman inside most creative people who knew the rules of behaviour: they said one thing, thought another and did a third. It was 'life in a lie' – a hard time for the creative intelligentsia, who had no place nor space for free speech in society (Solzhenitsyn 1991: 3–46).

The second interlude of the Soviet intelligentsia, the so-called 'thaw', was influenced by the political situation: Stalin's death, the Twentieth Congress of the CPSU and the de-stalinisation of Nikita Khrushchev. But other factors were important here as well – among them the protest of the Russian generation of the 1960s, 'the children of the 20th party congress' (see Vail and Genis 1996). During the 1930s and 1940s, the protest of the 'young' generation was slowed by terror and war, and found its first opportunity to express itself only during the 'thaw'. The atmosphere of Khrushchev's 'spring' was again, in the first instance, reflected in culture: in Evtushenko's poetry, in Marlen Khutsiev's famous movie about the Russian '60s' (*I Am 20 Years Old*) (1964), in *Ivan Denisovich* by Solzhenitsyn (1962). Shukshin, Tarkovskii and Vysotskii all appeared in the early 1960s as heroes of the new generation of students and youngsters (see Stranius 1998: 7–24; Viljanen and Stranius 1990).

The young professionals found their hero when Iurii Gagarin orbited the Earth and became a very peculiar film star. Even Andrei Sakharov appeared in 'The History of the CPSU', before being labelled a 'non-person'. This time the cultural dissent did not have its bases so much in the traditional groupings of the intelligentsia, but rather among the numerous new middle class of students and educated specialists.

In political terms the '60s' were often more to do with dreaming about 'socialism with a human face' than bringing down the whole system. But on the political field they found extremely little room to implement their ideas. For example, the emerging legal defence movement did not turn into an organised political opposition. What is important here is that certain civic and moral positions of the generation lived in the private or 'public–private' sphere (Duka and Zdravomyslova 1992: 14–27). Many literary and art works created in the 1960s survived outside the Soviet system, and played an important role in the new conditions that emerged during *perestroika*, under Gorbachev. Here I mean, for example, forbidden films and some *samizdat* newspapers and books. The same phenomenon can be detected on the level of human networks. I have noticed in my research that in in-depth interviews, members of the 'old' Russian '60s' often found each other again at the end of the 1980s.

The second interlude of the intelligentsia was interrupted by a *coup d'etat* from above and the reinforced censorship of all cultural life in society, at the behest of Brezhnev, Suslov and like-minded persons. The Moscow film historian Valerii Fomin refers to this ideological control very succinctly and pointedly as 'the aesthetics of shelving' (Fomin 1991: 42–7). In the USSR, for example, film production worked very slowly, even without censors. Most of those films that started production during Khrushchev's thaw were only finished under Brezhnev, in the late 1960s, when the political situation had changed. The era of stagnation had already begun. It is the main reason for there being so many shelved films in the years 1967–68. The tragedy was that the new generation, 'the children of the 20th party congress', tried to provide more space for public speech, literature and cinema, but their works were left unfinished or on their desks – and many films were put on the shelves (Fomin 1996).

The third interlude of the intelligentsia, *perestroika*, appeared at the same time to be (according to Iurii Levada) 'the swan song of the Soviet intelligentsia' (Levada 1994: 208–14). Under Gorbachev, the role of the cultural intelligentsia was noticeable. The generation of the 1960s were among the activists of the new movements and organisations, for example, in the popular fronts in St Petersburg and Petrozavodsk. This 'old' generation of the Soviet intelligentsia took its revenge when it saw its second historical chance in *perestroika* (see Tiriakian 1991: 26–34). Totalitarianism and stagnation especially impeded the cultural intelligentsia (writers, film makers, painters, scientists, journalists, actors, musicians, and so on) from living and working normally, and insulted their professional dignity. From about 1987 to 1991, Soviet publications printed a nearly complete collection of forbidden underground or secretly imported literature (*samizdat* and *tamizdat*). Banned discs (*magnizdat*), paintings and shelved films saw the light of day. This *'glasnost'* period' – before the collapse of the Soviet Union – seemed to be a real triumph of different avant-garde, counter cultures and those possessing 'cultural capital' on the whole.

It has been asked whether the people who came of age during the 'thaw' had a greater consciousness than the later generation of the years of stagnation? Did they have a deeper knowledge about such notions as 'human rights', 'freedom of speech and conscience', 'political pluralism', 'civil society'? Perhaps all these terms had already been in use among the '60s' generation, especially among those who obtained ideas from the West, the so-called *zapadniks* (Westernisers). Today we have witnessed how, after the collapse of the Soviet Union, the old conflict between Westernists and Slavophiles in Russian cultural life has been felt in the attitudes towards civil society and the so-called Russian idea or the Russian way. (See McDaniel 1996: 22–55; Patomäki and Pursiainen 1998: 1–56).

The *'glasnost'* period' did not last long: the historic moment passed again in the early 1990s. Some of the rebel intellectuals were co-opted with places in the new state machinery, some shifted from the popular fronts to new political parties and the State Duma or became leaders of new groups. Others found comfortable jobs in business, some emigrated, but the majority of the '60s' were again disappointed in the outcome of the system change, at least temporarily (see Gessen 1997; Kagarlitskii 1992; Siniavskii 1997).

From party-rule to market economy: education, literature, cinema

According to a general vision found among those Russian teachers, cultural workers, writers and film directors interviewed in this research, in the late 1990s all cultural life has been on the brink of destruction. Many of them assume that the intelligentsia is now 'dying' – after having again helped to create a false hero, the young profiteer of the market economy. The image of this hero, the 'New Russian', is now used to deprive the intelligentsia of its status. Old cultural values are crumbling and many of the cultural professions maintained by the Soviet system are becoming useless. In the public sphere, the intelligentsia remains remarkably quiet on the whole. One of the reasons for this silence may be the economic side of the question. During the Soviet period it was not considered good manners to speak openly about money among artists or teachers. Status – a self-image as the conscience of society, as the 'Great Educator' – was always more important than salary. Today the status of the intelligentsia has declined, and incomes have dropped drastically. Still the poorer intelligentsia – teachers, doctors and cultural workers – find it hard to make speeches or participate in demonstrations, even if they have not been paid for several months.

Little by little, however, this situation has been changing. In 1998–99, teachers from many schools went on strike in northwest Russia and the Republic of Karelia. Almost all schools in the district of Olonets were closed in September 1998 because the teachers got tired of waiting for their salaries. In Segezha teachers were on strike at the same time because the local administration mysteriously 'lost' the money sent from Petrozavodsk to pay months of back salaries to school workers. On the other hand, many schools in northwest Russia stand closed, under 'permanent' repair or in need of fundamental renovation. The classrooms are empty, without technical equipment or even desks, but the government and local administration do not have the finances for such needs. In Russian Karelia some parents refuse to send their children to schools in small villages because there is nothing to eat during the lunch break. The school kitchen can only offer the hungry children tea or, sometimes, tea and bread. In Lahdenpohja the teachers burnt the spelling-books as a protest against the financial situation in the local schools. On the road between Sortavala and Pitkäranta hundreds of teachers and cultural workers occupied the bridge near Laskela and stopped the traffic for many hours, and so on (see *Severnyi kurier* 29.8.98, *Karjalan Sanomat* 1.8.98, 5.8.98, 5.9.98, 12.9.98).

Going on strike is a big step for teachers, doctors and cultural workers. Usually feelings of professional pride are so high that teachers are ready to work for months without pay. On the one hand, such behaviour is a result of Soviet ethical and totalitarian education. On the other, the teachers do not have any choice: their opportunities to earn money in the commercial sector are limited.

One of my contacts – Valerii, the director of a private school in St Petersburg told me, half seriously, that in the Soviet era the technical opportunities of education were 50 years behind, but approaches to teaching and learning were 50 years ahead of the West. In his opinion, *perestroika* and the market economy have changed this situation, leaving Russian pedagogy, and education in general, 50 years behind.

By education, Valerii is an ethnographer. He is 46 years old and took an active part in *perestroika*. For a short time he even worked as an adviser to the Popular Front of St Petersburg. Now he is very disappointed in politics, and thinks it was a mistake to march to the barricades: education is his proper 'milieu' and it is through this sphere he participates in the development of a new society. In his own private school Valerii is trying to put into practice a new method of teaching, that he calls a 'method of dialogue'. He believes that in Soviet times the educational process was, on the whole, founded on the authority of the teachers. Not only schoolchildren, but even students in the universities had no chance of seriously discussing problems with adults – and thus developing into active citizens (Valerii, school director, St Petersburg, June 1997).

One of my informants, Marina, a young literature teacher from Petrozavodsk, was raped on the road home from school. The next morning she was again standing in front of her classroom. She says that she had no thought of leaving the children alone in the classroom, even during this kind of personal tragedy. Marina emphasised that she had always been a non-political person. However, in the course of telling me about her life story, 30-year-old Marina suddenly remembered that she was almost kicked out of the Komsomol because of her critical attitudes during her school years. Later, at the beginning of *perestroika*, she burnt her Komsomol membership card (Marina, school teacher, Petrozavodsk, December 1996).

Galina, a 55-year-old professor of medieval history at the State University of St Petersburg, is satisfied with the new administration in her faculty. No longer is there a party-state bureaucracy, a department of History of the CPSU. Very many other things have changed in the faculty – open archives, free discussion during seminars, no more 'black holes' in research themes, and so on. But Galina feels worried about the younger generation, about the students who cannot – or do not want to – go to the theatre or cinema, as she herself used to do in the 1960s. First, their parents are not able to pay for the tickets; second, the students prefer to watch such soap operas as the *The Bold and Beautiful*, or *Santa Barbara* on the television (Galina, professor, St Petersburg June 1997).

Notably, new popular culture or 'pulp culture' in Russia was criticised during my interviews by almost all members of the intelligentsia who were born in the 1950s or earlier. In particular, two 50-year-old writers – Viktor and Raisa, from St Petersburg and Petrozavodsk – are both bothered by the fact that the publishing and reading of serious literature is in continuous decline.

Viktor is a former dissident and poet who was one of the activists in the famous 'Club 81'. This intellectual club in St Petersburg united hundreds of informal writers, painters and cultural workers on the eve of *perestroika*. Many of them later joined the Popular Front and the new political parties. Now those times of civic activity have gone. Viktor is distinguished today as a non-political poet and journalist. He is a well-known and respected professional, and can earn money by translating or writing articles and columns for Western journals. However, he feels he is an outsider in his own town, St Petersburg, as he is almost without Russian readers (Viktor, poet and writer, St Petersburg, June 1995).

Raisa, a scriptwriter and journalist from Petrozavodsk, only once in her life took an active part in politics – in the action organised by the Karelian Popular Front. In August 1991 she went to the demonstration in Petrozavodsk to demonstrate her support for the continuation of *perestroika* and against the coup. Raisa noted that before and during *perestroika*, the reading of serious literature, not only forbidden *samizdat*, was a fearless civic act. Reading was a silent protest against the 'party-entertainment' of the CPSU (official newspapers like *Pravda*, party-programmes, declarations and orders). Even Soviet cinema sometimes conveyed elements of protest. There were hidden meanings which Soviet viewers tried to find behind the screen. Today film-making shows only what happens on the screen. In Raisa's opinion, American romantic and action films, or shallow detective stories in literature and cinema do not force the reader or viewer to think deeply and profoundly. This kind of pulp culture is a shock to most middle-aged Russians, who were used to reading moral narratives, and to seeing very long slow shots, and extended episodes on the screen (Raisa, scriptwriter and journalist, Petrozavodsk, June 1996).

For many decades, cinema was the most important sphere in the crucial role of both mass agitation and the education of ordinary citizens in the spirit of the state ideology, Marxism-Leninism. (As Lenin stated: 'Of all the arts, for us cinema is the most important'; while Stalin noted: 'Cinema is the greatest means of mass agitation'.) At the same time, in the Soviet Union literature and cinema were always considered to be 'Big Art', a part of high culture. Officially, Western or Russian popular culture was regarded as 'pulp culture', but inside the so-called 'second society' it sometimes played a very important uniting role. During NEP, the 'thaw' and *perestroika* we can even speak about a rise of alternative popular culture (see Stites 1992).

After the collapse of the Soviet Union (1991), Western popular culture captured most of the visual space – cinema, visual arts, fashion, advertisements, video and TV. It was an enormous shock after the years of 'party-entertainment'. Old cultural values and 'party truths' started to crumble. This was a death blow to Soviet-style cinema and TV entertainment. Middle-aged scriptwriters, film directors and TV-journalists either felt themselves useless, or tried to adapt to the new conditions, or were fired. Understandably, they are now thinking and speaking about the 'death' of the intelligentsia. The arena of culture they mastered has been ruined and it seems that the day of doom has come.

The Moscow film director Stanislav Govorukhin, who is also a representative of a small faction in the State Duma, remarks on the breakdown of Soviet cinema:

> in the heat of battle we managed to destroy the very best thing that we had in cinematography, the countrywide system of distributing and renting out films. Then you could see a film in any village, at any weather station. Now the two hundred odd films produced by Russian cinematographers have, for all intents and purposes, ended up on the shelf, because they do not get to the public. We have created a new phenomenon: movies without an audience. We began as revolutionaries and ended as a firing squad, as horrendous reactionaries.
>
> (Quoted in Siniavskii 1997: 45)

Another film director, 47-year-old Aleksandr from St Petersburg, prefers classic literature to cinema. In his opinion cinema is only taking its first steps as an art form and has not yet become a real 'fundamental art' like literature. Modern cinema all over the world is almost only about business and entertainment, not culture.

Aleksandr's first films were shelved, but he never felt like a dissident. On the contrary, during his student years, he was an activist in the Moscow Film Institute Komsomol – before being shelved, of course. After having several conflicts with the censors, Andrei Tarkovskii helped him to find his first job at Lenfilm, where he started to make very extraordinary cinema – a mix of documentary and fiction. He has filmed a well-known documentary sympathetic to Yeltsin. But now, after the war in Chechnia, all his illusions of the humane and wise leader and his power have disappeared. In recent years Aleksandr has had his own studio, and has been directing films with the financial co-operation of European and Japanese producers (Aleksandr, film director, St Petersburg, January 1996).

Aleksandr, like many of my informants, thinks that the crisis of cultural life in Russia has already dealt a 'mortal blow' to the old established intelligentsia close to the party-elite. The invasion of Western and new Russian popular culture appears to be a real threat to the so-called creative intelligentsia (cultural workers, writers, film directors) and to the Russian '60s', but not to the whole traditional culture, which has roots deep in Russian history.

The 'death' of the intelligentsia

To what degree can we speak about the 'death of intelligentsia' and the 'breakdown of culture'? According to the Soviet ideology, 'honourable' members of the established intelligentsia acted as a buffer between the party-state and the masses ('educator', 'conscience of society'). Sometimes this buffer was needed even for the purposes of agitation and education. Sometimes a part of the intelligentsia was even allowed to act as a symbol of freedom, but 'sacrificed' in the name of ideology if they went too far in utilising this freedom. This happened, for example, in the cases of Sakharov, Solzhenitsyn and Tarkovskii. Today, when there no longer is an ideological need for a 'buffer' or 'conscience' in Russian society, the status of this elite has disappeared. It is losing its face, prestige and faith – and is 'dying'.

On the other hand, the generation of the 1960s can no longer act as the 'agent of modernisation' inside the new Russia. These 'children of the 20th party congress' are becoming old: they underwent Khrushchev's 'thaw', Brezhnev's stagnation and started Gorbachev's *glasnost'* and *perestroika*, but their time has gone in Yeltsin's Russia. The political activity of this 'moral' generation lost its ground when the new symbols of 'private property' and 'market economy' started to crystallise in the new Russian reality (see Demidov 1993: 148–65, Stranius 1998).

The creative intelligentsia tried to fight for cultural values in society, but in the mid-1990s it has lost its illusions, such as the feeling that there were true representatives of the people in the Duma in Moscow. In their eyes, the market economy completely changed the sphere of culture, at the same time as the government was cutting funding for scholarships, publishing houses, cinema and culture. Finally, the 'Soviet' intelligentsia in the new Russia cannot play the role of the middle class in society. There are already new challengers waiting to assume this role: modern professionals and the educated new generation, who are breaking through into the public sphere as part of the new middle class. They are not always just 'those damned New Russians'. Many of them are interested in cultural values, in their own history and traditions, and they want to give their children a good education, too. Perhaps they are no longer representatives of the intelligentsia, but 'intellectuals' in the Western interpretation of this term? In this sense not only Russia but its intelligentsia is at a turning point in history.

References

Bourdieu, P. (1998). *Järjen käytännöllisyys*. Tampere: Vastapaino.
Demidov, A. (1993). 'Intelligentsia i vlast'' in V. Lisovskii, L. Koganovich and L. Riabov (eds) *Intelligentsia i nravstvennost'. Sotsiologicheskie ocherki*. Moscow: NIIVO, pp. 148–65.
Duka, A. and Zdravomyslova, E. (1992). 'Fazy razvitiia grazhdanskogo obshchestva' in A. Alekseev, E. Zdravomyslova and V. Kostiushev (eds) *Sotsiologiia obshchestvennykh dvizhenii: kontseptual'nye modeli issledovaniia 1989–1990*. St Petersburg: Institut sotsiologii, pp. 14–27.
Fomin, V. (1991). 'Hyllytysten estetiikka'. *Filmihullu 2/1991*, pp. 42–7.
Fomin, V. (1996). *Kino i vlast. Sovetskoe kino: 1965–1985 gody*. Moscow: Materik.
Gessen, M. (1997). *Dead Again. The Russian Intelligentsia After Communism*. London: Verso.
Kagarlitskii, B. (1992). *Hajonnut monoliitti*. Helsinki: Oy Orient Express.
Levada, I. (1994). 'Problema intelligentsii v sovremennoi Rossii' in T. Zaslavskaia and L. Arutunian (eds) *Kuda idet Rossiia?* Moscow: Interpraks, pp. 208–14.
Levinson, A. (1994). 'Intelligentsia v usloviiakh postsovetskogo obshchestva' in T. Zaslavskaia and L. Arutunian (eds) *Kuda idet Rossiia?* Moscow: Interpraks, pp. 110–14.
Lisovskii, V., Koganovich, L. and Riabov, L. (eds) (1993) *Intelligentsiia i nravstvennost'. Sotsiologicheskie ocherki*. Moscow: NIIVO.
McDaniel, T. (1996). *The Agony of the Russian Idea*. Princeton, New Jersey: Princeton University Press, pp. 22–55.
Patomäki, H. and Pursiainen, C. (1998). *Against the State, With(in) the State, or a Transnational Creation: Russian Civil Society in the Making?* Helsinki: Finnish Institute of International Affairs (UPI), pp. 1–56.
Shkaratan, O. and Gurenko, E. (1990). 'Ot etakratizma k stanovleniiu grazhdanskogo obshchestva' *Rabochii klass i sovremennyi mir 3/1990*, pp. 153–62.
Siniavskii, A. (1997). *The Russian Intelligentsia*. New York: Columbia University Press.
Solzhenitsyn, A. (1992). 'Odin den iz zhizni Ivana Denisovicha' *Novyi mir 11/1962*.
Solzhenitsyn, A. (1991). 'Na vozvrate dykhaniia i soznaniia' *Novyi mir 5/1991*, pp. 3–46.
Stites, R. (1992). *Russian Popular Culture. Entertainment and Society since 1900*. Cambridge: Cambridge University Press.

Stranius, P. (1997). 'Venäjän intelligentsija. Draama kolmessa näytöksessä' *Venäjän Aika 2/1997*, pp. 54–7.

Stranius, P. (1998). 'Venäjän intelligentsija – 60-lukulaiset ja 80-luvun murros' *Idäntutkimus 3/1998*, pp. 7–24.

Tiriakian, E. (1991). 'Ot 1968 k 1989: sotsiologiia i Annus Mirabilis' *Sotsiologicheskie issledovania 5/1991*, pp. 26–34.

Vail, P. and Genis, A. (1996). *60-e. Mir sovetskogo cheloveka*. Moscow: Novoe literaturnoe obozrenie.

Voronkov, V. (1996). 'Dissidenttien rooli kansalaisyhteiskunnan muotoutumisessa' in I. Liikanen and P. Stranius (eds) *Matkalla kansalaisyhteiskuntaan? Liikettä ja liikkeitä Luoteis-Venäjällä*. Joensuu: Joensuun yliopisto, Karjalan tutkimuslaitoksen julkaisuja No 115, pp. 143–9.

Interviews

Aleksandr – film director, St Petersburg, January 1996.

Galina – professor of history, St Petersburg, June 1997.

Marina – teacher, Petrozavodsk, December 1996.

Raisa – scriptwriter and journalist, Petrozavodsk, June 1996.

Valerii – school director, St Petersburg, June 1997.

Viktor – poet and writer, St Petersburg, May 1995.

Films

Iurina, T. (1987). 'Bez geroia'. A documentary film. Mosfilm 1987.

Khutsiev, M. (1964). 'Mne 20 let'. Mosfilm 1964.

Viljanen, M. and P. Stranius (1990). 'Elokuva vangitsee aikaa'. A documentary film in two parts. Shown on Finnish TV 26.10.1990 / 02.11.1990.

Part II
Nationality Reframed

5

National Schools and National Identity in and after the Soviet Union

Jeremy Smith

The existing literature on national schools since the Second World War contains a large number of contradictory facts and conclusions about the extent of provision of education in the mother tongue for non-Russians and the success or otherwise of numerous 'russifying' reforms in education. Official data on the extent of Russian language schools does not match up with anecdotal evidence or the census returns on language knowledge. This confused picture can only partly be explained by the lack of comprehensive and reliable data on national schools. I have tentatively concluded that the real situation is that national schools have continued to exist on a larger scale than has often been supposed, and that the compulsory learning of the Russian language has not been as successful as it should have been. These effects are most marked in remoter rural areas. While a number of causes may account for this, one possibility is that under communist rule there existed a certain level of civic organisation among rural communities of a homogenous, non-Russian ethnic make-up, which successfully resisted the russification of their schools.

Tsarist policies

> The final objective of education to be provided to the non-natives living in the far reaches of the empire is undoubtedly their russification and their fusion with the Russian people.
>
> (Count D.A. Tolstoi, 1870, from Carrère d'Encausse 1992: 6)

This comment on the part of the Minister for Public Education, makes crystal clear the basis of educational policies towards national minorities in late imperial Russia. Linguistic russification was one of the prime objectives of nationality policy, and this was to be achieved mostly through the education system. Russian was introduced as the official language of instruction at all levels in all Polish schools (apart from courses in Polish and the Catholic religion) in 1872. In Ukraine, the use of the Ukrainian language in any public setting was severely curtailed by decrees of 1863 and 1876 (Wilson 1997: 11). Russification intensified after the assassination of Tsar Alexander II in 1881, and measures included the introduction of Russian as a compulsory language for the first time in Finnish schools (Pipes 1964: 7). In practice, the shortage of qualified Russian-speaking teachers and the inability of Polish children to comprehend classes in a foreign tongue meant that Polish language schools continued to function, while elsewhere policies were unsuccessful in russifying significant numbers of non-Russians, and were to some extent abandoned after 1905. But the repressive measures did have the effect of restricting the development of an effective national movement in areas like Ukraine (Subtelny 1988: 54). Restrictions on the development of non-Russian national schools not only had a debilitating effect on national identity, but also meant a generally lower level of education for non-Russians. So according to the census of 1897, with the exception of some European nationalities and Jews, illiteracy was considerably more widespread among non-Russians than among Russians (Dimanshtein 1930: 273).

Early Soviet policies

These high levels of illiteracy contributed to the impression of the 'backwardness' of the non-Russians which underlay early Soviet national policies in general (Smith 1997: 62–84). For Lenin, the injustices of the Tsarist policy required a positive commitment to national education whatever the practical economic and cultural benefits of universal knowledge of Russian (Lenin 1958–65 vol. XXIV: 295). In the face of widespread opposition to his policies among the Bolshevik party rank and file membership, and notable leading Bolsheviks like Stepan Shaumian (Lenin 1958–65 XLVIII: 234), Lenin succeeded in having a commitment to 'the right of the population to receive instruction in their native tongue in schools at the expense of the state and local organs' included in the Bolshevik Party Programme of 1917 (Lenin 1958–65 XXXII: 154).

Of more immediate importance than Lenin's views, however, were the attitudes of the People's Commissariat of Nationality Affairs (Narkomnats), its commissar Iosif Stalin, the People's Commissariat of Enlightenment (Narkompros) of the RSFSR, and the governments and communist parties of the other Soviet republics. Narkomnats was initially organised into separate commissariats and departments for each nationality, and attached to every one was a cultural–educational section whose task was 'the reform of all existing schools to make sense for their own nationalities and the introduction of teaching in the native languages...' (*Zhizn' natsional'nostei* 24 November 1918: 8). *Narkomnats* was staffed, in part, by left-wing nationalists who had made common cause with the Bolsheviks in the hope of being able to promote the cultural and political distinctiveness of their own nationalities. But their aims coincided neatly with those of Stalin, who consistently put native-language education at the head of his list of functions of the newly formed autonomous territories of the RSFSR:

> the real sovietisation of these regions, their conversion into Soviet countries closely bound with central Russia into one integral state, is *inconceivable* without the widespread organisation of local schools, without the creation of courts, administrative bodies, organs of authority, etc., staffed with people acquainted with the life and language of the population.... this is precisely putting Soviet autonomy into practice; for Soviet autonomy is nothing but the sum total of all these institutions clothed in Ukrainian, Turkestan, Kirghiz etc. forms.
>
> (Stalin 1946 vol. IV: 372)

So in Stalin's view the creation of national schools was an essential step towards the sovietisation of the non-Russians.

At the most basic level, national schools were also needed in order to fulfil the Soviets' obligation to eradicate illiteracy, and this principle informed the strategy of Narkompros, which took over responsibility for national minority education from Narkomnats in July 1918. The Commissar for Enlightenment, A.V. Lunacharskii, was an avid champion of national education (Halevy 1976: 132) and a special Department for the Education of National Minorities was created under Narkompros to promote national schools (GARF, f. 1318, op. 1, d. 1, ll. pp. 46–7). Under Narkompros' proposals, national schools were to be not just confined to the autonomous national territories, but were to be opened 'wherever there exists a sufficient number of pupils of the nationality for the organisation of a school' – a number set at 25 pupils in each grade (*Izvestiia VTsIK* 31 October 1918: 4). Narkompros' practical approach to the education of national minorities was shared by most educationalists and teachers, who ridiculed the idea of 'internationalist' education (*Zhizn' natsional'nostei* 1 June 1919: 2) (though not by all parents, who saw advantages in a Russian language education).

The final group of people to leave their mark on early policies were the so-called 'national communists' – former members of national parties or groups who frequently carried with them a commitment to the Austro-Marxist notion of 'national-cultural autonomy' developed by Otto Bauer and Karl Renner around the turn of the century. Most significant of all were the members of the Jewish socialist Bund, who flocked to the Bolsheviks in their thousands after the revolution. Also influential were the Tatar Jadids centred in Kazan, who believed in the reform of the traditional Islamic education system in order to promote a reformed, secular vision of Islam.

Table 5.1   Native Language Education for Non-Russian Children in the Republic of their own Titular Nationality in December 1927

	Percentage taught only in native language
Soviet Republic	
Ukraine	93.9
Belorussia	90.2
Georgia[a]	98.1
Azerbaijan[a]	95.5
Armenia[a]	88.3
Uzbekistan	96.9
Turkmenistan	93.5
Autonomous Republic	
Kazakhstan	89.1
Kyrgiz	94.9
Bashkiriia	50.0
Buriat-Mongol	45.2
Dagestan (Gortsi)	15.4
Dagestan (Kumiks)	8.9
Karelia (Finnish)	42.2
Crimea (Tatars)	90.6
Volga German	98.2
Tatar	95.7
Chuvash	92.3

Note[a]: Figures are only given for each nationality in the whole of the Transcaucasian federation.

Source: S. M. Dimanshtein (ed.) (1930). *Natsional'naia politika VKP(b)*. Moscow, pp. 278–9.

The number of national schools grew rapidly after the formation of the USSR and the adoption of decisions on the national question at the XII Congress of the Russian Communist Party in 1923 (Dvenadtsatyi s'ezd 1963: 691–7). A flood of decrees forced the adoption of the 'native' language on the republican administration and education system (Martin 1996: 77). The extent of mother-tongue education for nationals living in the Union Republics of the USSR or Autonomous Republics of the RSFSR was considerable. Although some allowance should be made for distortions, deliberate or not, the official statistics shown in Table 5.1 indicate the impressive achievements in this area.

Almost all titular nationality children in the Union Republics were taught in their own language, and the same is true for many of the Autonomous Republics. In others, such as the Buriat Autonomous Republic, the shortage of resources may have contributed to the relatively low level of exclusively mother-tongue education, as would the reluctance of parents to send their children to Buriat-language schools. But the figures may also reflect the presence of a large number of bilingual schools, where children were taught in both the mother tongue and Russian. In the smaller republics where the Russian presence was strongest, a bilingual education accorded with the stated aim of Narkompros that 'the study of the language of the largest population of the given region is to be introduced in the Schools of National Minorities' (*Izvestiia VTsIK* 31 October 1918: 4). This principle was certainly more prevalent in the lower status Votiak, Komi and Mari Autonomous Regions, where bilingual education was at least as widespread as mother-tongue education in 1927 (Dimanshtein 1930: 278–9).

National schools were most widespread for children living in the republic or region named after their own nationality.[1] But Lenin's principle was that each child should receive education in his or her own language wherever he or she lived, and this principle had been affirmed by Narkompros on condition that sufficient children of the given nationality lived in the community. Some effort was made to provide mother-tongue education for such national minorities. From Table 5.1 it is clear that at least Georgians, Armenians and Azeris were all receiving widespread mother-tongue education in each others' republics, while considerable progress was also made for the Abkhaz, Adzhari, Ossetians and other significant nationalities of Transcaucasia. Table 5.2 shows the situation in the other Union Republics and main Autonomous Republics. Although the picture varies enormously, it is clear that in many areas provision of mother tongue education for national minorities was widespread.

In summary, three principles dominated the development of national schools in the 1920s:

1 The Leninist principle that each child should be able to (or, in some versions, should have to) study in his or her own mother tongue.
2 The territorial principle that education should be organised around the standardised language of the titular nationality of each national republic or region.
3 The principle that children should be taught in, or at least should learn up to the level of fluency, both the mother-tongue and the language of the majority nationality of the region.

The reforms of the Stalin years

The history of national schools from 1930 onwards can be seen in terms of the introduction of different overall priorities, which in turn affect the balance of these three principles. At least after 1938, a fourth principle needs to be added:

Table 5.2   Children of National Minorities Receiving Education in their own National Languages in December 1927 (percentage)

REPUBLIC Nationality	In national language	In own and 2nd language	In Russian only	Other
RSFSR				
Belorussians	0.9	7.1	90.5	1.5
Ukrainians	5.5	12.8	81.4	0.3
Latvians	19.6	15.5	61.8	3.1
Poles	4.5	1.4	92.5	1.6
Germans	84.2	5.0	10.5	0.3
Jews (Yiddish)	8.0	3.1	86.6	2.3
Tatars	82.3	8.6	7.5	1.6
Kazakhs	88.6	5.9	4.4	1.1
Kirghiz	90.5	0.2	4.6	4.7
Chuvash	77.6	16.7	5.2	0.5
UKRAINE SSR				
Russians	67.1	14.1	–	18.8
Poles	45.7	6.6	3.9	43.8
Germans	84.6	4.7	3.6	7.1
Jews (Yiddish)	49.6	3.4	19.6	27.4
Moldavians	49.0	14.2	6.2	30.6
BELORUSSIA SSR				
Russians	44.2	22.8	–	33.0
Poles	47.4	0.8	2.4	49.4
Jews (Yiddish)	55.5	1.6	11.5	31.4
UZBEK SSR				
Russians	94.6	4.8	–	0.6
Jews (Yiddish)	62.3	–	31.9	5.8
Tatars	30.4	9.1	25.2	35.3
Armenians	33.0	6.8	59.1	1.1
Turkmens	33.0	–	–	67.0
Kazakhs	63.7	1.4	1.1	33.8
Tadzhiks	74.1	4.7	0.2	21.0
TURKMEN SSR				
Russians	85.7	14.2	–	0.1
Armenians	25.6	20.5	49.1	4.8
Turks	72.9	9.6	1.7	15.8
Uzbeks	70.2	7.6	1.6	20.6
KYRGIZ ASSR				
Russians	97.7	1.7	–	0.6
Uzbeks	85.5	–	1.7	12.8
Ukrainians	–	–	98.3	1.7
CRIMEAN ASSR				
Tatars	90.6	7.4	1.9	0.1
Russians	93.6	4.3	–	2.1
Jews (Yiddish)	10.0	9.7	78.4	1.9

Ukrainians	1.9	–	96.6	1.5
TATAR ASSR				
Russians	96.6	2.8	–	0.6
Chuvash	71.7	20.6	6.4	1.3

Source: *Natsional'naia Politika VKP(b)*, pp. 278–9.

4 The demands of internationalism, Soviet patriotism and communication require each child to be fluent in, or taught exclusively in, the dominant Soviet language – Russian.

This change in direction can be traced to the late 1920s. In particular, the content of education, particularly in the history curriculum, had changed considerably, with attacks on the national intelligentsia and the rewriting of the history of Russian imperialism (for example, Subtelny 1988: 417).

But it was the compulsory introduction of the study of the Russian language in 1938 which is the clearest indication of a change in policy. The law 'On the compulsory study of the Russian language in schools of national republics and regions' which was passed by the Council of People's Commissars of the USSR on 13 March 1938, was a clear break with the Leninist principle that nobody should be forced to study the language of the dominant nationality, and has usually been identified as a russifying policy. Coming as it did on top of a whole range of reversals in national policies in the 1930s, the 1938 law certainly has to be seen as a step towards the promotion of a single, Russian-led Soviet identity. But the immediate impact of the law on national schools should not be exaggerated. Russian was being introduced as a subject of study, not the language of instruction (Konstantinov 1958: 11). The third 5-year-plan of 1939 allowed for the expansion of the network of national schools beyond that for Russians (Konstantinov 1958: 12). Implementation of the teaching of Russian at *all* grades was not immediate – in Armenia this took until 1957, while as late as 1975 only nine of the Union Republics of the USSR were teaching Russian from the first grade (Alpatov 1997: 104). There is some evidence of an early decline in the national school: according to Soviet sources, in 1934 school books were being produced in 104 languages (Konstantinov 1958: 11), but in 1955 instruction was being carried out in just 59 languages, 45 of them in the RSFSR (Lipset 1967: 181). Still, in the 1955–56 school year, the last for which comprehensive statistics are available for the Soviet Union as a whole, 35 per cent of pupils were being taught in languages other than Russian. But while in the RSFSR only 10 per cent of schools gave instruction in non-Russian languages to 6 per cent of the pupils, in the other Union Republics the levels of non-Russian education came much closer to the proportion of non-Russians in the population, as Table 5.3 illustrates.

Table 5.3   Instruction in Russian and other Languages in the 1955–56 School Year

	Percentage of schools with instruction in languages other than Russian	Percentage of pupils taught in Russian	Percentage taught in other languages	Number of languages used for instruction
USSR total	41	65	35	59
RSFSR	10	94	6	45
Ukrainian SSR	86	26	74	5
Belorussian SSR	95	22	78	2
Uzbek SSR	94	20	80	7
Kazakh SSR	57	66	34	6
Georgian SSR	93	20	80	6
Azerbaijan SSR	95	23	77	4
Lithuanian SSR	97	11	89	3
Moldavian SSR	73	33	67	3
Latvian SSR	79	33	67	2
Kyrgiz SSR	81	49	51	5
Tadzhik SSR	98	16	84	6
Armenian SSR	95	9	91	4
Turkmen SSR	93	21	79	4
Estonian SSR	94	22	78	2

Source: Harry Lipset (1967). 'The Status of National Minority Languages in Soviet Education' in *Soviet Studies*, vol. 21, no. 2, p. 181.

After this, the picture becomes murkier, with contradictory evidence pointing in different directions. Reliable data becomes remarkably scarce: so scant was information on national education that one Western writer could claim in the 1960s that 'it is very difficult to determine the language of instruction in universities and technical institutes' (Bilinsky 1962: 157, note 89). As late as 1984, there were official complaints at the highest levels about the lack of information regarding national schools (Kirkwood 1991: 68). On the one hand, sources point to the widespread decline and even disappearance of national schools for many national-ities. On the other hand, there are not only conflicting figures, but also continuing official pronouncements on the desirability of national schools, not least from the mouths of Brezhnev and Gorbachev, and census evidence on the perseverance of national languages and low levels of fluency in Russian. While the absence of official statistics and unofficial misinformation are mostly to blame for these contradictions, confusion and alternative interpretations regarding the extent of the decline of the national school can also be ascribed to lack of clarity arising from attempts to paint an overall picture without taking into account major differences:

- between schools for national groups inside and outside their own territories;
- between the RSFSR and the Union Republics;
- between different Union Republics;
- between town and country.

The 1958 education reform

The key piece of legislation affecting national schools in the postwar years is contained in the education reform of 1958–59. The nineteenth thesis on education approved by the Central Committee of the CPSU and the USSR Council of Ministers on 12 November 1958 includes the following recommendation:

> we must note that in the area of language study in the schools of the Union and autonomous republics children are considerably overloaded. It is a fact that in the nationality schools children study three languages – their native tongue, Russian and one of the foreign languages.
>
> The question ought to be considered of giving parents the right to send their children to a school where the language of their choice is used. If a child attends a school where instruction is conducted in the language of one of the Union or autonomous republics, he may, if he wishes, take up the Russian language. And vice versa, if a child attends a Russian school, he may, if he so desires, study the language of one of the Union or autonomous republics. To be sure, this step could only be taken if there is a sufficient number of children to form classes for instruction in a given language.
>
> To grant parents the right to decide what language a child should study as a compulsory subject would be a most democratic procedure. It would eliminate arbitrary decisions in this important matter and would make possible the termination of the practice of overloading children with language study. Permission should be granted not to include a foreign language among the required subjects in schools where appropriate conditions do not exist.
>
> (Bilinsky 1962: 139)

On the surface, this 'most democratic procedure' allowed parents the right for their children not to have to learn Russian any more, just as much as it gave them the right not to have to study in the local language. But the practical implication is clear: pupils who at present study three languages in the timetable are disadvantaged compared with those (Russians in Russia) who only study two. The study of a foreign language cannot be dropped (except where 'appropriate conditions do not exist') so for non-Russian children either the mother tongue or Russian ought to be dropped if the child is to get on level terms. This would certainly lead to a decline in the number of Russian children studying the titular language of their republic, and the same might be expected of non-Russians whose parents saw knowledge of Russian as essential to their children's advancement and access to higher education.

At least 'thesis 19' was regarded as an attack on the status of non-Russian languages in the Union republics themselves. In the debates surrounding the theses, representatives of the Transcaucasian and Baltic republics were strong enough in their opposition that these provisions were omitted from the all-Union law, and instead were left for the Union and Autonomous Republics to implement. The failure of Latvia and Azerbaijan to do so led to the direct intervention of Moscow and contributed to subsequent purges at the highest levels of the government and Communist Parties of those republics (Bilinsky 1962: 140–7).

The actual impact of the reform is a matter of controversy. There is clear evidence that the number of Russian-language schools increased shortly after the reforms at least in Ukraine and Kyrgizia (Bilinsky 1962: 151). Within the RSFSR, it is claimed that the number of languages of instruction declined from 47 in the early 1960s to 17 in 1982, 12 of which were only taught as far as the fourth grade (Alpatov 1997: 114). Among the nationalities to lose their schools entirely were significant territorial peoples such as Karelians (Finns), Kabardi, Balkars, Kalmyks, Adygei, Cherkess, and smaller peoples like Mansi and Eskimos (Lewis 1986: 83). Another source claims that in the whole of the North Caucasus non-Russian education persisted only in rural areas of Dagestan, and then only for the elementary grades (Alpatov 1997: 114). Of the nationalities of the RSFSR that continued to have national schools, only Bashkir and Tatar children were able to receive education across all ten grades; in the Tuva and Yakut Autonomous Republics, the national languages were in use up to the eighth grade; elsewhere, not beyond the fourth grade (Kuznetsov and Chekoeva 1982: 13). In all, by 1975 96 per cent of pupils in the RSFSR were being taught exclusively in Russian, according to official sources (Prokof'ev 1975: 20).

That entire sets of national schools should disappear as a result of parental choice in the wake of the 1958 reform not only goes against what would be expected, but defies the facts. Karelia lost its Karelian language schools in the war years, and Finnish schools in the two years immediately preceding the 1958 reform as a matter of specific policy unconnected to the reform (Austin 1992: 32–3). In the Kabardino-Balkar Autonomous Soviet Socialist Republic, all teaching was converted to Russian by decree, not parental choice in the 1965–66 school year (Lewis 1986: 81). The fact that Tatar education was not only left alone but, according to Soviet sources, more than tripled at the middle school level between 1965 and 1975 (Kuznetsov and Chekoeva 1982: 11), indicates that the attack on national schools was highly selective. If the 1958 reform was indeed aimed against the national school, it has to be seen as one part of a drawn out and more deliberate campaign as far as the RSFSR is concerned.

In the other Union Republics of the USSR, the picture is different. While the number of languages in use in schools declined (from 22 to seven in the Uzbek SSR between 1939 and 1962) (Alpatov 1997: 114), national schools for the titular nationalities continued to flourish in spite of some evidence of decline. Harry Lipset has produced figures based on the publication of school textbooks to show that not only were large numbers of pupils receiving mother-tongue education in the republican language at all grades in 1964, but that the number of Russian pupils studying the languages of the Union Republics actually increased between 1959 and 1964 (Lipset 1967: 183–4, 188). According to the then Minister of Education of the USSR in 1975, M. A. Prokof'ev, out of the 43.1 million pupils in the USSR, 35.7 per cent were receiving instruction in languages other than Russian (Prokof'ev 1975: 20), slightly up on the figure for 1955–56.

The state of the national school in the late Soviet period

While these sources are not altogether reliable, Western impressions of the decline of the national school in the Union Republics are likely to have been exaggerated, in the absence of overall statistics, by anecdotal evidence from particular regions. Most significantly, there is a clear difference in the persistence of national schools between urban and rural areas. Thus in the 1980s, 80 per cent of schools in the whole of Ukraine used Ukrainian as the main language of instruction against 20 per cent using Russian, but in the capital city of Kiev the proportions were reversed (Grant 1983: 28). As well as the preponderance of the ethnic Russian population in the major cities of Ukraine, we can also assume that the natural processes of assimilation would be more rapid in cities than in the countryside given parental choice and, in any case, a significant number of declared 'Ukrainian' city-dwellers already used Russian as their first language. A second factor producing a biased impression is the undue focus on the large Slavic nationalities – Ukrainians and Belarusans. It has been suggested that natural assimilationist tendencies will be strongest here, where the languages are closest to Russian (Alpatov 1997: 110–11) but, equally, it may reflect an official decision by the Soviet authorities to concentrate russifying efforts on the Slavic peoples while allowing the non-Slavs a freer national development. In any case, the Western visitor to one of the major cities of Ukraine or Belarus in the Brezhnev era may well have gained a false impression of the status of national schools in the USSR as a whole.

This is not to say that there was not a real decline in national schools in the Union Republics, and again there are contradictory statistics and the use of different languages of instruction at different levels clouds the picture – Alpatov claims that at the beginning of the 1980s only one middle school in the whole of the Belarusan SSR offered Belarusan language instruction across the whole cycle of education, but says nothing about the use of Belarusan only at early levels of the schools system (Alpatov 1997: 110). The same source points out the frequent changes in language policy which further cloud the picture – the language of advertisements on the Kiev metro was changed four times in the 1970s and 1980s (Alpatov 1997: 111).

But for most of the Brezhnev period at least the national school appears to have remained in favour. The official policy in the Union Republics was to promote bilingualism. Karen Collias has shown how in the Brezhnev era this was part of a broader policy of promoting national identities as a kind of subset and stepping stone towards a broader, multi-ethnic Soviet identity. The formal educational system was the primary vehicle by which Soviet patriotism and socialist internationalism were presented to youth during the Brezhnev era. The content of education, which was permeated with ritual, presented young people with the preferred behaviour patterns of the young patriot and internationalist in a personalised manner, emphasising the importance of a young person's local, ethnic, regional and republic identities as building blocks toward the desired goal of Soviet patriotism. Thus, patriotic and internationalist socialisation did not preclude the properly channelled expression of different ethnic identities within the framework of the Soviet identity it aimed to create (Collias 1990: 79–80).

This interpretation is in full accord with the public statements of leading politicians in the Brezhnev era. Brezhnev himself, speaking at a joint meeting of the Central Committee of the Communist Party of Kazakhstan and the Supreme Soviet of the Kazakh SSR in Alma-Ata in 1973, went out of his way to stress that the forging of a new Soviet people did not mean bringing an end to national development:

> our party reached an important conclusion, that as a result of the deep and all-embracing socio-political changes spanning half a century, a new historical community of peoples has been established here – the Soviet people (*sovetskii narod*). The history of the establishment and development of Soviet Kazakhstan is the clearest confirmation of that [prolonged applause]. When speaking of the new historical community of peoples, we do not mean at all that national differences are fading away here or, even more, that the fusion of nations has occurred. All nations and peoples inhabiting the Soviet Union preserve their distinctiveness, the traits of their national character, their language, their better traditions. They have at their disposal every possibility of securing the even greater flourishing of their national culture.
>
> (Brezhnev 1974: 242–3)

Accordingly, national schools were to be preserved, but the compulsory teaching of Russian as the common language of this 'new historical community of peoples' was to be strengthened. Table 5.4 shows the total number of classes per week, spread over all ten school grades, devoted to the study of Russian language and literature in national schools of some of the Union Republics in 1975.

Apart from the first grades in some republics, the number of classes was spread fairly evenly across grades, with the study of literature taking over from the study of language in the later grades – so roughly speaking four to five classes per grade per week for most children. By contrast, Ukrainian children had 61–2 classes per week over all 10 grades devoted to Ukrainian language and literature, while for Russian children 71 classes per week were devoted to the study of their own language and literature. Nevertheless, children in national schools were, in effect, studying one more major subject than their Russian counterparts, and this was made up for by a longer school week, longer school year (by one week), and slightly fewer hours devoted to less important subjects like nature study (Dunstan 1978: 35–7). Although the actual number of classes devoted to the study of Russian was not excessive by any means, the teaching of Russian in national schools was taken so seriously that a series of conferences on the subject were held in Tashkent (*Russkii iazyk v natsional'noi shkole* 1975: 2) and an entire journal, *Russkii iazik v natsional'noi shkole*, was devoted to it.

One innovative way of promoting the development of a combined national and Soviet identity among children was the creation of 'bilingual' or 'integrated' schools, popular in the 1960s. Russian children and children of the titular nationality would attend separate classes in the same school so, while all children were taught in their mother-tongue, they would mingle in

Table 5.4 Number of Classes per Week Devoted to the Study of Russian Language and Literature in National Schools of some of the Union Republics of the USSR, 1975

Union Republic	Classes/week (over all 10 grades)
Ukrainian SSR	40.5
Belarusan SSR	46.5
Moldovian SSR	41
Kyrgiz SSR	51.5
Latvian SSR	48*
Estonian SSR	43*
Lithuanian SSR	42*
All other SSRs	41–51

*Note:** in the Baltic Republics, classes spread over 11 grades.

Source: M. A. Prokof'ev (1975). 'Russkii iazyk v natsional'noi shkole i doshkol'nykh uchrezhdeniiakh' in *Russkii iazyk v natsional'noi shkole*, no.6, p. 21.

out-of-class activities and thereby develop a spirit of community at the same time as improving their skills in the other language. There were 247 such schools catering for one-third of children in Latvia in 1966; 24 per cent of children in Azerbaijan attended bilingual schools in 1968/69, and one-third of children in the Kyrgiz SSR in 1978. In practice, Russian was the only common language of the two groups of children, and the experiment did not succeed in promoting ethnic harmony and declined towards the beginning of the 1980s (Karklins 1986: 105–7, 124).

The number of hours devoted to the study of Russian, while not excessive, ought in certain circumstances to be sufficient for the pupil to have a good mastery of the language by the time of leaving school.[2] And yet standards of spoken and written Russian on the part of other nationalities were never as high as the authorities would have liked. No wonder, then, that the Red Army was seen as a 'second school' where non-Russian conscripts devoted a good deal of time to the study of Russian. An attempt was made to improve the situation by the centralisation of Russian-language teaching under one body (NII PRIaNSh – Research Institute for the Teaching of Russian Language in the National School) in 1975, and the production of a 'Model Programme of Russian Language for the Secondary National School' in 1979. This single programme replaced the language-specific ones developed over many years by linguistic specialists (Kirkwood 1991: 66).

These reforms, however, do not appear to have done much to improve levels of aptitude in the Russian language. In 1984 a further school reform aimed at producing school leavers who were all fluent in Russian was never really implemented (Kirkwood 1991: 67). In the Gorbachev era, there was no change away from the official policy of promoting bilingualism, but a more conciliatory tone was adopted. Thus, symbolically, the formula 'Russian-national bilingualism' was reversed in 1988 to 'national-Russian bilingualism' (Kirkwood 1991: 72). But in the more open atmosphere a whole range of criticisms were aired against the implementation of education in national schools as well as against the policy itself. In particular, complaints were made about the lack of comprehensive statistical information on national schools, and also about the lack of resources for teaching both the national language and Russian. For the first time, the whole principle of bilingualism came under fire: Mati Hint claimed that what was actually being produced was 'semilingualism' and 'semiculture'. Others argued that the policy was leading to lower levels of literacy in any language, and that a bilingual education from an early age could cause psychological difficulties in the child (Kirkwood 1991: 73).

What became clear in the *glasnost'* era was that the official policy in national schools was not altogether successful in producing bilingual children. But this should already have been obvious from the censuses of 1970 and 1979, and was reinforced by the census of 1989. Although there are clearly problems with the returns to these censuses (Tishkov 1997: 87–95),

Table 5.5 Percentage of Major Nationalities of the Soviet Union Claiming Fluency in Russian as a Second Language, and Proportion Giving Language of own Nationality as First Language, in 1970 and 1979

Nationality	Percentage claiming fluent Russian as second language		Percentage giving language of own nationality as first language	
	1970	*1979*	*1970*	*1979*
Russian	0.1	0.1	99.8	99.9
Ukrainian	36.3	49.8	85.7	82.8
Belarusan	49.0	57.0	80.6	74.2
Uzbek	14.5	49.3	98.6	98.5
Kazakh	41.8	52.3	98.0	97.5
Tadzhik	15.4	29.6	98.5	97.8
Turkmen	15.4	25.4	98.9	98.7
Kyrgiz	19.1	29.4	98.8	97.9
Azerbaijani	16.6	29.5	98.2	97.9
Armenian	30.1	38.6	91.4	90.7
Georgian	21.3	26.7	98.4	98.3
Lithuanian	35.9	52.1	97.9	97.9
Latvian	45.2	56.7	95.2	95.0
Estonian	29.0	24.2	95.5	95.3
Moldavian	36.1	47.4	95.0	93.2
Tatar	62.5	68.9	89.2	85.9
Chuvash	58.4	64.8	86.9	81.7
Dagestan peoples	41.7	60.3	96.5	95.9
Bashkir	53.3	64.9	66.2	67.2
Mordvin	65.7	65.5	77.8	78.6

Source: Grant, N. (1983). 'Linguistic and Ethnic Minorities in the USSR: Educational Policies and Developments' in J. J. Tomiak (ed.) *Soviet Education in the 1980s*. London and Canberra, p. 44.

they indicate much lower levels of knowledge of Russian than would have been expected. The successive reforms of 1938, 1958, 1975 and 1984 have all been interpreted as the product of russifying (or at least sovietising) policies which were restricting more and more the activities of national schools and promoting the Russian language at the expense of national languages. Undoubtedly, universal knowledge of Russian was the primary aim of these reforms. And yet, they seem to have failed: although declared fluency in Russian improved between 1970 and 1979 among the non-Russians of both the Union Republics and the RSFSR (Table 5.5), it declined again between 1979 and 1989. Thus the declared level of knowledge of fluent Russian amongst Uzbeks and Karakalpaks more than halved in this period – from 49.6 per cent to 23.8 per cent for Uzbeks, and from 41.1 per cent to 20.7 per cent for Karakalpaks (Alpatov 1997: 101).[3] However it is looked at, the levels of knowledge of Russian are lower than would be expected given not just the attention paid to Russian in the education system, but also the amount of day to day exposure to the Russian language through media such as television. The overall figures, if they are to be trusted, are remarkable. Of the titular nationalities of the Union Republics, only among the Ukrainians, Belarusans, Moldavians, Latvians and Kazakhs do more than half the titular population claim knowledge of Russian. Less than a third of Azerbaijanis, Georgians, Tajiks, Turkmens and Uzbeks living in their own republics claimed knowledge of Russian. Even inside the RSFSR, where the language of instruction is supposedly Russian in most grades outside of Tatarstan and Bashkortostan, a surprising number of people reported no knowledge of Russian – only among Karelians, Komi, Udmurts and Kalmyks did over 90 per cent of people in their own autonomous republics claim a knowledge of Russian (Tishkov 1997: 90–5, taken from *SSSR: Etnicheskii sostav naseleniia SSSR* 1991).

While allowance has to be made for the statistically significant older generations who are included in these figures but whose education predates one or more of the reforms, the fact is that the teaching of Russian to non-Russian children has been less effective than has generally been supposed. Certainly anecdotal accounts support this possibility. The ease with which the national language has been reintroduced to schools since the collapse of communism reinforces the belief that large numbers of national schools had persisted in areas where they were supposedly extinct. Already by 1992 it was reported that 70 per cent of elementary schools in the Kabardino-Balkar republic were operating in the national languages (Alpatov 1997: 142) – an astonishing achievement if it is really the case that no such schools operated between 1965 and 1991. A total of 48 languages are now being used as the language of instruction in the Russian Federation (one more than in 1960), and while most of the autonomous republics have maintained a commitment to bilingual education in schools, preference is generally given to the national languages, especially at the earliest levels (Guboglo 1994). In the Newly Independent States, the transition to a single language has not been a problem in terms of educational facilities for the titular nationalities (although it is a different story for the Russian population of the independent states).

Conclusion

A number of factors may account for the persistence of national schools. First, a false impression has been obtained by an exclusive focus on urban areas. Secondly, parent preference for native language schools has remained strong: an opinion survey of 1979 among Moldavians, Estonians, Uzbeks and Georgians showed that most members of each of these nationalities thought children should be taught only in the native language, especially so in rural areas (Karklins 1986: 105), while a 1994 survey found that 87 per cent of (North) Ossetians and 88 per cent of Tatars wanted their children to be taught in their national languages (Dimitrenko 1995: 198). Such attitudes on the part of parents are likely to rub off on children, whose approach to the study of Russian may therefore be unenthusiastic. Thirdly, there may have been a problem with the availability of qualified staff and materials contributing to a poor standard of teaching Russian. Bureaucratically decreeing a reform in education is a long way from implementing it, or providing the trained staff and textbook materials. Constant references in the later Soviet period to the need to train staff properly, and vociferous complaints in the era of *glasnost'* about the shortage of adequate teaching materials support this possibility. Fourthly, the reforms of the 1920s went so far that, once established, the national school would become a permanent feature. If Stalin's language law of 1938 was designed at weakening minority nationalism and promoting the dominant role of Russian, then it came too late. Within a few years the Soviet Union was at war, and the attitude towards non-Russians was relaxed considerably in order to secure support for the war effort. Subsequent reforms were aimed less at attacking the nationalities as promoting an all-Soviet identity held together by the Russian language, but were not implemented forcefully enough to overcome either direct resistance or the difficulties of reversing an established trend. Failure effectively to carry out these reforms at a local level implies a level of consensus and, moreover, organised opposition to them in smaller communities. Fifthly, by analogy with other aspects of the Soviet system, and in particular the economy, it is perfectly possible that local education officials, unable or unwilling to implement the required reforms in full, have misreported the true situation to their superiors. Thus the lack of official figures on national schools after the 1930s may in part be due to uncertainty on the part of the authorities as to the accuracy of their own data, and at any rate this factor makes official data unreliable.

Putting these possibilities together, we may conclude that national schools have continued to play a prominent part in the life of the nationalities of the Soviet Union, including the minorities within the RSFSR, throughout the Soviet period. They have played a major role in preserving the national languages and preventing the spread of the Russian language. This effect is mostly confined to compact rural communities. Data indicating that national identity and national language retention is much stronger in rural than in urban communities lends support to this hypothesis. The introduction of educational reforms in small, remote and homogenous communities would have been met by problems of a shortage of suitable personnel as well as parental and educational resistance – but such problems would not necessarily have been reported. Resistance to the perceived 'russification' of schools in such areas need not necessarily signify a high level of nationalism so much as a resistance to change and adherence to tradition. But the links with national identity, in both directions, are clear. Such communities may account for a relatively small part of the overall population of the Soviet Union, so that the statistical effect, while significant, is not massive. But, if these conclusions are correct, they would suggest a level of civic coherence and organisation at a very local level that is generally assumed not to have existed under communism.

Notes

1 Here I leave aside the more complex question of non-titular republics (Dagestan, Crimea) and the republics where the titular nationality was non-dominant numerically or subject to unclear definitions (Bashkiriia, Karelia).
2 By comparison, for example, with the teaching of the English language in Finland, where school teaching is reinforced by frequent exposure to the language out of school, most notably in the cinema and television.
3 Alpatov concurs with Baskakov in seeing the 1979 figures as too high.

References

Alpatov, V. (1997). *150 iazykov i politika 1917–1997*. Moscow: Institut Vostokovedeniia RAN.
Austin, P. (1992). 'Soviet Karelian: The Language That Failed' *Slavic Review*, vol. 51, no. 1, spring.
Bilinsky, Y. (1962). 'The Soviet Education Laws of 1958–59 and Soviet Nationality Policy' *Soviet Studies*, vol. 14, no. 2, pp. 138–57.
Brezhnev, L. (1974). *Leninskim kursom*, vol. 4, Moscow: Izdatel'stvo politicheskoi literatury.
Carrère d'Encausse, H. (1992). *The Great Challenge: Nationalities and the Bolshevik State, 1917–1930*. New York: Holmes and Meier.
Collias, K. (1990). 'Making Soviet Citizens: Patriotic and Internationalist Education in the Formation of a Soviet State Identity' in H. Huttenbach (ed.) *Soviet Nationality Policies: Ruling Ethnic Groups in the USSR*, pp. 73–93.
Dimanshtein, S. (ed.) (1930) *Natsional'naia politika VKP(b) v tsifrakh*. Moscow: Izdatel'stvo kommunisticheskoi akademii.
Dmitrenko, L. (1995). 'Ustanovki i real'noe iazykovoe povedenie molodezhi v respublikakh Rossiiskoi Federatsii (na primere Tatarstana i Severnoi Ossetii)' in L. Drobizheva and T. Guzenkova (eds) *Suverenitet i etnicheskoe samosoznanie: ideologiia i praktika*. Moscow: Institut etnologii i antropologii RAN, pp. 193–202.
Dunstan, J. (1978). *Paths to Excellence and the Soviet School*. Slough: Humanities Press.
Dvenadtsatyi s"ezd RKP(b), 17–25 aprelia goda 1923 – stenograficheskii otchet (1963) Moscow: Izdatel'stvo politicheskoi literatury, pp. 691–7.
Gosudarstvennyi Arkhiv Rossiiskoi Federatsii (GARF), f. 1318, op. 1, d. 1, ll. pp. 46–7.
Grant, N. (1983). 'Linguistic and Ethnic Minorities in the USSR: Educational Policies and Developments' in J. Tomiak (ed.) *Soviet Education in the 1980s*. London: Croom Helm, pp. 24–49.
Guboglo, M. (ed.) (1994). *Perelomnye gody. Tom 2. Iazykovaia reforma – 1989. Dokumenty i materialy*. Moscow: Institut etnologii i antropologii RAN.
Halevy, Z. (1976). *Jewish Schools under Czarism and Communism*. New York: Springer.
Izvestiia VTsIK, 31 October 1918.

Karklins, R. (1986). *Ethnic Relations in the USSR œ The Perspective from Below*. Boston: Allen and Unwin.

Kirkwood, M. (1991). '*Glasnost*', 'The National Question' and Soviet Language Policy' in *Soviet Studies*, vol. 43, no. 1, pp. 61–81.

Konstantinov, N. (1958). 'Osnovnye voprosy stroitel'stva natsional'noi shkoly za 40 let sovetskoi vlasti' in A. Burtakov (ed.) *Natsional'nye shkoly RSFSR za 40 let*. Moscow: Akademiia pedagogicheskikh nauk RSFSR, pp. 5–13.

Kuznetsov, G. and Chekoeva, S. (1982). 'Natsional'naia shkola RSFSR v sovremennykh usloviiakh' *Sovetskaia pedagogika*, no. 11, pp. 10–15.

Lenin, V. (1958–65). *Polnoe sobranie sochinenii*. (Fifth edition), vols. XXIV, XXXII and XLVIII, Moscow: Politizdat.

Lewis, G. (1986). 'Bilingualism as Language Planning in the Soviet Union' in J. Tomiak (ed.) *Western Perspectives on Soviet Education in the 1980s*. London: Macmillan (now Palgrave), pp. 75–96.

Lipset, H. (1967). 'The Status of National Minority Languages in Soviet Education' *Soviet Studies*, vol. 19, no. 2, pp. 181–9.

Martin, T. (1996). 'An Affirmative Action Empire: Ethnicity and the Soviet State, 1923–1938' unpublished PhD dissertation, University of Chicago.

Pipes, R. (1964). *The Formation of the Soviet Union: Communism and Nationalism 1917–1923*. Cambridge MA: Harvard University Press.

Prokof'ev, M. (1975). 'Russkii iazyk v natsional'noi shkole i doshkol'nykh uchrezhdeniiakh' *Russkii iazyk v natsional'noi shkole*, no. 6, pp. 18–26.

Russkii iaiyk v natsional'noi shkole, no. 6, 1975.

Smith, J. (1997). 'The Origins of Soviet National Autonomy' *Revolutionary Russia*, vol. 10, no. 2, December, pp. 62–84.

SSSR: Etnicheskii sostav naseleniia SSSR (1991). Moscow: Finansy i statistika.

Stalin, I. (1946 ff.). *Sochineniia*. vol. IV, Moscow: Politizdat.

Subtelny, O. (1988). *Ukraine: a History*. Toronto: University of Toronto Press.

Tishkov, V. (1997). *Ethnicity, Nationalism and Conflict in and after the Soviet Union: The Mind Aflame*. London: Sage.

Wilson, A. (1997). *Ukrainian Nationalism in the 1990s: A Minority Faith*. Cambridge: Cambridge University Press.

Zhizn' Natsional'nostei. (1918). no. 3, 24 November.

Zhizn' Natsional'nostei. (1919). no. 28, 1 June.

6
Ethnic Minorities in the Czech Education System: Before and After Transition (1945–97)[1]

David Čaněk

Introduction

The Czech lands (Bohemia, Moravia and Silesia) have a rich history of inter-ethnic conflicts over schooling, perhaps the most pronounced being that between Czechs and German-speakers in the nineteenth and first half of the twentieth centuries. The events of the Second World War, and the subsequent expulsion of practically the entire three-million strong community of Germans from Czechoslovakia, brought an end to the fragile coexistence of the two groups. This meant also an end to the highly developed German-language education system that had existed in inter-war Czechoslovakia (Mitter 1991: 214). The Holocaust and, to an even greater extent, the expulsion of Germans who resided mainly in the Czech lands, turned the latter into an almost ethnically homogenous region. Whereas in 1930 only 68.4 per cent of inhabitants of the Czech lands declared themselves to be ethnic Czechs, in 1950 as many as 93.8 per cent did so (*Demografická příručka* 1982: 48).

However, even such a dramatic decrease in the proportion of ethnic minorities in the general population did not make issues pertaining to their schooling disappear. In this chapter I will trace the position of the Polish, Slovak, German and Romany minorities in the Czech education system from 1945 to roughly 1997, and focus on the specific educational policies developed for them by the state (if applicable) as well as on the educational accomplishments of members of the named minorities. Particular attention is paid to the ways in which the four minorities were affected by the democratic transition of 1989.

Ethnic minorities of the Czech lands: recognition and policies of the state

In this section I give a brief account of public policies developed for particular ethnic minorities. It is clear that the attitude of the state towards minorities is of vital importance, if one intends to study their position in the education system. In a highly centralised education system of a country such as the former Czechoslovak Socialist Republic, or even the independent Czech Republic, the power of the state in education was and continues to be very significant.

The Second World War represented a major rupture in many respects, and it obviously also affected minorities in postwar Czechoslovakia. In the Czech lands, the German and Polish ethnic groups were perceived as traitors by many, due perhaps to the fact that both minorities were used by Germany and Poland respectively to help dismantle pre-war Czechoslovakia. Thus, Czech politicians after liberation stressed that in the new state, members of minorities would no longer have any special rights that they had held in pre-war Czechoslovakia (Staněk 1991: 260).

Indeed, the 1948 Constitution stated that socialist Czechoslovakia was a state of the Czech and Slovak nations, making no reference to minorities. In the Czech lands these were the remnant of the German ethnic group and the Poles, as far as the 'historical' minorities are concerned. In addition, there were the (mainly) immigrant Slovak and Romany minority groups, whose members came from Slovakia to find housing and employment in industrial centres located mainly in the border areas of the Czech lands left depopulated after the expulsion of the Sudeten Germans.

The restrictive approach of the state administration to ethnic minorities, however, soon gave way to a policy that was, at least to a limited extent, more welcoming. This concerned mainly the Polish, but partly also the German, minorities. As far as the former is concerned, the rebuilding of schools with Polish as the language of instruction started as early as 1945. By the mid-1950s, Polish-speakers could communicate in their mother tongue with local authorities of the Těšín region (in which they were concentrated) (Borák 1997: 29).

The remnant of the German minority was in a much more difficult situation. It was as late as 1953 that all persons of German ethnic origin who permanently resided on Czechoslovak territory were re-granted Czechoslovak citizenship. Unlike the Polish minority, it was out of the question that German speakers would be allowed to communicate in their mother tongue with local authorities. On the other hand, in some areas special German-language courses were offered to pupils of German nationality from the early 1950s, which signified a partial departure from an overtly assimilationist policy in regard to this minority.

With the federalisation of Czechoslovakia and its subdivision into the Czech and Slovak Socialist Republics in 1969, a new constitutional act on national minorities came into force (Borák 1997: 29). The German minority was granted official recognition and the official status of the Polish, Hungarian and Ukrainian (Russyn) minorities was reconfirmed.[2] The act signified a certain rupture with the previous approach. From 1969 on, national minorities were granted collective rights. These concerned the areas of education, language and culture as well as proportional representation in elected bodies. On the level of practical policy the change was not as dramatic, however, since special linguistic measures accommodating the specific needs of the Polish minority in the Czech lands and the Hungarian and Ukrainian (Russyn) minorities in Slovakia were implemented from the early 1950s onward.

Ironically, the Slovak minority in the Czech lands – the greatest ethnic minority there (see Table 6.1) – had never been officially recognised as a national minority by Czechoslovak authorities. Its members had to wait for such a status until 1993, when the independent Czech Republic was established. The Romany ethnic group was granted official recognition as a national minority only after the democratic changes of 1989. The communist authorities treated Roma as a backward social group and attempted to assimilate them completely with the dominant population.

The collective character of minority rights was abandoned with the democratic changes, and formally cancelled in 1991. Instead, the individual rights of members of national minorities were introduced. The effects of this particular change for the education of minority pupils were not very significant. This does not mean, of course, that ethnic minorities – at least some of them – were not critically affected by the democratic changes, or later by the dissolution of Czechoslovakia, as far as their schooling is concerned.

The Polish minority

The resurrection of Polish minority schools in northern Moravia was started in the immediate postwar period. After the settlement of some bilateral controversies over the Těšín region between Poland and Czechoslovakia, a

Table 6.1   Main Nationalities in the Czech Lands (per cent)

Year	Czech	Slovak	Polish	German	Romany[3]
1930	68.4	0.4	0.9	29.5	0.0
1950	93.8	2.9	0.8	1.8	–
1970	94.5	3.3	0.7	0.8	–
1991	94.8	3.1	0.6	0.5	0.3

Source: *Demografická příručka* (1982), p. 48 and from Frištenská and Sulitka (1994), pp. 13–14.

Treaty on Friendship and Mutual Aid was signed by the two countries in 1947, which also enhanced the progress of Polish minority schools (Šindelka 1975: 118–23). The diverse structure of these schools, ranging from kindergartens to educational institutions at the secondary level, was not an invention of the communist regime itself: the tradition of highly developed schooling in Polish language reaches back into the Czechoslovak state of the inter-war period (Šrajerová 1996: 143). In any case, communist officials started to promote Polish minority schools after 1948 when they seized power in Czechoslovakia.

The Polish ethnic group of northern Moravia is concentrated mainly in the Těšín region, which borders on Poland, and can be described as an historical (autochthonous) minority residing on an enclosed territory. The fact that members of the Polish minority in the Těšín region live next to Poland helps them to maintain their ethnic culture, yet this has also, in the past, been the cause of a constant security risk for the Czechoslovak state. In the same way that Nazi Germany used Sudeten Germans to help it destroy Czechoslovakia, Poland used the Polish minority for its efforts to annex the Těšín region. The dispute over the Těšín area, which in the end stayed Czechoslovak, and later Czech territory, was settled only after the diplomatic intervention of the Soviet Union following the Second World War.

The prevalence of friendly relations between the two neighbouring states of the communist bloc, Poland and Czechoslovakia, from the 1950s on was also reflected in the generous treatment of the Polish minority in northern Moravia, as far as education is concerned. The Czechoslovak and, after the federalisation of 1969, Czech Ministry of Education funded not only kindergartens, elementary[4] and secondary schools with Polish as the language of instruction, but also appropriate textbooks and periodicals for use in the classroom. Naturally, the price was complete loyalty to the communist regime (as was the case in regular Czech schools).

Polish minority schools had the highest postwar enrolment in 1961, that is, even prior to the new legislation on national minorities and the introduction of collective rights for them. Since 1961, Polish medium schools have experienced a steady decline in the numbers of both schools and pupils. Its main cause has been the insufficient reproduction of the Polish minority. Other, minor, factors that influenced the structure of Polish-language schools were of an administrative kind. Thus, there were two causes of the setback of Polish minority schools in the postwar period: a) demographic; b) administrative. These are now addressed briefly.

Whereas before the Second World War almost 80 per cent of marriages entered into by persons of Polish nationality were ethnically homogenous in the Czech lands, in the early 1950s intermarriages prevailed (standing at 54.6 per cent) (Šrajerová 1996: 143). Ever since, the proportion of Poles who entered a mixed marriage has been – with the exception of single years – steadily rising. In 1990, only 22.5 per cent of marriages that Poles entered were ethnically homogenous (Sokolová 1994: 272). Obviously, mixed marriages prove to be a powerful means of assimilation, affecting not only the spouses themselves, but also their offspring. It also follows that assimilation towards the dominant culture, i.e. Czech, is more frequent than towards its minority counterpart. Thus, generally, mixed marriages bring about a reduction of a minority and the Polish ethnic group in the Czech lands is no exception therein.

Between 1950 and 1991 the Polish minority declined by 16.1 per cent, and the proportion of children within this ethnic group dropped from 21 to 10.3 per cent between 1961 and 1991 (Šrajerová 1996: 145). Between 1966 and 1970 women of Polish nationality gave birth to 5121 children. A census carried out in 1970 recorded, however, only 2558 children of Polish nationality between 0 and 4 years of age. The rest went by other than Polish nationality. The most recent 1991 census recorded that 90.4 per cent of children (in the Czech lands) of Polish parents who had intermarried had Czech nationality.[5] School statistics recorded that between 1961 and 1997 the number of pupils of Polish nationality in all elementary schools of the Czech lands dropped from 9544 to 2951 (see Table 6.2). The high rate of intermarriages, with their powerful effects of assimilation, can be seen as the main cause for the general decline of pupils of Polish nationality in the Czech lands including the setback of Polish minority schools.

While demographic factors are decisive, I believe, in the steady decrease of Polish minority schools in the Czech lands, administrative measures may slow down or enhance the process. It has to be stressed that the system of Polish minority schooling was extraordinarily well developed in socialist Czechoslovakia, and it continues to operate smoothly in the independent Czech Republic. However, school statistics reveal that the number of Polish-language elementary schools dropped abruptly in the second half of the 1970s. It is clear that the decrease exceeded the demographic decline of children of Polish nationality at that time (see Table 6.2). The setback cannot be interpreted as an attack on Polish medium schools – it resulted from a government decision on the gradual abolition of small schools, among which were several with Polish as the language of instruction (Jasinsky 1997: 199–202).[6]

It is interesting to see how pupils of Polish nationality and their parents struggled with the decrease of Polish medium schools in the second half of the 1970s. While the proportion of pupils of Polish nationality educated in Polish decreased in 1975 and 1976, in 1977 it increased again and almost reached the position it had held in the early 1970s. Thus, from the statistical evidence available it can be concluded that pupils from those Polish medium schools that were closed down transferred in most cases to those Polish minority schools that remained in operation. This must have meant an increased necessity to commute for the affected pupils, since the network of Polish minority schools lost its previous density. The fact that pupils of

Table 6.2 The Elementary Education System in the Czech Lands and Polish Minority Pupils

Year	All pupils of Polish nationality	Pupils educated in Polish	Ratio between columns 2 and 3	Number of Polish-language schools
1945	7609	7550	1:0.99	83
1947	7712	6835	1:0.89	71
1948	8163	7438	1:0.91	77
1961	9544	8961	1:0.94	84
1971	6212	5572	1:0.90	69
1972	5904	5305	1:0.90	67
1973	5594	4978	1:0.89	64
1974	5471	4846	1:0.89	59
1975	6022	4700	1:0.78	54
1976	5718	4451	1:0.78	54
1977	4997	4289	1:0.86	43
1978	4819	4127	1:0.86	36
1989	3808	3355	1:0.88	28
1990	3648	3231	1:0.88	28
1993	3090	2818	1:0.91	29
1997	2951	2690	1:0.91	28

Polish nationality and their parents did not turn their backs on Polish minority schools brings further evidence of the powerful ability of Polish minority members to resist assimilation.

The democratic revolution of 1989 affected the educational system significantly in a number of aspects. Polish-language elementary schools remained, however, intact. The proportion of pupils of Polish nationality who were educated before and after 1989 in Polish-language elementary schools has basically stayed the same, and the number of these schools has not decreased since 1989. The negative demographic development of the Polish minority in the Czech lands, however, persists, and the number of pupils of Polish nationality in the entire education system is constantly decreasing.

It also seems that individual members of the Polish minority did not suffer any particular harm in the course of the transition period, in comparison, for instance, to the Romany minority (see below). The educational achievements of pupils and students of Polish nationality have been for some 20 years or so comparable to the accomplishments of the general population. Thus, the Polish minority – in particular its members born after the 1960s – were no less prepared for the transition to market economy than the general population as far as their educational status is concerned (Hernová 1997b: 59).

That the system of Polish minority schooling under communism was – at least formally – well developed is clear from the fact that most children of

Polish nationality attended kindergartens (Sokolová 1987: 102) and elementary schools with Polish as the language of instruction, and not its Czech alternatives. In spite of having been educated in a minority school, their educational achievements were comparable to those of the general population and their transition to Czech-language institutions of higher education was unproblematic. After 1989, the dramatic changes that affected almost all spheres of social and political life left the Polish minority schools basically intact in the Czech lands. The breakup of Czechoslovakia at the turn of 1992 and 1993 left them unaffected as well.

The Slovak minority

Unlike the Polish and German minorities, the Slovak ethnic group cannot be characterised as a historical minority of the Czech lands. The Slovak community comprises more or less recent immigrants and their descendants. As an immigrant group, and given the similarity of the Czech and Slovak languages, many Slovaks in the Czech lands have assimilated very quickly and with great ease into the host society.

While their proportion within the general population was insignificant before the Second World War in the Czech lands, after 1945 immigration from Slovakia accelerated and Slovaks soon became the greatest ethnic minority in the Czech part of Czechoslovakia. The initial reasons for their migration were economic – the search for employment and housing – and they often moved to the border areas of the Czech lands where there was plenty of both after the departure of the three-million-strong community of Sudeten Germans. Later, with the industrialisation of Slovakia, Slovak migrants came to the Czech lands with other motives, for instance, to join relatives, and in the most recent period a number of Slovak intellectuals moved to the Czech Republic even for political reasons.

The position of Slovaks permanently residing in the Czech lands was, until 1993 when Czechoslovakia broke up, quite ambivalent. While the Slovak nation in the newly established Slovak Socialist Republic received powerful and equal rights with the 1969 federalisation of Czechoslovakia, Slovaks permanently residing in the Czech Socialist Republic did not enjoy the status of a national minority (in a situation in which even the German ethnic group had finally been recognised as one by the authorities). It must be stressed, however, that Slovaks in the Czech lands were in some important areas (such as education) actually treated as if they were an officially recognised national minority.

Unlike the Polish minority, with its rich tradition of minority schools in the Czech lands, the Slovak ethnic group, an immigrant community, did not have a similar tradition of its own. Thus, while re-opening Polish-language schools after the liberation meant simply a restoration of the pre-war state, the concept of Slovak-language schools in the Czech lands had yet to be developed. The first Slovak minority school was opened in the city of Karviná in northern Moravia. Its establishment took the following course. First, in 1956 two classes were opened for Slovak pupils within a regular Czech school. In 1957 parents of Slovak nationality filed a request with the local authority to establish a separate Slovak-language school, but the request was turned down. After a repeated demand, the first Slovak-language school was finally established in Karviná in 1958 (Šrajerová 1996: 145).

In 1969, a second Slovak minority school opened in Karviná, and by 1971 the number of pupils enrolled in Slovak-language schools – and there were only those two in Karviná – reached its highest ever in the Czech lands, with 1349 pupils. Around this time there were efforts to establish Slovak minority schools in other cities of the Czech Socialist Republic as well, including Prague with its relatively populous community of Slovaks. The attempts were, however, either unsuccessful or their results were short-lived. Moreover, the second Slovak-language school of Karviná closed down in 1983, leaving the Czech lands with only one school of this kind, also situated in Karviná (Šrajerová 1997a: 107–8).

One can, indeed, speak of a decline of Slovak minority schooling which commenced in the second half of the 1970s and resulted in the closing of the second Karviná Slovak-language school. One has to bear in mind, however, that in the Czech lands there had never been a strong and well-developed network of Slovak minority schools in the first place. When the number of pupils enrolled in Slovak-language schools reached its highest point in 1971, with 1349 pupils, it was still negligible compared with the total of 40 190 pupils of Slovak nationality in the entire elementary education system of the Czech lands.

Although the data available do not allow for the calculation of an exact percentage, it can be concluded with certainty that in 1971 over 96 per cent of Slovak pupils attended regular Czech elementary schools. Here a comparison with the Polish minority is interesting. In 1961, when Polish-language schools had reached their highest enrolment, over 93 per cent of pupils of Polish nationality actually attended these schools. Even after the absolute number of Polish pupils dropped in Polish-language schools, the proportional enrolment in these schools has remained very high, that is, the vast majority of pupils of Polish nationality attended Polish medium schools at any time after 1945. In 1997 it was still approximately 91 per cent.

The position of both the Slovak and Polish ethnic groups in minority schools was affected by assimilation, though in different ways. The Polish minority has not been able to reproduce itself to a sufficient extent owing to assimilation, and thus the number of pupils of Polish nationality has been more or less gradually decreasing since the mid-1960s, inevitably resulting in a corresponding decline of their enrolment in Polish minority schools. The pupils of the Slovak minority also bear the imprint of assimilation, which has meant they have not attended Slovak-language schools even in the first place.

It would be wrong to think that central and local authorities in the Czech lands engaged in some kind of project of forced assimilation and refused to open Slovak-language schools. Although the Slovak ethnic group had not been recognised officially as a national minority until 1993, its members were actually treated as belonging to one in the Czech lands even before then as far as education is concerned. For instance, a 1971 order of the Czech Ministry of Education on minority schooling applies not only to the officially recognised minorities but also, and equally, to pupils of Slovak nationality.[7]

The Slovak minority is dispersed literally all over the Czech lands, making Slovak medium schooling difficult from a technical point of view. Territorial diffusion may not be decisive, however, since in some locations, for instance in Prague, the number of pupils of Slovak nationality would theoretically suffice to establish a Slovak medium school. Past and present efforts to run a Slovak-language school in the Czech capital have, however, been futile in spite of the fact that the main, if not all, Slovak minority organisations have a seat there and their activity is concentrated in Prague to a significant extent. Indeed, it takes a fair amount of commitment to send one's children to a minority school. In a situation where there is a long tradition of Slovak migration to, and assimilation in, the Czech lands, together with the wide acceptance of Slovaks by the majority society, and given the similarity of Czech and Slovak languages, there is no wonder that Slovak parents have been content with sending their children to regular Czech schools.

The situation in education corresponds to the high proportion of inter-marriages that Slovaks have entered throughout the postwar period in the Czech lands, with the number rising constantly. While in 1951 the proportion of intermarriages was 53.9 per cent, in 1971 it had risen to 77.4 per cent, and has increased further in the course of the 1990s: it reached 83.8 per cent in 1994, for instance (Hernová and Sokolová 1977: 205; Hernová 1997a: 23). The absolute majority of spouses who Slovaks intermarried with were, of course, Czechs. It perhaps does not need to be stressed that such marital bonds are powerful vehicles of assimilation which affect mainly the off-spring. However, even 48 per cent of children who were born to a Slovak mother and father went by Czech nationality as a 1994 survey detected. It also recorded that 68.5 per cent of children in these homogenous marriages only speak Czech, 24 per cent are bilingual and only 5.1 per cent of them speak just Slovak (Šrajerová 1997b: 73).

Educational achievements of pupils and students of Slovak nationality seem to have been partly influenced by the specific conditions of their migration to the Czech lands. In particular, the early migrants from Slovakia of the 1950s and early 1960s were mostly manual workers, which decreased the average educational status of Slovaks in the Czech lands to a level lower than that of population in general. It was only later that Slovaks with higher educational qualifications migrated in greater numbers to the Czech lands.

However, even among younger persons of Slovak nationality there is a significantly larger proportion of those with only low educational status. This may be caused by the above-mentioned historical reasons of Slovak migration to the Czech lands, or it may also be connected with the fact that a significant proportion of Roma – who have very low educational status on average – go by Slovak nationality in censuses. The proportion of Slovaks under 30 years of age who have a university degree is, on the other hand, almost identical with that of the general population (Hernová 1997b: 59).

It seems that the effects of the transition period on Slovaks in the Czech lands differed little from those felt by the majority.[8] They were hit more significantly, however, by the breakup of Czechoslovakia at the end of 1992, in particular by the difficulties with obtaining new Czech citizenship, for which the Czech Republic was criticised heavily. One of its consequences was that it made it quite complicated, in some cases, for Slovaks who permanently resided, or had even been born in the Czech lands to acquire the new Czech citizenship. Over 300 000 Czechoslovaks who lived permanently in the Czech lands became foreigners (with Slovak citizenship) on 1 January, 1993. The difference between a national and a foreigner is substantial in a number of aspects of everyday life.

As far as education is concerned, the potentially dramatic consequences were diminished by an inter-state agreement on education between the Czech and Slovak Republics which came into force on the first day of the new states' existence (Agreement no. 203/1993: 29 October 1992). The agreement set a one-year transition period during which Slovak citizens who attended Czech schools at the time of the federation's breakup were allowed to proceed as if they were nationals. Since then, Slovak citizens with long term or permanent residence in the Czech Republic have been allowed to enrol in any school as if they were nationals, although some people have had difficulties obtaining residency permits. One has to recognize, however,

Table 6.3 The Elementary Education System in the Czech Lands and Pupils of Slovak Nationality

Year	All pupils of Slovak nationality	Pupils educated in Slovak	Ratio between columns 2 and 3
1961	46 682	510	1:0.011
1971	40 190	1349	1:0.034
1976	33 103	1122	1:0.034
1978	27 185	802	1:0.030
1981	20 571	503	1:0.024
1989	14 848	174	1:0.012
1993	8 712	98	1:0.011
1997	6 348	56	1:0.009

that the new states made substantial effort to make it possible for citizens of the other state to attend educational institutions under convenient conditions.

Moreover, under the Czech educational act Czech *or* Slovak may be used as a language of communication in elementary and secondary schools (Law no. 29/1984 as amended). Institutions of higher education do not discriminate against Slovak-speaking and -writing students in the Czech Republic either. The wide acceptance of Slovak pupils and students in regular Czech educational institutions is very significant, since they attend these almost exclusively at present (see Table 6.3).

The German minority

There were over three million Czechoslovak citizens of German nationality in the Czech lands before the Second World War. In 1950 there were only 159 000 left. The members of the German ethnic group in the Czech lands – as in several other east European states – were perceived to have been traitors and supporters of the Nazis during as well as after the war. With the defeat of Nazi Germany, and after the Allies granted their consent, Czechoslovak authorities 'transferred' most members of the German minority, who resided mainly in the Czech lands, to the neighbouring German-speaking countries in the course of 1946.

Czech resistance activists and politicians, for instance Edvard Beneš, who was later to become Czechoslovak president, had already laid plans for the expulsion of the German minority during the war. Beneš, who was in British exile, prepared a number of documents on the postwar status of the German minority. Beside the demand for expulsion of a part of the German ethnic group – which later turned out to be the vast majority – they also dealt with the linguistic and educational status of the prospective remnant of this minority.

It had become clear already during the war that the relatively extensive linguistic and educational rights of the German minority from before the Second World War would not be renewed after liberation. Postwar Czechoslovakia was – at least initially – conceived as a state of the Czech and Slovak nations only. Although the legal system of prewar Czechoslovakia was resurrected as a whole after 1945, provisions granting educational and linguistic rights to the German minority were not enforced (Staněk 1993: 52) and with the new communist constitution of 1948 they were deleted formally.

The different memoranda that Beneš submitted to the Allies during the war varied with regard to suggestions concerning the education of the remaining German-speakers. In a 1943 document handed over to Soviet officials, it was stated that the languages of instruction in postwar Czechoslovakia would be Czech, Slovak and Ukrainian. A memorandum submitted to the Western Allies in 1944, on the other hand, suggested that children of German nationality would be educated in their mother tongue in elementary schools in postwar Czechoslovakia (Staněk 1991: 33, 44–5). This, however, did not materialise.

On 7 June 1945, the closure of all German-language schools, including institutions for the physically and mentally handicapped, was announced by the Czechoslovak Ministry of Education (Staněk 1991: 80). Most children of German nationality were, of course, expelled with their parents. As for those pupils of German nationality who were allowed to stay in the Czech lands, the whole situation was quite chaotic in the first postwar years. Some of the remaining German-speakers were concentrated in various types of camps in which education was sometimes provided to their offspring. Children of those who stayed outside these camps would attend regular Czech schools. In any case, education in German language was not provided.

In 1947, after the completion of the 'transfer' of Sudeten Germans, there were 16 077 pupils of German nationality in elementary schools of the Czech lands (*Zprávy státního úřadu statistického republiky Československé* 1948: 1099–101). This was, of course just a tiny fraction of its prewar equivalent, which had amounted to 315 581 in 1935 (Mitter 1991: 217). Indeed, as Wolfgang Mitter points out, there is actually no continuity between the pre-war and postwar German minority in the Czech lands (Mitter 1991: 211). And there is, consequently, no continuity between the pre-war system of elementary, secondary schools, colleges and a university with German as the language of instruction, and the postwar optional courses in German language that pupils of German nationality could attend from the early 1950s in regular Czech elementary schools.

While official attitudes towards the remaining members of the German minority were rather hostile, and their assimilation was openly promoted after 1945, the authorities modified their policy in the 1950s. One of the incentives for the change was perhaps the establishment of diplomatic relations with the German Democratic Republic in 1949. The improvement was not dramatic, however. The plan to assimilate the German minority had not been abandoned, but it was no longer actively promoted.

The societal climate in the postwar period was anything but supportive of the preservation, let alone reproduction, of the German minority and its culture. The relatively high degree of dispersal of this ethnic group – a result of postwar administrative measures – made the situation for the German minority even more difficult. Children of German nationality soon ceased to be bilingual, let alone monolingual, and their knowledge of German gradually evaporated or decreased. By the 1960s, the demographic structure of the German minority was extremely unfavourable to its reproduction. Many young people of German nationality left Czechoslovakia for one of the German-speaking countries. Between 1950 and 1980 the number of Germans decreased by 103 988 in the whole of Czechoslovakia, with 48 per cent of this drop accounted for by emigration.

The recognition of the German ethnic group as a national minority, which came into effect in 1969, had almost no practical consequences as far as education is concerned. Although guidelines issued by the Czech Ministry of Education in 1971 regulated the details of establishing German medium schools and classes, neither could be instituted. The necessary minimum of 30 parents that would have to apply for the establishment of a German medium class was not reached anywhere in the Czech lands (Staněk 1993: 185). Thus, optional courses in which German language was taught to those interested remained the only choice for pupils of German nationality in elementary schools.

While the German ethnic group was the largest minority until 1946 in the Czech lands, by the mid-1990s it had almost ceased to exist. For instance, by 1994, 97 per cent of its members entered a mixed marriage (Hernová 1997a: 23). Consequently, the number of pupils of German nationality in Czech elementary schools is very low. In 1997 there were 762 of them – more or less dispersed over several regions of the Czech lands (*Statistická ročenka školství* 1998: Table C-46). The German minority had suffered a series of interventions of state administration after 1945 that eventually led to its inability to reproduce itself and to the destruction of its minority schools. The resulting assimilation of the German minority was, obviously, of a fundamentally different kind than that of, for instance, the Slovak ethnic group.

While the Slovak minority is an immigrant community, dispersed all over the Czech Republic, and one that exercises only very limited efforts to preserve its ethnic culture, the German minority was a historical group of people concentrated in an enclosed territory and with a tradition of highly developed educational and cultural institutions in its own language. It was the state administration that transformed it into a dispersed community, deprived it of its minority schooling and rendered it incapable of resisting assimilation.

The Romany minority

The Romany ethnic group represents a specific case among the minorities dealt with in this chapter in a number of respects, as I will show later. Similarities exist, of course, as well. The postwar Romany population in the Czech lands is, like the Slovak minority, an immigrant community. There was only a very small number of Roma before the war in the Czech lands. The majority of them – about six thousand – were exterminated during the Second World War. After liberation the Czech lands were left with only about one thousand Roma (Srb and Andrle 1994; 286).

Their number has grown steadily, however, since 1945 owing to their migration from Slovakia and the relatively high fertility of Romany women combined with a low number of intermarriages (see Table 6.4). As early as the 1950s, the communist authorities considered Roma a significant enough group to adopt an official policy in regard to them. Subsequently, various

Table 6.4   Roma in the Czech Lands

Year	1945	1966	1970	1980	1985	1991[10]
Number	1 000	56 519	60 279	88 587	132 167	32 903

Source: Srb and Andrle (1994), p. 286.

resolutions, measures, instructions and directions were introduced, yet the question of the Romany minority has remained a constant issue in politics and in other areas, including education.

In 1958 the central committee of the communist party decided that the 'gypsy question', as it used to be called, would not be tackled within the legal and political framework designed for national minorities since, according to the former, Roma were not a national minority and could not become one. The essence of the 'gypsy question' was, then, the contradiction between 'the high cultural level of a socialist society on the one hand and the exceptionally low level of social life of the population of gypsy origin'. This contradiction was to be tackled by an intentional policy of assimilation (Sus 1961: 11).

Since Roma were not recognised as a national minority under communism and, given the official policy of assimilation, schools with Romany as the language of instruction were out of the question – regardless of whether Roma would actually wish to attend such schools. Slovak Roma who migrated to the Czech lands after the war came usually from very poor backgrounds with very little or no education at all. Thus, the issue of schooling Romany children appeared very soon after the end of war in the Czech lands.

It seems that the default option after 1945 through to the 1950s was to place Romany children (in particular, those many who came from not-yet-assimilated families) in schools for pupils with intellectual deficiencies. Some teachers criticised this practice as 'discrimination', pointing out that the affected Romany children were, in most cases, not intellectually deficient. The reasons why they were placed in such a school were perhaps the following: their knowledge of Czech was poor and/or they lacked various basic skills that other children had upon enrolment in an elementary school. In addition, their class attendance was reported to be irregular. The contemporary term used to describe their condition was to say that they were 'neglected' children (Říhová-Kunová 1949: 187).

To meet the challenge that Romany children represented for the Czech educational system, schools and classes for Roma were established in several towns in the early 1950s. These schools or classes were, however, not comparable to other minority educational institutions. The language of instruction was Czech, and the reason for their establishment was to collect 'neglected' Romany children in order to teach them some basic skills considered necessary for school attendance. These schools and classes were conceived as a temporary measure, and their pupils were to be placed in regular schools later on. These educational institutions, however, remained in operation in a limited number until the 1980s.

Until 1958, Romany pupils could be placed in schools for the intellectually deficient even if they actually did not meet the definition for enrolment in such institutions. After that date, such practice was no longer legal (Predmerský 1961: 97). The significantly overproportional enrolment of Roma in these (so-called) specialised schools did not end with 1958, however. It has remained an unresolved issue to the present time.

It would be wrong to think that the communist authorities disregarded the problem of educating Roma children. In the course of the communist period, a number of measures were adopted that were intended to improve the position of Roma in the education system. For instance, it was believed that placing Romany children in kindergartens prior to their enrolment in a school would increase their future educational chances. Thus, preference to be placed in a kindergarten was granted to children from Romany families in some areas and, as far as pre-school education is concerned, some significant achievements were made. Generally, however, the situation was not good at all.

Statistical evidence from 1970 shows that the proportion of Roma aged between 25 and 29 with complete secondary education was well below one per cent (Srb and Job 1974: 179). Many Romany pupils were not even able to complete a regular elementary school. In 1970 only about 15 per cent of them reached the last (9th) grade, the remainder dropping out before that. A significant proportion of Roma was enrolled in specialised schools. Comprehensive statistical evidence documenting this is available from the early 1970s to 1990 (see Table 6.5).

A dramatic increase – proportional as well as absolute – of Roma in specialised schools in the course of the late 1970s and the 1980s was due to a major educational reform introduced in 1976. The duration of the elementary school was cut by one year to eight years total. Consequently, demands on pupils increased and those who could barely make it through in the elementary school before 1976 were, after this reform, often sent to a specialised school. Whereas before the reform the proportion of Roma in schools for the intellectually deficient was actually decreasing, with its inception it started rising dramatically. By the mid-1980s almost every other Romany child attended a specialised school while before the reform it was not even every fourth.

The proportion of Roma in schools for the intellectually deficient was enormous by the mid-1980s. One has to inquire into the significance that education actually held under communism. Although the communist authorities stressed the importance of a highly educated society as a whole, from the economic point of view it made only very little, or no difference at

Table 6.5 Roma in the Czech Elementary School System

Year	In regular schools	In schools for the intellectually deficient	Ratio between columns 2 and 3
1971	–	5341	–
1972	12 810	5866	2.18:1
1973	13 272	6445	2.06:1
1974	13 301	6709	1.98:1
1975	14 105	5105	2.76:1
1976	14 076	4829	2.92:1
1977	13 650	5993	2.28:1
1978	13 477	6812	1.98:1
1979	13 254	7792	1.70:1
1984	13 611	12 615	1.08:1
1989	15 483	13 196	1.17:1
1990	15 207	12 444	1.22:1

Source: *Statistika školství*, respective years.

all, whether an individual had a university degree or was a graduate of a specialised school.

With, on average, very low educational status, Roma were not ready for the democratic changes of 1989 which introduced capitalism into the Czech lands. After 1989 many Roma were forced out from the construction business by guest workers from the Ukraine, for instance, who were willing to work for very little. The Romany community was simply very harshly hit by the changes, thanks to which the educated gained and those with little education lost.

The arrival of democracy, however, also brought about the official recognition of Roma as a national minority in the Czech lands (Resolution no. 463: 13 November 1991). Those who supposed that such a step would initiate some kind of great revival of Romany culture and language within the community were wrong. In the 1991 census on national minorities there were only about 33 000 persons who declared themselves to be of Romany nationality in the Czech lands. Meanwhile, estimates of the total size of the Romany community in 1991 were around 150 000. Some Romany leaders suggested even much higher numbers.

In my opinion, the census may suggest that the majority of Roma more or less accepted the policy of assimilation promoted by the communist regime. This was, of course, in stark contradiction to the efforts of many prominent Romany intellectuals who, immediately after 1989, emphasised the need to introduce classes in which the language of instruction would be Romany.[9] Promoters of this policy sometimes admitted that it would not in fact be well received by most Roma (Bánom 1990: 7).

To date there is not a single Romany elementary school in the Czech Republic, and no efforts are made to establish one – neither by government, nor by Romany leaders. What Romany leaders, along with some international organisations, have criticised, however, is the high proportion of Roma in specialised schools. This problem persists in spite of the new selection procedure introduced after 1989. While under communism a district authority had the decisive power in the process of placing a child in a specialised school, since 1991 parents have had the last word in the procedure (Announcement of the Czech Ministry of Education no. 399/1991: 13 September 1991). Still, the problem persists and seems to be a complex one; that is, it cannot be blamed only on racial prejudice among Czech teachers. In 1997 the Czech Minister of Education was assigned the task of stopping the over-placement of Romany pupils in specialised schools (Resolution of Czech government no. 686: 29 October 1997). Its effects have yet to be examined.

To improve the educational status of the Romany minority, the Ministry of Education also set up several preparatory classes in which Romany pupils are prepared for their enrolment in an elementary school (in 1995/96 there were 36 of them). Since the communist and post-communist statistics on Roma in schools are not comparable, it is impossible to determine exactly what happened after 1989 with the Romany community in schools. Data based on the subjective declaration of Romany nationality show that in 1995/96 there were no Roma at institutions of higher education, 580 were in elementary schools and 1176 in all special schools (the majority, with certainty, in schools for the intellectually deficient) (Srb 1997: 40).

After 1989, all parents were empowered in the selection procedure in which it is determined whether special education would be more suitable for their child. When it is recommended to Romany parents to have their offspring enrolled in a specialised school, they do not have to follow the recommendation – although coercion may be exercised over them, of course. A precise standing and new developments concerning the Romany community in the educational system after 1989 have yet to be examined. At present it is clear that the Romany community suffered enormously from the dramatic changes that took place after 1989 – in particular, from the ever increasing value of education combined with the inability of many Roma to meet this challenge.

Conclusion

Although the postwar Czech lands, and later the Czech Republic, could almost be described as an ethnically homogenous country, the history of ethnic minorities in Czech schools offers not only a wide array of public policies that tackled ethnic diversity, but also different reactions to them by the concerned minorities.

In this chapter I have examined two autochthonous ethnic groups – the Polish and German minorities – whose members faced radically different public policies in the education system. While the Polish minority soon came to be treated very generously, with the state providing it with an extensive network of Polish medium schools, the German minority – its majority – was physically removed from Czechoslovak territory so that the issue of schooling did not even appear for this group of people. The remnant of the German minority faced a number of measures of state administration, aimed at complete assimilation of this ethnic group.

I also examined two more or less recent immigrant groups in the Czech lands – Slovaks and Roma, both of which also faced differing public policies in education. Although Slovaks were treated to some extent as an autochthonous group and not as an immigrant community by the officials, most Slovak pupils did not make use of the opportunity to be educated in Slovak and chose (or their parents did) to be educated in regular Czech schools. Roma, on the other hand, had faced until 1989 an overt policy of assimilation. As in the case of underprivileged immigrant groups in other European countries (the Turkish minority in Germany, for instance) the educational achievements of Roma are very much below those of the general population.

It was Roma who suffered most from the changes that took place after 1989. First, many of them experienced a dramatic economic setback caused by the new value of education in a market economy. Second, as immigrants from Slovakia (or as their descendants) they faced substantial difficulties with receiving the new Czech citizenship that only worsened their already underprivileged status. In view of the present condition of the other three minorities, it appears that improving educational achievements of Roma remains the greatest and perhaps the only challenge for Czech officials as far as the situation of ethnic minorities in Czech schools is concerned. This challenge seems to be an extremely difficult task – one that Czech authorities have not yet fully begun to tackle.

Notes

1 This paper has been written with the generous support of the International Policy Fellowship Program sponsored by the Open Society Institute, Budapest.

2 These three minorities had been granted the official status of a minority already by the Czechoslovak Constitution of 1960.

3 Under communism Roma were not allowed to declare Romany nationality in a census. In the first post-communist census of 1991, only a fraction of them gave Romany nationality. Most entered Slovak or Czech nationalities. It is estimated that there were over 150 000 Roma in the Czech Republic in 1991. See Srb and Andrle (1994), p. 286.

4 The designation *elementary school* included nine grades (reduced to 8 from 1978, restored to 9 from 1990).

5   Calculated from data given in *Národnostní složení obyvatelstva České republiky* (1994), pp. 77–8.
6   See Resolution of Czech government no. 301/1972 of November 8, 1972.
7   Guidelines of the Czech Ministry of Education of 11 October, 1971.
8   This applies to non-Romany Slovaks in particular. On the situation of Roma see the appropriate section.
9   The demand for the introduction of the Romany language into schools was also raised by the Romany Civic Initiative in its 1992 election prospectus.
10   The number of Roma is so low in 1991 because, for the first time after 1945, it is based upon a subjective declaration of Romany nationality by individuals. Every census before that recorded Roma on the basis of external criteria.

References

Bánom, J. (1990). 'Budoucnost pro Romy' in *Mladá fronta Dnes*. March, p. 7.

Borák, M. (1997). 'Z historie Poláků v České republice' in G. Sokolová *et al.* (eds) *Češi Slováci a Poláci na Těšínsku a jejich vzájemné vztahy*. Opava.

Demografická příručka (1982). Prague.

Frištenská, H. and Sulitka, A. (1994). *Průvodce právy příslušníků národnostních menšin v České republice*. Prague.

Hernová, Š. and Sokolová, G. (1977). 'Národnostně smíšená manželství jako činitel společenské integrace' *Slezský sborník*, no. 3, pp. 201–21.

Hernová, Š. (1997a). 'Národnostní heterogamie a její vliv na skladbu obyvatelstva ČR' *Slezský sborník*, no. 1–2, pp. 20–9.

Hernová, Š. (1997b). 'Sociálně ekonomická charakteristika základního a výběrového souboru' in G. Sokolová (ed.) *Češi Slováci a Poláci na Těšínsku a jejich vzájemné vztahy*. Opava, pp. 52–63.

Jasinsky, Z. (1997). 'Školství' in K. Kadlubiec (ed.) *Polská národní menšina na Těšínsku v České republice (1920–1995)*. Ostrava, pp. 184–213.

Mitter, W. (1991). 'German Schools in Czechoslovakia 1918–1938' in J. Tomiak (ed.) *Schooling Educational Policy and Ethnic Identity. Comparative Studies on Governments and Non-Dominant Ethnic Groups in Europe 1850–1940*. vol. 1, Aldershot and New York, pp. 211–33.

Národnostní složení obyvatelstva České republiky (1994). Prague.

Predmerský, V. (1961). *Rastú nám noví ľudia. Problémy detí cigánskeho pôvodu*. Bratislava.

Říhová-Kunová, J. (1949). 'Cikánské děti ve zvláštní škole' in *Nápravná pedagogika*. Prague, pp. 187–9.

Šindelka, J. (1975). *Národnostní politika v ČSSR*. Prague.

Sokolová, G. *et al.* (1987). *Soudobé tendence vývoje národností v ČSSR*. Prague.

Sokolová, G. (1994). 'Národnostní heterogamie v soužití obyvatel etnicky smíšených regionů České republiky' *Slezský sborník*, no. 3–4, pp. 270–6.

Šrajerová, O. (1996). 'Národnostné školstvo na Těšínsku' *Slezský sborník*, no. 2, pp. 142–57.

Šrajerová, O. (1997a). 'Národnostné školstvo na Těšínsku' in G. Sokolová (ed.) *Češi Slováci a Poláci na Těšínsku a jejich vzájemné vztahy*. Opava, pp. 103–22.

Šrajerová, O. (1997b). 'Slováci v českých krajinách včera a dnes' *Slezský sborník*, nos. 1–2, pp. 68–75.

Srb, V. and Job, J. (1974). 'Některé demografické ekonomické a kulturní charakteristiky romského obyvatelstva v ČSSR 1970' in *Demografie*, no. 2, pp. 172–83.

Srb, V. and Andrle, A. (1994). 'Romské obyvatelstvo v České republice podle sčítální lidu 1991' in *Slezský sborník*, no. 3–4, pp. 285–96.

Srb, V. (1997). 'Skolarizace romské mládeže' in *Demografie*, no. 1, pp. 40–1.

Staněk, T. (1991). *Odsun Němců z Československa 1945–1947*. Prague.

Staněk, T. (1993). *Německá menšina v českých zemích 1948–1989*. Prague.

Statistika školství. (1962–1991). Prague.

Statistická ročenka školství. (1992–1998). Prague.

Sus, J. (1961). *Cikánská otázka v ČSSR*. Prague.

Zprávy státního úřadu statistického republiky Československé (1947–1949).

7

New Paradigms of National Education in Multi-Ethnic Russia

Gerlind Schmidt

Introduction

Developments in Russia in the area of ethnic-national education need to be discussed in the context of the breakdown of the old ideological system and the re-emergence of Russia in 'pedagogical world culture' (*mirovaia pedago-gicheskaia kul'tura*). The search for identity on the part of more than 120 ethnic groups that make up the Russian population does not fit easily with the aim of redefining inter-ethnic relations in a country that regards itself as a multinational state with a pluralistic conception of society. While ethnic Russians account for the overwhelming majority (now over 81 per cent of the population, compared with just over 50 per cent of the Soviet popula-tion), according to the preamble to the 1993 constitution, Russia is a 'multi-national body of people' (*mnogonatsional'nyi narod*).

In this context I shall be dealing with two questions. First, what attempts are being made – in view of efforts to achieve an ethnic renaissance of individual ethnic groups (this includes the Russians) – to safeguard a third entity, embracing those of other backgrounds, and involving the integration of basic values and the cohesion of nation and state in a common educa-tional space (*edinoe obrazovatel'noe prostranstvo*)? Second, what particular features arise from changes in the system and from the propagated process of democratisation, especially with reference to the 'bottom up' initiatives arising from a pluralistic civil society, which may be postulated program-matically but which, in reality, exists only at a rudimentary level?

Education, ethnic-national diversity and unity in historical and present-day change

Even today, many discussions of issues of ethnic-national education in Russia are dominated by ideas of a linguistic, cultural and ethnic homogen-eity of ethnic groups that rarely correspond to reality.[1] One of the origins of this situation lies in the structure of the Soviet Union. Developed in the

1920s as a multinational state with a *territorially* defined Soviet concept of federalism and a corresponding concept of autonomy for minorities, this structure had little to do with the patchwork-like settlement structure of the past. Today, political, economic and social relations between ethnic groups, between majorities and minorities – this includes the demarcations between them – have begun to change and are being overlapped by the development of new regional identities. None the less, it is the understanding of ethnicity as a homogeneous category determined by objective factors which prevails; attempts by Russian ethnologists to introduce a constructivist concept of ethnicity linked to the voluntary decision of the individual (Drobizheva 1996: 196), have so far met with little approval in educational discussions. This needs to be emphasised as freedom of declaring (or not) one's national identity is guaranteed in Article 26, Paragraph 1 of the Constitution of the Russian Federation of 1993 (see Schmidt 1994).

In the Soviet era, education was defined and exploited as an instrument for reconciling economic, social and cultural differences between ethnic groups, or for preventing or eliminating inter-ethnic tensions. Following this tradition, concepts of harmony for inter-ethnic contact or for the inter-action of members of different ethnic groups still often dominate educational theory and practice. The contradictions and concrete problems currently emerging in the education system of Russia as a federal state are influenced by historical continuities going back to the Tsarist empire. During the Soviet period, developments culminated in the promotion period when the merging of peoples to a community of Soviet people was propagated, along with an interpretation of Soviet patriotism that has been called mono-ethnic (cf. Taylor 1992: 83). The hierarchy in the status of ethnic groups or nationalities, languages and cultures was politically defined, although it did also take historical and cultural considerations into account. This state of affairs outlasted the end of the Soviet system but is often ignored in debates even today. With the establishment of new independent states outside and the new federalism and regionalism inside Russia, this hierarchy is likewise in the process of change.

The fact that the Russians are in the majority *vis-à-vis* the other nationalities, a fact reflected in the dominant position of its culture and its language as the *lingua franca* and common official language (Brunner 1996: 302), has led to the assertion of a position of superiority, to paternalism and cultural imperialism. This is in line with the tradition of Russian and Soviet history. In the current debate it is concealed behind the slogan *primus inter pares* and is often not an issue for discussion. Indeed, it is often claimed that the negative effects of the Soviet system and its ideology on the different languages and cultures also apply to the Russian language and culture. Thus, with the consent of other ethnic groups (for example, the Minister of Education in Tatarstan referred to the 'derussification' of the Russian people) (Gaifullin 1995: 78), the Russian majority joins the victims of the totalitarian regime of the past.

This can be particularly observed in the education system. The institution of the minority school handed down from the Soviet education system – the 'national school' geared to teaching the native language and literature along with national customs, which was, at times, characterised by its bilingualism – is no longer regarded as an appropriate instrument for solving present tasks and problems.

A survey of current activities in education with regard to the issue of nationality

Against the background of a federal educational policy of preserving a common education space (*edinoe obrazovatel'noe prostranstvo*), characterised by principles such as diversity and competition of educational provision as well as by the consideration of *plural* educational needs in society, Russia has seen the development of a diversity of ethnically-nationally oriented educational concepts and provision in the last few years.

First, following a series of declarations of sovereignty, the 21 national republics have pushed through a number of special, political rights against the other territorially defined subjects of the federation, including the introduction of a second official language. Some of the national ministries of education concerned have taken measures affecting the restriction of the Russian language and the contents of the humanities (*predmety gumanitarnogo tsikla*). These appear to be unilaterally and, as it were, 'monoculturally' characterised by the political as well as the ethnic-national or even religiously embedded educational needs of the *titular* (*eponymous*) nationalities. In some republics and autonomous entities, this has led to a situation which is regarded as running counter to the objectives of a 'common education space' formulated on the federal level (Kuz'min 1997). It remains to be seen, however, whether these changes come about as quickly as is feared by the Russians.

Second, the – as yet uncompleted – rehabilitation of the peoples suppressed or linguistically and culturally marginalised in the Soviet system remains on the agenda. Among these, the small indigenous peoples of the north receive special attention, and there are experiments aimed at bringing about an ethnic renaissance through the schools, without isolating the students in their multinational school environment (Gromyko 1996). To this purpose, comparative cultural approaches of a 'dialogue' or a 'polilogue' of cultures (*Bakhtin*) are being developed. To meet the educational needs of scattered ethnic groups that have no territory of their own, a law on national cultural autonomy was introduced in 1996 ('O natsional'no kul'turnoi avtonomii' 1996). According to this law, scattered ethnic groups and nationalities can establish their own *non-state* education system or apply for support for their ethnic-national educational needs within the public education system.

Third, pressure groups from the national minorities of historically separate waves of immigration have developed in the urban centres of Moscow and St Petersburg as well as in other cities. Their aim is to establish 'national schools' from below; in Moscow, such schools are labelled as establishments with an 'ethnocultural (national) component'. Both Russian and multinational schools have recently been set up alongside Tatar, Jewish, Armenian and other schools (see below).

New streams of migrants have lead to an increase in or an open emergence of xenophobia and ethnic discrimination in the old 'centres' as well as on the periphery, a fact which results in corresponding challenges for the education system. The urgency of this problem is a result of the increasing immigration from the CIS-states, the main political responsibility in Russia being focused on the 25 million ethnic Russians who live outside the country and partly have (re)immigrated.

Existing concepts, then, are based partly on the regulations of the federal government or those of the federational subjects (in the national republics); others have also developed 'bottom up' from educational practice, from society (for instance, the national schools in Moscow), or they are pilot projects of educationalists. In future, account will also have to be taken of schools that are established on the initiative of associations of cultural autonomy.

To some extent, the development has already evolved its own, historically-shaped political and social impetus. However, in the present financial situation room for manoeuvre exists only:

- in economically strong national republics or regions;
- when foreign states provide financial and/or personal assistance; or
- occasionally in the case of protective measures for the small peoples of the north (apparently also in 'rich regions', as in the case of the Khanty and Mansi in Tiumen').

National education in Moscow

Owing to its centuries-old function as a capital city, the general situation in Moscow, and therefore its education system and educational policy as well, is characterised by distinctive political, demographic and social features. The centralisation of political power within a giant European–Asian area, the co-opting of non-Russian elites and the opening of the city to a 'foreign' (*inostrannyi*) multi-ethnic and multi-religious immigrant population are part of Moscow's history (Kappeler 1992: 130).

With a population of currently around 9 million (12 million if the Greater Moscow area is included), Moscow is regarded as a multinational and multi-denominational megalopolis. The proportion of the non-Russian population has not significantly increased since the nineteenth century and has remained relatively stable over the last decades. Standing at 9.5 per cent in 1994 (Saidbaev 1997: 8), it is approximately half as high as in the rest of the Russian Federation and includes Jews (175 000), Tatars (157 000), Belorussians (73 000) and Armenians (44 000) as the four largest minority groups (*'Sostoianie i perspektivy...'* 1995: 25).

With regard to the issues of integration or assimilation, the non-Russian part of the population has become increasingly diverse and heterogeneous over the last few years. Integration processes are, for example, shaped by the growing number of illegal and often socially uprooted immigrants (*zhiteli bez propiski*) (Kezina 1996; Saidbaev 1997). Moreover, there are strong indications that the proportion of the Muslim population – which is increasingly regarded as foreign by the Russian majority – has been growing for some time now (Saidbaev 1997). The length of the period of residence, a most important factor for integration, is not often regarded as a relevant criterion of differentiation (for an exception, see St Petersburg) (Vershlovskii 1997). This is surprising, considering the current increase in migration occurring during a period of far-reaching social and political transformation.

As a political and cultural centre, Moscow on the other hand continues to play the role of the temporary or permanent home of sections of the elites from CIS countries and from the so-called 'national centres' of Russia, even though its function as a 'centre' has been affected by regionalisation and decentralisation. Some of these elites are in political exile, some are responsible for the political contacts of the appropriate governments, some are living in Moscow to acquire special academic and artistic qualifications or are there on business missions, while others living there are socially uprooted. Lately, the term non-Russian 'diasporas' has been adopted to describe these groups. On the Federation level the city is the focus of the nationality policy and thus the place to find those who, on behalf of their governments or numerous social 'movements' (*dvizheniia*), potentially support a renaissance of their own specific national education and culture.

As a political subject within the new Russian Federation, the city of Moscow is attempting to maintain and to consolidate its position of power as a capital and as the 'centre' against the advances of the periphery (almost as a 'state within the state'). Education policy with regard to national schools is therefore used by the local Moscow government as an instrument to develop both its own activities within the new federal state system and its corresponding 'common education space' alongside the activities of the Federal ministry of education. The Committee for Education of the Moscow government has received the support of Mayor Luzhkov in this matter.[2]

Both the official education policy and the work of educationalists and other experts reflect the fact that the contacts with international organisations and 'distant' countries – these include West European countries (*dal'nee zarubezh'e*) – still play a role in Moscow. Special attention, yet, is paid to 'closer' countries of the 'near abroad' (*blizhnee zarubezh'e*), especially those belonging to the CIS. These claims, which have been made so frequently in the field of national education are also reflected in the debates. Certain terms and concrete proposals are in line with Western paradigms while, at the same time, co-existing with the 'old' paradigms of Soviet national schooling and education, as in the case of 'bilingualism', for instance.[3] The basic positions fit well with the idea of 'patriotic consensus', whereby the movement 'Education – Future of Russia' attempts to maintain a rather moderate national stance. Meanwhile, there are numerous other groups, among them the Zemstvo Association (closely connected to Solzhenitsyn) or the movement 'Russian Schooling' (headed by Professor Goncharov, of St Petersburg, with a strict Russian national position) and many other groups of merely regional importance.

Among the corresponding activities within the education system of Moscow mention should be made of the following: the implementation of UNESCO schools (this goes back to the Soviet era!) and Council of Europe projects in support of minorities in the education system, the setting up of joint Russian–Turkish, Russian–Korean, Jewish and other schools, with the support of the respective foreign countries. Contacts with CIS countries include the provision of textbooks (from the Moscow Education Committee, not from the Federal Ministry of Education!) for schools in Georgia and Tadzhikistan (Ushakova 1997). Existing contacts with Russian and national-language institutions in thirty regions of Russia, including the national republics, have also been consolidated (an excellent example is the experiment in Khanty-Mansiisk; see Gromyko 1996).

To show that, when compared to other similar cities in the (Western) world, present day Moscow is a 'multi-cultural and multi-denominational' centre, it is pointed out that in all Moscow schools the composition of the student body is 'multinational' (Semenov 1997: 4). In 1997, the Moscow Committee of Education identified 42 educational institutions with a national orientation (out of a total of 1300 schools) in the city, among them 17 (i.e., around 40 per cent) 'Russian schools', nursery schools or education 'centres' and one multinational school, founded as early as 1989 as an Armenian Sunday school (Kuznetsov 1997: 89; *Sostoianie i perspektivy...* 1995: 31). In 1998, the total figure had gone up to 47 (Holdsworth 1998). Among these are several educational institutions called *kompleksy*, i.e. schools comprising pre-schools and Sunday schools, colleges and 'complementary' education (*dopolnitel'noe obrazovanie*). This so-called 'subsystem' of educational institutions with a national focus is subject to a set of financial and legal regulations and activities as well as to measures designed for the promotion of developmental work. These cover educational programmes, the production of textbooks (by the institute MIROS, Moscow Institute for the Development of Education Systems), the initial and in-service training of teachers.

The framework laid out in the 'Programme for the Development of National Education in the City of Moscow' of 9 December, 1994, and the accompanying 'Conception of the Educational Content of Moscow Schools with an Ethno-cultural (National) Component' (*Sostoianie i perspektivy*... 1995) still applies in its basic principles. However, there have been shifts of emphasis, for example, as a result of the adoption of the Religion Act of 1997. The idea of civil society, which seems most likely to encourage an educational policy in favour of national minorities, remains important. However, the main trend is to strengthen the opportunities for state regulation and control.

The setting up of a 'Russian national' school indicates a shift in the type of paradigm in favour of the Soviet tradition of the 'national school', as is revealed particularly in its concept of minorities. The increase of Russian national ideas among many teachers and parents, endorsing the 'patriotic consensus' in society, made it appropriate for a place to be found for the 'Russian national school' within a so called 'subsystem' of national education. This is counterbalanced by state protection and support, including that of the capital, Moscow, for the national minorities, which in the past were discriminated against in various ways. Models of 'Russian national education' compete with the 'national schools' of other ethnic groups for promotion and support from parents and society. They sometimes also cushion educational policy arguments, characterised by the fear of infiltration from foreign cultures and often, but not only, voiced by people from communist party circles. However, in order to ensure agreement on basic values, tolerance of other nationalities, and the cohesion of society as a whole, extreme developments with a fundamentalist orientation are supposed to be avoided. This applies not only to schools with a Muslim ethnocultural component, as was demonstrated by the recent debate on the Religion Act.

Recent developments have led to the logical demand for the introduction of state-approved timetables in the national schools, not only on the local Moscow level but on the Federation level as well. The corresponding proposal immediately met with severe criticism on the part of the liberal reformers among the pedagogues; in their opinion, the initiative for the establishment of national educational institutions should come from the minorities (Adamskii 1998). At the same time, encouraged now by the state, the risk of a social fragmentation 'into ethnic districts' (*kvartiry*) is conjured up as a possible negative result of the new conception (Gershunskii 1997).

When assessing these developmental processes, it should be born in mind that a pluralistic civil society has not yet developed within the existing governmental, political and social structures of Moscow. A pluralisation of society arouses numerous anxieties among the Russian majority. Attempts to achieve the intended development of democratisation and political emancipation of the minorities are observed with mixed feelings by this group. On the other hand, the risk of the re-emergence of a Pan-Russian chauvinism is regarded by supporters of the Russian national school as slight.

Schools or classes with a 'national component' are frequently confronted with an overload of subject matter as they usually have to cope with two educational programmes: the minimum of the obligatory educational standards applying to the whole country along with the supplementary 'ethno-cultural programme' of the individual school (Ushakova 1997). Some of the 'ethno-national' schools, which came into being in the 'diaspora' situation of the nationalities, have developed into larger state-run (or private) complexes. They may appeal to parents as attractive institutions characterised by a spirit of educational innovation and a wide range of facilities with an outstanding range of courses. This gives these schools a socially elitist character by comparison with average schools (see also a survey in St Petersburg; Vershlovskii 1997). Owing to the complex factors of structure, content and organisation described above, these schools no longer tend to be regarded as open towards the remaining part of the education system but rather as cut-off from it.

Developments in the practical implementation affect all the basic principles of the Russian Law on Education of 1992. This applies to the question of the official language and the national languages, the issue of the separation of state and religion and of school and church, but also to the equality of educational opportunity and the issue of the privatisation of educational institutions. In the Moscow concept, too, the main tensions and contradictions, as well as potential areas of future conflict, are based on issues of common basic values and the safeguarding of regional and federal cohesion, as well as on the interaction between state and society, between 'top' and 'bottom' in this 'subsystem' of schooling and education.

Until now, there has been little evidence that there will be any withdrawal from the idea of homogeneity of ethnic groups, the potential harmony of their co-existence or the particular position of the Russian ethnic group as *primus inter pares* (Zorin 1996: 28). However, teaching staff will soon be confronted with the problems resulting from this situation in everyday school life. The basic position is that education focusing on a successful ethnic self-identification will guarantee inter-ethnic communication characterized by tolerance and harmony and peaceful co-existence in school and society, a position that is soon likely to be made aware of its limits in everyday school life. What is more, the interest taken by young people at school in ethnic issues has not proved to be very great in recent years.

Chances and risks of the new approaches

Although Russia officially defines itself as a multinational state, multi-nationalism as a common third factor encompassing this ethnic diversity seems to be characterised by a reversion to Soviet patterns of thinking. For the educational policy of the state as a whole, the Russian Federation, it is the idea of a political process of nation-building, together with a reorganisation of education opportunities, which seems most appropriate for taking account of the educational needs of individual ethnic groups. This finds expression in the notion of a Russian 'super'-nation (*superetnos*) incorporating the ethnic groups at least in the political sphere, if not in language and culture (Simon 1997: 1176), and including those fellow countrymen living outside Russia (*sootechestvenniki*). This incorporates a patriotism focused on the Russian Federation ('Ob utverzhdenii Kontseptsii' 1996) and the construct of a 'spiritual community' (*dukhovnaia obshchnost'*) of ethnic groups, which, historically, came about during the building of the Russian empire and which still exists today. The reappraisal of the common multinational history demanded in education appears in the shape of an indispensable pedagogical project for the future, which in the long run may help to reduce the differences and conflicts between the ethnic groups and to strengthen national cohesion. Thus, the objective of achieving a general assimilation of language and culture is relinquished, and the task of providing value-free information on all ethnic groups likewise remains on the agenda.

On the other hand, it is the Russian language and culture which is continually stressed as the *lingua franca* and as the primary or even sole medium providing access to the cultures and languages of the world. It remains to be seen whether the bilingualism of Russian and national language/mother tongue will remain essentially a matter of the minorities, a one-way street (Taylor 1992: 88); a concept which is, indeed, increasingly being recognised as such by the ethnic Russians in the national republics. (For example, in Tatarstan an increasing number of Russian parents display an interest in their children receiving instruction in the Tatar language (Drobisheva 1996: 286)). It is also uncertain what long-term effects will result from the reassessment of the hierarchy of languages in the so-called 'national centres' with regard to the advance of the English language as a world-wide *lingua franca*. Insofar as the pedagogical debate is dominated by concepts of cultural (and also language) comparison, the traditional hierarchy of languages and cultures would appear to have moved backstage for the time being. At the same time that a Russian-national school system catering for the language and culture of the majority is beginning to emerge in the sense of a quest for ethnic identity, opportunities for a renewed assimilation in the sense of Russification are also appearing. This may, however, also result in the isolation or even exclusion of ethnic groups, thus opening the door into national chauvinism, xenophobia and ethnic discrimination in education.

However, the following should be mentioned as remarkable new approaches, which might prove to be desirable steps towards a solution of the multinational issue and which are of international interest. Russia's education system is in principle open to social initiatives in the area of ethnic-national education, with the claims of ethnic groups being regarded as worthy of protection even if they do *not* correspond to the interests of the state as a whole. However, one should not forget the ambivalence of state support, which can also function as state control (Kuz'min 1994, 1997). Likewise, there is still no right to the support of language or ethno-cultural education that can be claimed in a court of law. At the same time, the fundamental openness should be emphasised with which the consequences of the violent subjugation and colonisation of ethnic groups in the tsarist regime are taken into consideration, as are the effects of the marginalisation, and even extermination, of these groups in the Stalin era.

Sooner or later it will become indispensable for the various new approaches for the specifically ethnically-oriented educational institutions described above to be joined together in educational policies and to be linked to the concept of the 'ordinary school' (*obychnaia shkola*), which has no particular new ethnic orientation. Many problems remain unsolved with regard to the didactic and educational implementation of these approaches. For instance, the new concepts are strongly oriented towards the acquisition of knowledge of language and ethno-cultural contents; educational tasks other than the imparting of knowledge are not a subject for debate. This illustrates that, on the whole, the new concepts continue to be firmly embedded in the Soviet tradition of educational thinking and indicates how significant is the mixing of the traditional lines of thought and theoretical fragments with highly topical ideas from Western discussions.

Notes

1 Drobizheva (1996: 186) mentions an 'ethnic nature' which does not depend on 'concrete historic circumstances' of society. In this sense there exists an understanding of ethnic homogeneity, which neglects existing differences of race, language or cultural assimilation among people belonging to an ethnic group.
2 In issues of national education, the Moscow Education Committee co-operates with a group of researchers originally coming from the Soviet Academy of Pedagogical Sciences and from E. Dneprov's 1988 group of reformers 'VNIK Shkola'; today it is also supported by members of the Education Commission of the State Duma.
3 Bilingualism and bi-culturalism in the new post-Soviet circumstances are still considered to contribute a positive dimension to the education process and its aims (e.g. *Sostoianie i perspektivy...* 1995: 44).

Bibliography

Adamskii, A. (1998). 'Pokhozhe, chto mnogie segodnia uzhe ne proch' sdelat' obrazovanie chast'iu natsional'noi ideologii' *Pervoe sentiabria*, no. 69, 30 June, p. 1.
Brunner, G. (1996). 'Minderheitenrechte in der Rußländischen Föderation' in A. Kappeler (ed.) *Regionalismus und Nationalismus in Rußland*. Baden-Baden: Beck, pp. 289–308.
Drobisheva [Drobizheva], L. (1996). 'Neue Minderheiten: Die Russen in den Republiken der Rußländischen Föderation' in A. Kappeler (ed.) *Regionalismus und Nationalismus in Rußland*. Baden-Baden: Beck, pp. 275–88.
Drobizheva, L. (1996). 'Ethnizität und Nationalismus in der post-sowjetischen Gesellschaft. Diskussionsschwerpunkte der 90er Jahre' in *Sozialwissenschaft in*

Rußland, vol. 2, Deutsch–Russisches Monitoring. Berlin: Berliner Debatte Wissenschaftsverlag, pp. 184–204.

'Eksperimental'nyi bazisnyi uchebnyi plan obshcheobrazovatel'nykh uchrezhdenii Rossiiskoi Federatsii (postroennyi na kul'turologicheskikh printsipakh). Ob utverzhdenii bazisnogo uchebnogo plana obshcheobrazovatel'nykh uchrezhdenii Rossiiskoi Federatsii' (1998). Uchitel'skaia gazeta, no. 10, 17 March, supplement, p. 6.

'Föderales Gesetz: Über Gewissensfreiheit und religiöse Vereinigungen. Verabschiedet von der Staatsduma am 19 September 1997. Bestätigt vom Föderationsrat am 24 September 1997' (1998). Osteuropa, vol. 48, A 274–86.

Gaifullin, V. (1995). 'Obrazovanie v Tatarstane: Problemy i perspektivy' Narodnoe obrazovanie, vol. 7, pp. 78–82.

Gershunskii, B. (1997). 'Drugoi zhanr' Uchitel'skaia gazeta, no. 50, December 16, p. 8.

Gosudarstvennaia shkola mnogonatsional'noi i polikonfessional'noi Moskvy (1997). Moskva: Moskovskii institut povysheniia kvalifikatsii rabotnikov obrazovaniia, Tsentr mezhnatsional'nogo obrazovaniia.

Gromyko, I. (1996). 'Nationalitätenfragen im russischen Bildungswesen: Neue Ansätze und Projekte' Tertium Comparationis, no. 2, pp. 82–92.

Holdsworth, N. (1998). 'Ethnic groups to get own schooling' Times Educational Supplement, no. 4263, 13 March, p. 29.

Kappeler, A. (1992). Rußland als Vielvölkerreich. München: Beck.

Kezina, L. (1996). 'Na kakom iazyke govorit shkola' Rossiiskaia gazeta, no. 166, 31 August, p. 2.

Kuz'min, M., A.A. Sasokolov, V.B. Bacyn and M.B. Estrich (1994). Kontseptsiia natsional'noi shkoly: Tseli i prioritety soderzhaniia obrazovaniia. Moskva: Ministerstvo obrazovaniia Rossiiskoi Federatsii. Institut natsional'nykh problem obrazovaniia.

Kuz'min, M. (1997). Natsional'naia shkola Rossii v kontekste gosudarstvennoi obrazovatel'noi i natsional'noi politiki. Moskva: Ministerstvo obshchego i professional'nogo obrazovaniia Rossiiskoi Federatsii, Institut natsional'nykh problem obrazovaniia.

Kuzmin [Kuz'min], M. (1992). 'The Rebirth of the National School in Russia' Soviet Education Study Bulletin, vol. 10, no.1, pp. 17–23.

Kuznetsov G. (ed.) (1997). Natsional'noe obrazovanie v Moskve. Moskva: Moskovskii komitet obrazovaniia, Tsentr innovatsii v pedagogike. Normativnopravovoe obespechenie soderzhaniia obrazovaniia v Moskve. 4.

'O natsional'no-kul'turnoi avtonomii. Federal'nyi zakon. Priniat 22-go maia 1996 g' (1996). Rossiiskaia gazeta, no. 118, 25 June, p. 3. (German translation in G. Schmidt and M. Krüger-Potratz (eds) (1999). Bildung und nationale Identität aus russischer und rußlanddeutscher Perspektive. Münster, New York: Waxmann, pp. 62–81).

'Ob utverzhdenii Kontseptsii gosudarstvennoi natsional'noi politiki Rossiiskoi Federatsii. Ukaz prezidenta Rossiiskoi Federatsii. June 15, 1996' (1996). Sobranie zakonodatel'stva Rossiiskoi Federatsii, no. 25, June 17, pp. 6225–36. (German translation in G. Schmidt and M. Krüger-Potratz (eds) (1999). Bildung und nationale Identität aus russischer und rußlanddeutscher Perspektive. Münster, New York: Waxmann, pp. 47–61).

Saidbaev, T. (1997). 'Vospitanie tolerantnosti – vazhnoe napravlenie gumanizatsii obucheniia i vospitaniia' in Gosudarstvennaia shkola mnogonatsional'noi i polikonfessional'noi Moskvy. Moskva: Moskovskii institut povysheniia kvalifikatsii rabotnikov obrazovaniia, Tsentr mezhnatsional'nogo obrazovaniia, pp. 7–14.

Schmidt, C. (1994). Der Minderheitenschutz in der Rußländischen Föderation, Ukraine und Republik Weißrußland – Dokumentation und Analyse. Bonn: Kulturstiftung der Deutschen Vertriebenen.

Schmidt, G. (1998). 'Kontinuität und Wandel im Bildungswesen Rußlands' *Die Deutsche Schule*, no. 90, pp. 231–47.

Schmidt, G. and M. Krüger-Potratz (eds) (1999). *Bildung und nationale Identität aus russischer und rußlanddeutscher Perspektive.* Münster, New York: Waxmann.

Schmidt, G. (1999). 'Bildungssysteme nach dem Zerfall der Sowjetunion – Probleme des Umbruchs in den neuen Staaten' in W. Hörner, F. Kuebart and D. Schulz (eds) *'Bildungseinheit' und 'Systemtransformation' – Beiträge zur bildungspolitischen Entwicklung in den neuen Bundesländern und im östlichen Europa.* Berlin: Berlin Verlag Arno Spitz, pp. 95–113.

Semenov, A. (1997). 'Predislovie' in *Gosudarstvennaia shkola mnogonatsional'noi i polikonfessional'noi Moskvy.* Moskva: Moskovskii institut povysheniia kvalifikatsii rabotnikov obrazovaniia, Tsentr mezhnatsional'nogo obrazovaniia, pp. 3–4.

Simon, G. (1997). 'Auf der Suche nach der "Idee für Rußland"' *Osteuropa*, vol. 47, pp. 1176–90.

Sostoianie i perspektivy uchrezhdenii natsional'nogo obrazovaniia g. Moskvy. (1995). Vypusk 2. Moskva: Moskovskii Departament Obrazovaniia.

Taylor, B. (1992). 'Multicultural Education in the Former Soviet Union and the United Kingdom: the language factor' *Compare*, vol. 22, pp. 81–90.

Ushakova, V. (1997). 'Innovatsionnye protsessy v natsional'nom obrazovanii' in *Gosudarstvennaia shkola mnogonatsional'noi i polikonfessional'noi Moskvy.* Moskva: Moskovskii institut povysheniia kvalifikatsii rabotnikov obrazovaniia, Tsentr mezhnatsional'nogo obrazovaniia, pp. 14–18.

Vershlovskii, S. (ed.) (1997). *Natsional'naia shkola: Sotsial'no-pedagogicheskie problemy.* Sankt Peterburg: Komitet po obrazovaniiu Sankt Peterburga.

Zorin, V. (1996). 'Natsional'nye aspekty rossiiskogo federalizma' *Svobodnaia mysl'*, no. 10, pp. 19–30.

Part III
Identity Matters

8

Ethnographical Activism as a Form of Civic Education: a Case Study on School Museums in North-West Russia

Kaija Heikkinen

This chapter studies certain issues of post-Soviet education in the light of ethnicity construction. I will focus, on the one hand, on official or semi-official ethnic identity politics, especially concerning the Vepsians living in north-west Russia, in the Karelian Republic and the Leningrad *oblast'*. My main interest is in issues of learning, preserving and developing local language and ethnic traditions, and in the practices of remembering the ethnic past (which may be more or less mythologised). I will also examine the production of historical consciousness at the local level, in the form of case studies on local school museums.[1] The main actors in this process are both professional and non-professional people (university lecturers, school teachers, ethnic activists etc.). Educational activities in museums involve both children and adults, and combine academic and elementary school instruction with voluntary activism. In this sense such activities can, indeed, be called civic education.

Remembering history

Soviet historiography did not allow much space for specific local and ethnic history. It is well known that Soviet history teaching emphasised revolutionary events and topics important to communist ideology, with the conscious aim of unifying the multi-ethnic Soviet people and consolidating the Soviet Union as a state. This can be seen in museological principles, as well as in the philosophy behind building monuments, creating common festivals, and even in the naming of streets. In every city, town and village a 'Leninskii Prospekt' can be found.

On the other hand, after the revolution an equally important ideological and practical aim was to transform the country, as quickly as possible, into a modern, urbanised, industrial state (see Hosking 1985: 137, 149). From the history of sociology we know that the concept of modernity has from the beginning been, and still is, extremely hostile to everything viewed as traditional. In Soviet Russia the official atheistic ideology followed this line. It can even be considered as an extreme form of rationalism and materialistic techno-scientific thinking. For example, the closing of churches in the late 1920s and early 1930s was closely related to the collectivisation of agriculture (Fitzpatrick 1994: 33–7, 204–13; Luukkanen 1997: 51, 56–7; Viola 1996: 39, 66, 144, 185). Collectivisation, for its part, was regarded as a means of transforming agriculture into something resembling modern industrial production (Hosking 1985: 125). Recent research has demonstrated the variety of ways in which people attempted to oppose these plans by sticking to their traditional culture (eg. Fitzpatrick 1994; Viola 1996). Officially, mythologies and traditions in general were limited solely to the realm of folklore and poetry. This was the framework given by Soviet nationality policy in its positive description of these topics.

Soviet historiography, and the educational principles of history teaching, followed these lines. In the heart of (Soviet) modernity was a determination to eliminate cultural models that were different (a case in point was nomadism, which existed among many peoples in Soviet Asia and Siberia). The dichotomy of two antagonistic modes of culture – one primitive and the other civilised – is deeply rooted in both the Russian concept of history, and in the Western as well.

The idea of a civilising process, in Soviet thought associated with that of Russia, has deep roots in earlier Russian ethnography. Russian language, literacy, high culture, technology and Christianisation have also in the past been regarded as civilising factors. It is easy to find examples of this in texts on Karelians written by Russian travellers (see Taroeva 1965: 17–18). Similarly, Finnish authors and early ethnographers used to observe and evaluate Finnish influences as civilising elements (see Heikkinen 1989: 14–18; Kupiainen 1998: 178–86).

The study of so-called primitive or pre-modern life-style was subsequently professionalised by ethnographers. In the Karelian and Vepsian cases this has meant that both Finnish and Russian scholars have collected materials (folklore, antiquities, oral history, and so on) and continuously published 'readings' of this material. In Finland, the interpretation process has been closely linked with the question of Finnish national identity and nation-building. In Russian texts the position of writers can either be described as having a 'big brother' attitude towards the small minorities, or as openly chauvinistic slavophilism. In Russian texts (written by both Russians and members of other ethnos) the term 'national minority' (*nat'sional'naia gruppa*) is used rather than 'ethnic group'. This seems to be a reflection of the subordinated meaning that the word 'ethnic' carries. I think it is necessary to make a division between 'national' and 'ethnic'.

The scholarly tradition has left only a few possibilities for the small non-Russian peoples to have their voice heard. Sometimes the old history and traditions are, however, still seen in different spheres of everyday culture. For instance, geographical names often carry traces of old pre-Soviet and even pre-Russian history: *Chudskoe ozero* (Lake of the Cuds) near St Petersburg bears the name of an ancient Baltic-Finnic people (the Chuds). In everyday life, its traditions have unconsciously been preserved in many ethnically coloured customs (foods, communication habits, and so on). The old graves (*kurgans*) are still there, but they have to be found, otherwise they will remain just ordinary hills. The point is that we have to be able to 'read' these marks of local history, and, of course, education is one of the most important channels for teaching this reading.

The Karelians, Vepsians and Finns

Before giving concrete examples of the ethnic revival of the small Finno-Ugrian minorities in Russia, namely the Karelians, Vepsians and Finns, I will sketch briefly their history and the patterns of nationality policy that was applied to them during the Soviet period. The Karelians, Vepsians and Finns belong to the same linguistic group: the Baltic-Finnic branch of the Finno-Ugrian peoples. To understand the complicated way in which these Finno-Ugrian peoples are connected with each other – with the Finns in Finland and with the Russians – it is necessary to provide some basic information on these groups.

The population of the Karelian Republic in 1989 was about 790 000. Its ethnic composition in the same year (later statistics do not exist) was as follows: Russians 581 571 (73.6 per cent), Karelians 78 928 (10.0 per cent), Belorussians 55 530 (7.0 per cent), Ukrainians 28 242 (3.6 per cent), Finns 18 420 (2.3 per cent) Vepsians 5954 (0.8 per cent), Poles 4077 (0.5 per cent) Tatars 2992 (0.4 per cent), Chuvash 1763 (0.2 per cent), Lithuanians 1458 (0.2 per cent) Jews 1203 (0.2 per cent), Mordvinians 1179 (0.1 per cent) (Klement'ev 1991: 59–60). The number of Finns has diminished dramatically during the 1990s, since the government of Finland declared them Finnish remigrants and allowed them to move to Finland (Virtanen 1996: 138).

The Karelians and Vepsians can be defined as indigenous peoples. Today, gaining the status of an indigenous people in accordance with international law and its modifications is important to these groups. In present-day Russia this status provides some guarantees – at least in theory – about developing the national language and culture of the group. In this international legal sense language is one of the main criteria for defining a group.

The total number of Karelians in the Soviet Union in 1989 was about 100 000. Most of them lived in the Karelian Republic, but there was also a Karelian settlement in the Kalinin district, so-called Tver Karelia (23 200). By religion the Karelians are Russian Orthodox (Klement'ev 1991: 59–60; Taroeva 1965: 5–6). The Karelian language is divided into three main dialects: North Karelian, spoken in the northern area (closely related to Finnish), and the Livonian and Lydian dialects spoken in the south. The dialects are still quite distant from each other, a factor that has made it difficult to develop one unified written language.

It would offer a distorted picture to examine the Karelians in Russia without mentioning the Karelians on the other side of the border, the Finnish Karelians. Today they are for the most part linguistically and culturally assimilated into the Finnish culture and way of life, even if many of them still consider themselves Karelians.

The Vepsians in Russia live in three different administrative units in the Republic of Karelia, in the Leningrad region and in the Vologda region. According to the latest census figures they number 12 000, 5954 of whom live in the Karelian Republic (1989). Traditionally the different groupings have used different ethnonyms: *Lydikel* (in the Karelian Republic), *Vepsläine* (in the Leningrad region), *Chuhar* in the Vologda region. Vepsian first became a common term for all three groups in the late 1920s, during the process of administrative and literary reconditioning (Pimenov and Strogal'shchikova 1989: 6–7).

The Finns in Russian Karelia are not a homogeneous group, but consist of very different types of people. The largest group consists of descendants of Finns who moved from Finland in the seventeenth century to an area near present-day St Petersburg (Ingria/*Inkerinmaa* in Finnish). They are called 'Ingrians' or 'Ingrian Finns' (*Inkeriläiset* in Finnish). Until the revolution they had their own Finnish culture, and Finnish literary and cultural institutions, which were often organised around the Finnish Lutheran church (Fishman *et al.* 1996: 71–80; Nevalainen 1996: 57–9). Many of the Ingrians were deported to Siberia, first as a result of 'dekulakisation', and later on the eve of the Second World War and in 1941 and 1942. Those who lived in the area occupied by the Germans were removed to Finland in 1943. After the war these Ingrian Finns were returned to the Soviet Union, and were deported. Since the late 1940s the Ingrian Finns have been allowed to move to the Karelian Republic. In 1949 21 000 moved to Karelia (Laine 1999; Lallukka 1998: 55–8).

Ingrian Finns speak the Eastern dialect of the Finnish language as their mother tongue. Many of them have been linguistically assimilated into the Russian population. One of the strongest factors differentiating them ethnically from the Russian and Karelian population is religion. Ingrian Finns are Lutherans, which has been, and which remains, a significant factor in the formation of their ethnic identity in the contemporary situation (Virtanen 1996: 139–40).

A second group of Finns are the descendants of the 'Red' emigrants who escaped from Finland after the abortive revolution of 1918. In the 1930s more Finns moved to the Soviet Union illegally (Laine 1996: 80–3), and large groups of Finns from Canada and the United States moved to Soviet Karelia by invitation of the Soviet government. As in the case of the Reds, and most of the defectors, the ideological and political orientation of the American Finns was – at least in the beginning – pro-Soviet (Sevander 1993: 66–99).

Politically and ethno-historically, the Karelians and Finns have a special, highly complicated place on the ethnic map of Russian Karelia. The position of the Karelians has been greatly affected by the fact that, since the 1930s, Finnish has been considered to be equal to Russian as the 'national languages' of the republic. An attempt to constitute Karelian literary language was made only during a short period in the late 1930s, when the Finnish Red elite was liquidated. This exceptional relationship between the Karelians and Finns in Russia, and to some extent the bonds between the Karelians, the Finns and the so-called Finnish-Karelians (in Finland) as well, has deeply influenced the contemporary ethnic atmosphere in Russia. The creation of a Karelian literary language in the 1990s has to be examined in connection to Finnish and its status in the Soviet Union. Since 1923, the Finnish language has for the most part had the status of a 'national language' in (Soviet) Karelia, and in the northern parts of the republic Finnish has been used as the language of instruction in the so-called national schools.

The history of the Vepsian literary language has been less complicated. In the early 1930s a literary language was created and the teaching of Vepsian started in the schools in 1932. This only occurred in the schools of the Leningrad region, not in Soviet Karelia. Literature was also published in Vepsian, but again, the centre of these ethno-cultural activities was not in Soviet Karelia. In Karelia the question of the Vepsian language gained little attention, and the 1937 law concerning the position of minority languages put an end to the development of Vepsian culture in the Leningrad district as well (Pimenov and Strogal'shchikova 1989: 21; Zaitseva 1989: 97–100; Zaitseva 1994: 53–4).

The history of the Karelian and Vepsian literary languages is of prime importance in understanding contemporary ethnic movements. In spite of the difficulties encountered, earlier attempts to create a literary language provided a basis for further linguistic and socio-cultural development. However, in the conditions of current ethnic activism it has been easy both to criticise and underestimate the short history of the Karelian and Vepsian literary languages. Ethnic activists understand their value, but criticise the bureaucratic manner in which they are created. It has been seen as a linguistic 'revolution' from above and, in this sense, contrary to contemporary tendencies (see Zaitseva 1994: 14). The relative positions held by the Karelian and Vepsian languages during the Soviet period *vis à vis* the more developed Finnish language raised problems that are both linguistic and political, and which still exist in contemporary post-communist Russia.

Ethnic organisations

Since the end of the 1980s, ethnic minority groups in the former Soviet Union have been active in creating organisations of their own. The first new voluntary associations in the Karelian Republic in the 1980s consisted of different types of cultural associations. However, the first wave of organisations at the end of the 1980s was more inspired by ethnic associations and 'new' trade unions (see Birin 1996: 28–40; Druzhinin and Morozova 1996: 59–65; Klement'ev 1996: 43–6).

At the turn of the decade the first formal ethnic organisations were founded. In 1989, the government permitted the establishment of the Ingrian National Revival Movement (later the League of Ingrian Finns). The Tallinna Union and the Leningrad Union of the Ingrian Finns had already been founded in 1988 and 1989, and served as prototypes (Birin 1996: 30–2; Klement'ev 1996: 143–4). During the same year, the Society for Vepsian Culture and the Society for Karelian Culture (since 1990, the Union of Karelian People) were established. The leaders of the societies were mostly scholars from the Karelian branch of the Academy of Sciences (Birin 1996: 29–34; Heikkinen 1994: 287–8).

Since then, Vepsian and Karelian literary languages (actually two) have been created. Linguistic primers, other elementary books and the first translations of the Bible into the national languages were published in the early 1990s. In 1992, the Petrozavodsk Centre for National Cultures (that is, for Karelians, Vepsians and Finns and other non-Russian ethnic groups) was opened. The organisations of the Karelians, Vepsians and Ingrians have adopted their own flag for public use, new Karelian and Vepsian newspapers have been founded, and the national languages have been approved as school subjects in a number of schools in the Karelian Republic and the Leningrad region. In 1993 the Faculty of Baltic-Finnish Languages and Cultures at the University of Petrozavodsk was established, and in 1994 new Departments for Karelian and Vepsian Languages and Cultures were created at the University of Petrozavodsk and the Pedagogical University of Petrozavodsk. During the summer, national folklore festivals are now held, new programmes in Karelian and Vepsian have been launched on television and radio, and even novels and poetry have been published in the newly developed national languages, though thus far with very limited circulation. Finally, Vepsian and Karelian national administrative units have been formed in the Karelian Republic (Birin 1996: 34; Heikkinen 1994: 287–8).

During this ethnic cultural revival, organisational and financial support from Finland has been important. Part of it has been channelled through the government budget, while the remainder has been donated by individuals and voluntary groups. To some extent, this has influenced the role that these movements have played in the renewal of the political system.

School museums as incarnations of remembering history

Museums are not only collections of handmade things and folk art, they are predominantly incarnations of historical memories. The process of transforming the culture and the everyday life of an 'underdeveloped' (not industrialised) people into a museum is a multi-faceted and sensitive operation. On the one hand, folk cultures have been categorised as old-fashioned and backward. As part of a museum they are there to be seen as things from the past, and perhaps criticised or laughed at by the audience. From the socialisation point of view it must be humiliating for children to see items of their own culture exhibited as an example of undeveloped (primitive) culture. At the same time, such exhibitions always honour the mundane cleverness, handicraft skills and aesthetics of these peoples. It is common to talk of folk art when dealing with handcrafts.

There is, of course, an ongoing debate with regard to how to interpret museum exhibitions, whether it is 'right', for example, to emphasise differentiating or unifying ethnic features. During the post-socialist period, such debates have intensified, and have reached both official main museums and small local ones.

Local museums, many of which are to be found in schools, have a long history. They cannot be regarded as contemporary, post-communist phenomena but, in the contemporary ethnically active period, they are achieving more and more ethnic significance. School museums have inherited from the Soviet period well-established forms, a visual lay-out, an organisational structure under the local school system, and they are often a part of the institutionalised educational, leisure time and social activities of the school children. Previously, the Pioneer and Komsomol organisations played the main role in their organisation; now a new type of organisation has been founded to further these institutions: the so-called children's historical clubs that have been established in the late 1990s. This organisation is led by the Ministry of Education (at least in Petrozavodsk) and in this way it is more closely connected with formal education. These clubs are not always ethnically based (this is true in Petrozavodsk, for instance) but, in localities that are more ethnically 'loaded', this is the case.

Museums are chiefly divided into two or three parts: an historical, an ethnographical and sometimes a natural science department (or a room or a corner). The historical department represents politically important events, principally the Second World War. Local war veterans, heroes, partisans and, of course, those killed in the war are remembered here, through their personal effects (letters home, party cards, and so on) and photographs of them. Army relics (helmets, parts of mines, weapons) are also exhibited. In many places they belonged to the veterans and the fallen in the Afghanistan War. The revolutionaries, party activists and heroes may have lost their glory, but the Great Patriotic War has retained its place. This war seems to be almost the only unifying factor in contemporary Russia.

The ethnographical section consists of typical ethnographical items, such as tools, handicraft products (of wood, birch bark, textiles, more seldom items of village smiths), beautiful folk dresses, and embroidered textiles (in particular ritual towels). In many localities it is quite difficult to find any folk antiquities. They were collected and taken away by ethnographers and educational officers from St Petersburg or Finland during the Second World War (and later in the 1960s by Estonian ethnographers). This state of affairs raises bitterness among contemporary ethnic activists. For them the beauty of handmade wood and textile products has great significance in raising ethnic consciousness.

As a case study we can look closer at a village called Kurba, which is located in the Leningrad region. Kurba is a typical forestry settlement, a forest workers' community built rapidly after the Second World War. At that time it attracted a young labour force (for a general description of a forestry settlement see Klement'ev 1996: 191). Because of its character as a modern settlement based on the forestry industry, Kurba is multi-ethnic. There is a substantial Vepsian population, from Vepsian peasant *sovkhoz* villages in the area, but there is nothing ethnically Vepsian in Kurba. There are, or were some years ago, a school, a cultural club, some shops, a common sauna-bath, and other services.

The school and the club can be regarded as the cultural and educational centre of Kurba. The school is also an active agent of Vepsian culture and language. The Vepsian language is only a voluntary subject at the school, but it is quite popular and non-Vepsian children like to study it as well. Studying the language is connected with folklore activities. There is a children's folklore group which performs Vepsian, Russian and Karelian dances and songs. This stimulates children to study the Vepsian language.

There is a museum in the school and its collections of Vepsian folk culture are rich. In particular, the beautiful collection of textile items astonishes outsiders. The language teacher, who is Vepsian by birth, and the headmistress, who is Russian German and who emigrated from Uzbekistan, are enthusiastic in their mission. The Vepsian Cultural Society and Finnish voluntary organisations try to provide teaching material (textbooks in Vepsian, video tapes, Vepsian newspapers, and so on). In contrast to the Karelian Republic, the administration of the Leningrad region has shown no interest in developing ethnic minority cultures, which causes the ethnic movement many problems. As a result, ethnic activities in Kurba are based mostly on voluntary work.

In the museum, pupils eagerly guided us, showing us the various items in the museum and telling us about them. Some of the exhibited pieces belonged to their grandparents, as they would note by telling us: 'This is my grandma's spinning wheel or ritual towel'. This direct relationship to the material world obviously raises a particular type of (ethnic) awareness in them. Collections of such items can be a very effective bridge not only to family history, but to history on a larger scale. We can compare this situation with that in most museums, where visitors see things that are 'just like their grandma's'.

Handicraft is typically one of the cultural features which along with folklore, folk music and dances, and (national) dresses has been heavily marked by ethnicity. In many countries (in Finland as well as in Russia) ethnology has defined it as folk art. In this way it has in one sense been 'ennobled'. At the same time, the interpretation and evaluation of the functionalism of peasant culture has been emphasised. In Finland this mundane and practical cleverness has often been graciously praised. Handiwork has become a symbol of ethnicity in Russia too but, in fact, most of the models, patterns, types, and techniques presented are common to all peoples in northern Europe (including the Russians).

In many schools and children's clubs (*doma detskogo tvorchsestva*) handiwork lessons have once again become popular. In Kurba, as well as in the so-called national, Finno-Ugrian, elementary school in Petrozavodsk, children can learn handiwork in addition to Finnish, Karelian and Vepsian. Wood carving, birch bark twining, weaving, spinning by hand, embroidering, and lace-making are regarded as something typically national. The models for textiles and dresses are taken from the museum collections and from ethnographical books. Paradoxically, in ethnographic studies, embroidering and making lace are not considered as something typical of Finnish culture (Talve 1997: 150–62). On the other hand, knitting is absent in the Petrozavodsk Finno-Ugrian school, even though it is the most popular type of handiwork in Finland today.

Marking some types of handiwork as something ethnically special is a good example of Hobsbawm's theory of 'inventing' traditions (Hobsbawm 1993). More precisely, one can add that it is a process that can be defined as reinventing traditions. In this process something becomes ethnically loaded, even if objectively speaking it is not at all unique but belongs only in a relative sense to some ethnic (or national) group.

The Vepsian language

Under Vepsian language lessons the pupils are taught hints of Vepsian folklore, ethnic history and the material and spiritual culture. However, the language seems to be rather difficult for the children. Many of them can speak it only with their grandparents, but not normally at home.

Reactions to the potential death of their mother tongue depend on the age of the representatives of the Veps population. Surprisingly, it seems to depend less on the actual knowledge of the language. Vladimir Pimenov and Zinaida Strogal'shchikova made an empirical study of the linguistic situation among the Veps in 1983, in which some statistical and value-oriented information was included. Among those who regarded themselves as Veps, 70 per cent stated that Vepsian was their mother tongue, and a half stated that they spoke Vepsian better than Russian. These were elderly people. But if we look at this group from the point of view of ethnic consciousness, we find an interesting paradox. It is mainly the older people who do not see any special value in their national language: in this 1983 study they did not regard it as useful for young people.

Among the younger generation the situation was different. According to the results of Pimenov and Strogal'shchikova's study, more than half of the younger informants who considered themselves to be Veps regarded Russian as their mother tongue, one-third Vepsian, and the rest felt that they were bilingual, having both as mother tongues. In young families Russian was normally used. The reasons for giving up the national language were often: 'It's more convenient to be Russian', 'They [the Russians] do not respect Veps and they do not like them', 'Veps themselves feel ashamed of being Veps' (Pimenov and Strogal'shchikova 1994: 34). More practical reasons were also given, such as: 'it is necessary to speak perfect Russian in order to get ahead in economic and cultural life.' It is obvious that the oppressive national politics of the Soviet government made it extremely difficult to preserve their ethnic self-respect (Pimenov and Strogal'shchikova 1994: 35).

Today, however, we can see an ethnic paradox among the young Veps. On the one hand, they are losing their language and assimilating with the Russians, while at the same time there is a new desire to keep the language alive and to develop it. Young, mostly urbanised and educated Veps are the main activists in the Vepsian movement, which has developed during the recent years. They respect the language, which, as a matter of fact, they do not know very well. They are, however, often eager to organise more teaching of Vepsian in the schools. To some degree, the same kind of process has been observed among Karelians (see Pyöli 1996: 329–34). In fact, a similar process can be detected in many other countries all over the world.

Unshared history of the Karelians and the Finns

Vepsian history and some of its material manifestations must be seen in the context of the Russian (Soviet) state and the fact that Vepsian ethnicity is related to Russian. By means of cultural and linguistic differences, Vepsian activists are able to produce a special form of identification. When we turn to the Karelians and Finns in Russia the situation becomes much more compli-cated, even ideologically and politically marked. Negotiations on ethnic origins, genetics, the meaning of historical events, ethnic and political sig-nificance and the substance of culture and the form of language are taking place in Russia as well as in Finland – and not always in a very calm atmos-phere.

Karelians living on both sides of the state border consist at the same time of many categories: Finnish/Russian Karelians in the ethnic sense of the word, Finnish/Russian Karelians in its geographical sense, and the Karelian evacuees living in Finland. One example of the difficulties in negotiating the mythical ethnic history of the Karelians is the *Kalevala*. In Finland it is categorised as the Finnish national epic, but in Russia (and in the former Soviet Union) the definition 'Finnish-Karelian national epic' has been employed. The origin of the *Kalevala* poems, most of which were collected in Russian Karelia, and the interpretation of the story have been a vehicle for furious political and ideological struggle in politically difficult periods (see Wilson 1976). In short, the history, culture and language of the Russian Karelians and the Finnish Karelians have been endlessly debated, defined and redefined.

Half a million (ethnic) Finns and (ethnic) Karelians lived in the area which was ceded after the Second World War to the Soviet Union. The population left the area and was resettled in Finland. The area included a part of the Karelian Isthmus, the north-east shore of Lake Ladoga and some areas in northern Finland (today part of the Murmansk Region). In Finland the area is often called 'lost Karelia' or 'the Karelia of Memories'. After the war the emptied settlements, rural villages and towns were settled, by the decree of the Soviet administration, with Russians and Belorussians. Karelians and Finns were not allowed to move there. Until the *perestroika* period the new settlers in these localities were not very well aware of the 'Finnish' past of their, by then, native places.

In the 1990s, the Finns started to arrange pilgrimage-type excursions to their or their parents' native lands. These trips have given birth to mythologised narratives which are full of emotion and mystical recognition of these locations. People bring back earth from their former home districts, or water from Lake Ladoga. Often these pilgrims try to find old graveyards and signs of the life and death of their ancestors (Raninen-Siiskonen 1996). On the Russian side, such visits by foreigners are something novel, and by observing and sometimes even hosting these travellers, Russians learn something new about the 'Finnish' history of their area.

In towns like Sortavala or Vyborg the old urban architecture, which had been built by Finns at the beginning of this century or in the 1920s and 1930s (functionalist in style), has begun to be seen by Russians as something specifically Finnish. The well-known library in Vyborg, designed by Alvar Aalto, is one example of modern architecture in 1930s Finland. Even if the Russian commemoration of this old Finnish culture is often connected with a search for sponsorship, it brings the Finnish cultural heritage and the former Finnish presence to public consciousness.

The Finnish heritage has also been utilised in the sphere of civic culture. For instance, Russian and Finnish partners have established a women's organisation, the Marthas, in Russia (the first unit was registered in 1992 in Kurkijoki). The birthplace of the association, Kurkijoki, carries a special significance as its status as a former Finnish territory links it to Finnish traditions (Boichenko and Heikkinen 1998).

Even ideologically more sensitive co-operation exists. Since the war, the Finnish Karelians and the Finnish evacuees from 'ceded Karelia' have established associations, cultural clubs and semi-formal organisations in Finland which are well organised and fairly well financed. They have now started, sometimes with other Finnish non-governmental associations, to co-operate actively with Russian partners. The most emotional activities are searches for signs of fallen Finnish soldiers, hidden and forgotten graves, and erecting memorials to the Finnish fallen.

This kind of shared remembrance of history breaks down ideological and political barriers, which have been deeply seated in the Finnish and Russian mentalities. For instance, in Salmi (in the Pitkäranta district) three different monuments to fallen soldiers and wartime heroism have been erected near one another. A point to note is that they have, thus far, been undisturbed by 'patriotic' hooliganism.

Although it is too early to say whether some sort of shared history is developing among Finns (Karelians) and Russians, we can see some elements of them getting together. The radical changes in historical remembrance are quite promising. From the perspectives of local and ethnic identity, and from the pedagogical perspective, such new changes make the situation more confusing but at the same time stimulating.

The former Russian Finns have found themselves in a very confusing and reverse ethnic position. In the new political situation, in which they have the status of remigrants, they have to reassess their personal historical memories, and their knowledge of their origin, of a long or short history in Russia (and in the Soviet Union). They have to identify themselves in a society where there are Finnish Finns (who are different from Russian Finns), Karelians and Russians. The repressions of the Stalin era, the Ingrian deportation to Siberia and resettlement in Karelia, rather than to native districts near Leningrad, shaped their identity and sharpened differences between Ingrians, politically active (communist) Finns and other groups.

Conclusions

Ethnic differentiation is important as part of the identification process of small minority groups in Russia. There is, however, reason to set this in a larger context for comparison. The Karelians, the Finns and the Vepsians have different histories; their ethnic status varies and their 'nearness' to Finnish Finns is a source of differentiation. Today, this last factor seems to be the most significant in the process of remembering history.

Marking not only spiritual culture but also material culture as ethnically significant is one feature of contemporary ethnic movements. Even if many features of the Karelian, Vepsian and the Finnish folk culture are similar to those of the culture of northern Russia, they can be loaded as ethnically unique. For instance, even though the famous museum on Kizi Island is a, more or less, typical example of northern Russian wooden architecture, the place is today seen as something Karelian. In fact, in the museum there is only one truly Karelian peasant house, removed from a Karelian village in Olonets. Obviously, the word 'Karelian' has a new kind of geographical connotation here.

Creating ethnicity in schools in language lessons, in folklore groups, in handiwork, and taking care of school museums is closely connected with old women (*babushka*). *Baba*-women have always been associated with the countryside and peasant culture (see Dal' 1978: 32–3; Viola 1996). In many ways ethnic identity is produced in connection to everyday life. As a result, its dimensions are more unconscious. It is connected with language, with speaking and communicating, but also with everyday food, housing, interiors as well as feasts.

Problems of everyday domestic life are often more a concern of women, thus making rurality, femininity and domesticity such a strong triangle in ethnography. It binds the various elements of ethnicity into an intimate mosaic. Inside this feminine triangle, a large part of amateur ethnographical work finds its place. Through their domesticity, old women are capable of creating an emotionally positive atmosphere for learning minority languages. The Vepsian poet A.B. Petuhov, who started writing poetry in Vepsian in the early 1990s, remarked how 'deep in his soul there is his childhood's language, his grandma's voice'. Julia Kristeva's conception of semiotic 'chora' is to be found here.

Note

1 The analysis is based on my observations and notes on visits to Kurba school museum (Leningrad *oblast'*) 18.6.1991, Shugozero school museum (Leningrad *oblast'*) 21.8.1993, Pandala museum (under construction, Karelian Republic, Vepsian national *raion*) 23.8.1995, Primorsk museum (Leningrad *oblast'*) 15.8.1998.

References

Birin, V. (1996). 'Kansalliset liikkeet Karjalan tasavallan yhteiskunnallisessa murroksessa' in I. Liikanen and P. Stranius (eds) *Matkalla kansalaisyhteiskuntaan? Liikettä ja liikkeitä Luoteis-Venäjällä. Joensuun* yliopisto: Karjalan tutkimuslaitoksen julkaisuja, no. 115, pp. 27–42.

Boichenko, L. and Heikkinen, K. (1998). 'Cross-Border Cooperation of Women's Organisations. The Case of the Karelian Republic' in H. Eskelinen, I. Liikanen and J. Oksa (eds) *Curtains of Iron and Gold. Reconstructing Borders and Scales of Interaction.* Aldershot: Ashgate, pp. 347–56.

Dal', V. (1978). *Tolkovyi slovar' zhivogo velikorusskogo iazyka. Tom 1.* Moscow: Russkii iazyk.

Druzhinin, P. and Morozova, T. (1996). 'Karjalan ammattiyhdistysliike murrosvaiheessa' in I. Liikanen and P. Stranius (eds) *Matkalla kansalaisyhteiskuntaan? Liikettä ja liikkeitä Luoteis-Venäjällä.* Joensuun yliopisto: Karjalan tutkimuslaitoksen julkaisuja, no. 115, pp. 59–66.

Fishman, O., Juhnjova, N., Shangina, I., Konkova, O. and Zadneprovskaia, A. (1996). 'Historical Ethnographic Composition of St. Petersburg and the Leningrad Region' in E. Varis and S. Porter (eds) *Karelia and St. Petersburg. From Lakeland Interior to European Metropolis.* Jyväskylä: Joensuu University Press Oy, pp. 71–103.

Fitzpatrick, S. (1994). *Stalin's Peasants. Resistence & Survival in the Russian Village After Collectivisation.* New York: Oxford University Press.

Heikkinen, K. (1989). *Karjalaisuus ja etninen itsetajunta. Salmin siirtokarjalaisia koskeva tutkimus.* Joensuun yliopiston humanistisia julkaisuja No 9. Joensuu.

Heikkinen, K. (1994). *Mahtuvatko vepsäläiset kansalaisyhteiskuntaan?* in T. Hämynen (ed.) *Kahden Karjalan välillä, kahden Riikin riitamaalla.* Joensuun yliopiston humanistinen tiedekunta, pp. 279–89.

Hobsbawm, E. (1993). 'Introduction: Inventing Traditions' in E. Hobsbawm and T. Ranger (eds) *The Invention of Tradition.* Cambridge: Cambridge University Press.

Hosking, G. (1985) *The First Socialist Society. A History of the Soviet Union from Within.* Cambridge MA: Harvard University Press.

Klement'ev, E. (1991). *Karely. Karialazhet. Etnograficheskii ocherk.* Petrozavodsk: Kareliia.

Klement'ev, E. (1996). 'Formation of a Civil Society and National Movement in the Republic of Karelia (some problems of research methodology)' in K. Heikkinen and E. Zdravomyslova (eds) *Civil Society in the European North. Concept and Context.* St Petersburg: Centre for Independent Social Research, pp. 142–5.

Kupiainen, T. (1998). 'Runoja keräämässä ja kansaa tarkkailemassa. Suomalainen katse 1800-luvun lopun Karjalassa ja Inkerissä' in M-L. Hakkarainen and T. Koistinen (eds) *Matkakirja. Artikkeleita kirjallisista matkoista mieleen ja maailmaan.* Kirjallisuuden ja kulttuurin tutkimuksia No 9, pp. 172–97.

Laine, A. (1996). 'Suomalaiset Karjalassa – kaksi nousua ja syvenevä assimilaatio.' in I. Liikanen and P. Stranius (eds.) *Matkalla kansalaisyhteiskuntaan? Liikettä ja liikkeitä Luoteis-Venäjällä.* Joensuun yliopisto, Karjalan tutkimuslaitoksen julkaisuja no 115, pp. 77–91.

Lallukka, S. (1998). 'Shtrikhi k etnicheskoi karte severo-zapada Rossii' in T. Vihavainen and I. Takala (eds) *V sem'e edinoi: Natsonal'naia politika partii bolshevikov i ee osushchestvlenie na Severo-Zapade Rossii v 1920–1950-e gody.* Petrozavodsk: Izdatel'stvo Petrozavodskogo Universiteta. Kikimora Publications Series B. Aleksanteri-instituutti, pp. 42–65.

Luukkanen, A. (1997). 'The Religious Policy of the Stalinist State. A Case Study: The Central Standing Commission on Religious Questions, 1929–1938' SHS. *Studia Historica* 57. Tampere.

Nevalainen, P. (1996). 'Historical connections of the economy and population of eastern Finland and St. Petersburg' in E. Varis and S. Porter (eds) *Karelia and St. Petersburg. From Lakeland Interior to European Metropolis.* Jyväskylä: Joensuu University Press Oy, pp. 57–69.

Pimenov, V. and Strogal'shchikova, Z. (1989). 'Vepsy: rasselenie, istoriia, problemy etnicheskogo razvitiia' in V. Pimenov, Z. Strogal'shchikova and J. Surhasko (eds) *Problemy istorii i kul'tury vepsskoi narodnosti.* Petrozavodsk: Karel'skii filial AN SSSR. pp. 4–26.

Pimenov, V. and Strogal'shchikova, Z. (1994). 'Vepsäläisten etnisen kehityksen ongelmista' in K. Heikkinen and I. Mullonen (eds) *Vepsäläiset tutuiksi.* Joensuun yliopisto, Karjalan tutkimuslaitoksen julkaisuja no 108, pp. 19–40.

Pyöli, R. (1996). *Venäläistyvä Aunuksenkarjala. Kielenulkoiset ja -sisäiset indikaattorit kielenvaihtotilanteessa.* Joensuun yliopiston humanistisia julkaisuja no 18.

Raninen-Siiskonen, T. (1996). 'A Postwar Finnish Story. A Case Study of the Evacuated Karelians' *Ethnologia Fennica, Finnish Studies in Ethnology,* Vol. 24, pp. 31–42.

Sevander, M. (1993). *Red Exodus. Finnish-American Emigration to Russia.* Michigan: OSCAT.

Talve, I. (1997). *Finnish Folk Culture. Studia Fennica. Ethnologica 4.* Helsinki: Finnish Literature Society.

Taroeva, R.F. (1965). *Material'naia kul'tura karel.* Moscow / Leningrad: Nauka.

Viola, L. (1996). *Peasant Rebels under Stalin. Collectivisation and the Culture of Peasant Resistance.* Oxford: Oxford University Press.

Virtanen, T. (1996). 'The Ingrian Product: Processes and Projects. An Ethnological View to the Levels of Activity' in K. Heikkinen and E. Zdravomyslova (eds) *Civil Society in the European North. Concept and Context.* St Petersburg: Centre for Independent Social Research, pp. 137–41.

Wilson, W.A. (1976). *Folklore and Nationalism in Modern Finland.* Bloomington and London.

Zaitseva, N. (1989). 'Vepsskii iazyk i problemy ego razvitiia' in V. Pimenov, Z. Strogal'shchikova and J. Surhasko (eds) *Problemy istorii i kul'tury vepsskoi narodnosti.* Petrozavodsk: Karel'skii filial AN SSSR, pp. 95–101.

Zaitseva, N. (1994). 'Vepsän kieli ja sen kehitysnäkymiä' in K. Heikkinen and I. Mullonen (eds) *Vepsäläiset tutuiksi. Kirjoituksia vepsäläisten kulttuurista.* Joensuun yliopisto, Karjalan tutkimuslaitoksen julkaisuja no 108. pp. 51–62.

9

Gender Representation in Educational Materials in the Period of Transition in Hungary

Eva Thun

Gender in Hungarian society

When discussing the socio-cultural situation in Hungary, as is the case throughout the Central Eastern European region today, we find an extremely complex network of formative forces. Individuals are overwhelmed with various ideological and economic trends that consist of elements borrowed from historic Hungarian traditions, from the routines of the socialist-communist past and from interaction with the Western part of the world. In the turmoil of economic and political changes an ethical, normative and cultural transformation is also taking place in Hungary, leaving many Hungarian citizens insecure, hesitant and doubting. They are searching for a new identity and they are desperately trying to rid themselves of the inherited social structure.

Unregulated 'wild capitalism' produces a series of unforeseen social problems. Those areas of the government budget which do not produce economic growth, for example, healthcare and education, are not prioritised (Lévai and Tóth 1997: 68–83). The political–governmental treatment of women's issues has become a 'victim' of opportunistic attitudes that seek short-term solutions for long-term problems.

The position of Hungarian women is rapidly deteriorating. Many women are losing their jobs, the once elaborate social welfare system (including day care, maternity leave and other benefits) is falling apart. The significant cutbacks in education will have an impact on women's advancement in the workplace by denying them access to the necessary job skills and training needed to maintain competence in the working environment. The absence of programmes on personal and social education and civic education leaves women with no opportunity to learn to identify their needs, to make informed choices, and to make their voice heard in the political arena – a place where it needs to be heard most.

The discussion of women's issues in a systematic and responsible way has not yet begun. Government policies tend to treat women's issues as something unpleasant but necessary in order to be able to meet the requirements of the EU law-harmonisation processes (Bollobás 1993: 201–6; Neményi 1996: 83–9).

The lack of a feminist construct in current Hungarian society is often justified with the 'there is no need' argument: feminism is not needed, because of the negative experience of the communist 'solution to the woman question' (the political–ideological term used to refer to women's issues). The socialist–communist system discredited emancipation and the 'woman question' when, through the implementation of bureaucratic measures, they forced women into 'equality' against their own will thereby creating women-monsters, who want to dominate, who do not want to go back to where they belong, the home. This new mutant woman sabotages the so-called valid, historic social order. This approach successfully manipulates women's awareness of their social status (which is defined in the confines of the male viewpoint of the world) (Gal 1996: 75–81).

It is also vitally important that we recognise that the communist system distorted and violated men's lives as well. Men suffer just as much from the struggle for gaining back their identity and their self-importance. The problem is that in doing so, they often seem to accuse women for many of the wrong doings of a past system, thus blurring several issues in one big surrealistic picture, instead of analysing the different issues separately. We might categorise these issues as follows:

1   issues concerning the definition of an individual's identity;
2   issues concerning the definition of national identity;
3   issues concerning the analysis of the impact of the communist system on men's and women's lives; and
4   issues concerning the position of women in present-day society.

It is the belief of an emerging women's movement in Hungary that women's issues such as discrimination against women – especially in the crucial areas of employment and education, and women's health issues – violence against women, and social welfare issues need to be identified and discussed as part of public socio-political discourse. Through raising the public awareness of these problems, through education, through the fostering of self-help groups and the networking among women, and through the initiation of an academic university programme for women, we might well be able to stem the tide of this unfavourable process and contribute to the emergence of a significantly healthier Hungarian society (Adamik 1993: 207–12; Einhorn 1993: 181–215).

The educational scene

Structural changes

During the past few years, a wide variety of scholastic structures have been reintroduced into the Hungarian school system. Instead of the old structural rigidity of state-controlled educational institutions, now students and parents can select from a wide range of structures and institutions. Most of the structural changes have occurred at the elementary and secondary level (Glenn 1995: 199–225; Kozma 1992: 135–96). Heated debates still continue over which structure best fits the needs of Hungarian students.

National curriculum and local decision making

Despite the already demonstrated increasing need for high quality education in the newly emergent Hungarian socio-political climate, and despite the fact that experts proclaim the need for the modification of educational content and methods so as to meet these escalating needs, and despite the need for increased fiscal support for the educational welfare of the country as a whole, the reality of everyday teaching has not changed a great deal.

A National Curriculum has been designed that describes the core knowledge content, requirements and teaching methodologies mandatory for every Hungarian school. Such areas of general knowledge as learning about social and economic processes, learning about one's own personality, and learning life skills and the rights of citizens are included to a certain extent. However, the new National Curriculum is still very much traditional in the sense that the emphasis is distinctly on the teaching and learning of facts and data, rather than gaining knowledge through activities and developing the skills of how to learn. The creativity and the contribution of the students in the learning process is not a crucial requirement.

The philosophy of the National Curriculum is guided by the Constitution, by the Law on Public Education and by international treaties about human rights. The National Curriculum promotes those human values that have developed as a result of European social cultural processes. It also invites the educators to promote traditional Hungarian national values.

The gender issues of either economic or social development, and the traditional and stereotypical values that came to existence as a result are completely absent from the concerns of the National Curriculum. Gender issues are not discussed even in such specific areas as 'People and Society', and even under the heading 'Equality and Equity'.

We should note, however, that in several aspects the ideals and guidelines described in the National Curriculum seem to be wishful thinking. There is such a huge gap between the values and human qualities favoured in the harsh world of 'new capitalism': the desired qualities to have in social interactions and relations are: being able to adapt, honesty, fidelity, generosity, serving others, solidarity, respect for others, patience, and politeness. In reality 'the survival of the fittest' attitude prevails.

The National Curriculum is designed in such a way that the actual local versions for the individual schools are to be drafted by the local authorities and by the teachers working in those schools. (However, the fact that 70 per cent of the knowledge content is prescribed, as is the amount of time to be spent on the different areas of knowledge, seems to contradict the declared flexibility.) The local school districts do not receive much professional assistance with the methods of designing and methods of teaching the new local syllabuses. Further, the financing of the development and introduction of new local syllabuses is the responsibility of the local council. Local authorities tend to function similarly to the government: education and healthcare are the areas that are the first to suffer cutbacks when money is tight and needed for immediate survival purposes.

In summary, there is no guarantee that at the local level the National Curriculum would be implemented in a professional way, to the benefit of the students and teachers. Decision making in reality is not in the hands of local educational experts, but 'at the mercy' of local fiscal officials.

Unchallenged issues in the educational arena

Several aspects of the school structure and educational practices have remained intact and unchallenged, one of them being the representation and discussion of the two genders. Schools still reflect the patriarchal-traditional heritage of views and attitudes towards gender. Among the many illustrative examples are:

- Men are much more likely to be found in leading positions within the schools. The feminisation of the teaching profession, coupled with the low social status of teaching as a profession, and of knowledge/education as a whole is more apparent than ever.
- Most schools' curricula are still result-oriented and tend to disregard the importance of the process of learning. Additionally, teachers are not aware of the different instructional and learning style needs of the different sexes.
- Apart from the work of a small number of experimental institutions, the majority of Hungarian schools do not question the validity of their teaching methods, or their relevance to the development of the individual students, the content of the schoolbooks. Although nearly all textbooks have been rewritten since 1989, they have been recast in such a way as to still concentrate on memorisation of data, rather than on the development of creative thinking and daily life skills, as well as issues of ethics, morality, and social sensitivity.
- Although teachers are encouraged to familiarise themselves with democratic, learner-centred teaching styles, they find it hard to abandon the

less demanding and therefore more convenient authoritarian teaching style. Most of them are still convinced that the old style of teaching is more effective and more appreciated by parents and students alike. These teachers feel uncomfortable about those trends in education that foster the creativity and independence of the students. They deem it a waste of time and an ideological approach that gives way to individuality, diversity, and variety, and to chaos and disruptive behaviour. The newest trends in teacher education, teaching for learner autonomy, are still alien to Hungarian educational theory and practice.

• Current Hungarian educational theory literature does not discuss the gender aspects of education. Hungarian feminism is still in its infant stage of defining its personality and its role in both the Hungarian social climate and the global feminist climate. It is also trying to survive the myriad philosophical, ideological, and gender-based (read here, male) assaults of traditional thinkers in a generally old-fashioned and patriarchal society. As a consequence, it has not got to the point of a finer delineation of the subtleties of its character, namely, what fields should be analysed from a feminist point of view.

Analysis of educational materials

Three readers

Very little is known about those processes through which the network of social institutions and, in particular, the educational institutions prescribe and shape male and female social roles and rules of behaviour and the ways in which gender identities and roles are acquired (Houston 1996: 51–63; Thun 1996: 404–16). Gender identity acquisition and gender role acquisition in the educational context appear to be extremely complex processes nestled in the social, psychological and cognitive development of children. The analysis of these processes is made even more difficult by the fact that many of the formative elements are not explicitly present in the educational curricula; rather, they have the tendency to lurk in the 'hidden curriculum' of education.

We intend to examine one significant and influential element of this process of gender identity formation, namely, how the network of society is described and social behaviour is prescribed in school readers for six-year-olds. We will analyse three textbooks that are the most widely used in the Hungarian elementary schools:

1 Romankovics, A., Romankovics, T.K. and Meixner, I. (1996). *Olvasni tanulok. ÁBÉCÉSKÖNYV a szóképes előprogramra épülő elemző-összevető eljáráshoz.* 20. Kiadás. Mogyoród.
2 Ivánné Sélley, E. (1995). *Szótagoló ábécéskönyv.* Budapest.
3. Esztergályosné Földesi, K. (1995). *Az én ABC-m.* Celldömölk.

The social institution of schools seems to be one of the most decisive formative influences aimed at the young in a society, second to the family environment. The intensity of this influence is often explained by the fact that schools represent a form of power over students in terms of power of knowledge, power of discipline, and the ethical power of deciding what is right or wrong (Ferge 1976: 54–65; Martin 1994: 133–53). The behavioural and life-style models conveyed by the educational materials and by the teachers' attitudes and expectations are an imperative, they are extremely pervasive, and they are most often presented as unquestionable.

Issues to consider

Purposes and intentions

Textbooks are designed primarily to convey a certain amount of knowledge to the students which is relevant and appropriate to their educational needs. One would suppose that the content and the form of the educational materials are intentional and they are designed and structured in a professional fashion. Further, they are meant to utilise a specific, clearly identifiable teaching method.

In the case of readers the intended educational purpose is the teaching and learning of reading and writing, that is the acquisition of basic skills. Consequently, providing knowledge about the world seems to be of secondary importance. Yet the content through which the skills are presented cannot help but convey a certain set of values and expectations of activities and behaviours to the students. The following questions could be raised:

1 How relevant and important is it to design and organise the materials carefully through which these skills (reading and writing) are presented and practised?
2 How relevant is it through what kind of knowledge content the children learn these skills?
3 What influence does the content have on the character formation of the students?
4 What knowledge is provided for them about the world?
5 Does the knowledge provided belong to well-definable subject knowledge or is it set out to provide general knowledge about the world for 6-year-olds?
6 How relevant is the knowledge about gender – if provided at all – to the purposes of the reader?

Knowledge content (What is presented about the world in these readers?)

After even a cursory examination of the readers one can conclude that the knowledge presented in the readers belongs to the category of general knowledge. In the introduction sections of the books the authors discuss the choice of teaching methods, but they do not offer information on their choice of the content through which they intend to present the skills.

Since the content through which they present reading and writing is not of primary importance, the authors do not devote conscious attention to what appears in the books. It may be postulated that the readers reflect their own convictions, attitudes, expectations – or at least reflect those expectations of theirs which they consider to be everyday knowledge appropriate for six-year-olds – but presented without careful and thorough preparation. As a result the presented images of the social world are extremely general and unpretentious.

Characteristically, most of the textbooks utilise a lot of images – pictures and drawings – to illustrate and convey their purposes. The subject matter of these drawings is limited in many ways: (1) most often they depict the most likely everyday surroundings of the children; (2) they portray the most usual activities that the children perform or are expected to perform; (3) children are depicted in the company of other children almost all the time, or in the company of parents and teachers.

The texts of the reader follow a very similar pattern. The scope of texts is slightly wider than that of the illustrations, in that they introduce expected character traits and expected behavioural patterns more explicitly than in the case of the drawings. There is more interaction presented between characters in the texts. However, the pictures and drawings dominate the readers compared with the texts available.

Textbooks as autonomous symbolic systems

Textbooks could be interpreted similarly to a piece of art from the point of view of representation and expression. The moment the textbooks come out of the printing house they start to live their own lives as an organised set of representations, presentations and reflections of the culture and society in which they were created. They do not necessarily convey the intended messages of the authors only but, by obeying the rules of their inner auto-organisational forces, the textbooks create a symbolic system, which will become the vehicles of the 'hidden curriculum' (Szabó 1985: 25–34).

Users of the textbooks – teachers

It is reasonable to think that the teachers themselves interpret and evaluate the textbooks they are using in a complex manner, on the basis of their own:

1 knowledge and convictions concerning their profession;
2 views on society and culture;
3 convictions and expectations of what constitutes an educated and cultured person; and
4 attitudes and expectations towards social roles in general and gender roles in particular.

Furthermore, this act of interpretation and evaluation is present in all other activities included in the teaching process, such as interaction with students in the classroom, feedback on and evaluation of the students' work, requirement and expectations set for the students (Golombok and Fivush 1994: 169–88).

Teachers are considered to be influential agents of transmitting knowledge to the children; however, during this process they deliver their knowledge of the world already filtered through the prism of their own social status and social and psychological identity – including gender identity.

Users of the textbooks – students

Children also actively and significantly contribute to the shaping of their own learning. Children do not approach the textbook images and texts from/in a position of *tabula rasa*. By the time they come to reading and writing they have already accumulated a reasonable amount of experience about the world around them, that is, their understanding of the material presented in the textbooks will be influenced by their previous knowledge.

Reader 1 – *Olvasni tanulok* (Romankovics) (Figure 9.1)

Olvasni Tanulok has been one of the most widely used readers in the Hungarian elementary schools for twenty years. In spite of the fact that the edition of the textbook observed claims to be a revised edition, the outdatedness of the textbook is obvious in terms of the content, illustrations and texts and in the poor quality of the layout, and especially the crude and undemanding quality of drawings and their organisation.

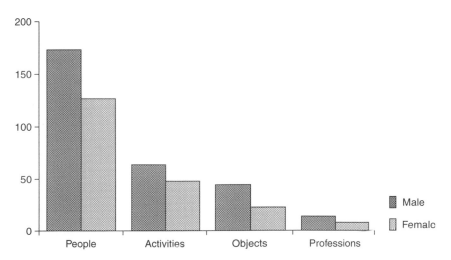

Figure 9.1 Distribution of Representation of People, Activities, Objects and Professions by Gender: Textbook 1

The difference between the number of males and females shown in illustrations is not outrageously huge. It is in accordance with previous findings in other Hungarian textbooks. Háber and Sas carried out the content analysis of school readers in 1980. They observed 67.9 per cent male–42.1 per cent female ratio of the characters (Háber and Sas 1980: 65–114; Horváth and Andor 1980: 104–26).

Characters depicted – adults–children ratio

As one would expect, the majority of illustrations depict children engaged in various activities – most often connected with playing and studying. Adults are most often represented as parents or appearing in a limited number of professions. Stereotypical male professions, such as doctors, postmen, car mechanics, firemen, policemen are described, while women can be found in an even more limited number of professions: schoolteachers, typists and shop assistants. Old people are under-represented in the illustrations and they occur in the home environment, most often in a village home environment, engaged in such activities as grandmothers knitting and grandfathers smoking a pipe, or looking after farm animals.

In the visual illustrations both males and females are depicted in terms of traditional gender-role stereotypes without exception.

Environment

The majority of the characters are found in the home and school environment. Other far less frequently presented places typically are shops (grocery, market place, clothes, technical equipment), work environment, playgrounds, and village scenes. However, women's space seems to be a lot more restricted than men's space. Men are seen in the streets, in the shops (as shop assistants), in the playground, in the park, in the workplace (car mechanic's shop) and in the home, while women are found most often at home or in school (as schoolteachers), in shops (while doing the shopping), and grandmothers in the gardens of their houses in the village. Boys' and girls' spatial worlds do not differ much. They are also seen in the school and home environment most often. Additional places are the playground, zoo and circus.

Within these limited circumstances the women's and girls' activities and spaces are even further limited, almost stiflingly restricted.

Activities

The number of activities engaged in by male and female characters reflects a very similar ratio to that of the total number of male and female characters. The activities described could be easily associated with stereotypically-determined male and female agents. Women teach, do the shopping, do the vacuum cleaning, do the sewing, and grandmothers knit; men work as shop assistants, car mechanics, they sit and watch TV, read a sports paper, travel, and ride a cart.

The girls' and boys' activities similarly fulfil all the stereotypical expectations. Girls play with dolls, watch the fashion show on TV, play with a ball, draw and do the washing, while boys build castles, watch a football match on TV, play football, climb trees, play with toy aeroplanes and cars, play with the dog and help grandmother with the shopping.

Interaction

It is very characteristic of the images and characters of this reader that they are pictured most often as living next to each other, engaged in solitary activities, and without any sign of interaction with the other characters. This is especially true when we consider the children–adult and adult–adult interactions depicted. Even when families are presented in their home environment they do not speak to each other or they do not do activities together. The adult–adult interactions are strictly professional ones. In the children–adult interactions women are more often seen with children than men. There are a few exceptions, however, when men take part in the activities, but on these occasions they are always accompanied by women as well. (See Table 9.1.)

Values and expectations

Apart from looking for the bare facts and investigating the state of affairs, (numbers of characters and activities and places described) the researcher looks for the representation of values attached to the characters (that is, whether the illustration itself conveys any aesthetic or emotional and social value message connected to the character or the activity described). In the case of the present reader very little value judgement was observed. Most of the illustrations are alarmingly blank, barren, shallow and emotionless, with one peculiar exception: old women are most often pictured in an unfavourable way, they are ragged and ugly witch-like figures.

Table 9.1 Representation of Interaction between Characters: Reader 1

Type of interaction	Number of occasions presented in reader
Children with mother	6
Children with father	3
Father and son	1
Mother and daughter	1
Father and daughter	1
Mother and son	2
Mother, father and children	3
Children with grandmother	2
Children with teacher	3

It describes the world for six-year-olds as a very bleak and barren place, where the characters perform robot-like activities of everyday life. It provides the students with simplistic, almost cartoon-like characters and, in general, there is a lack of clearly-defined values expressed in the images presented in the reader. The influential value-loaded elements that would support the affective components of the learning–teaching process are almost entirely missing from this reader.

Reader 2 – *Szótagóló ábécéskönyv* (Sélley) (Figure 9.2)

Szótagoló ábécéskönyv was published in 1995 approximately 20 years after the Romankovics book. The images and pictures are more detailed, more colourful and more friendly, and one would assume that they are more appealing to children. The overall workload for children is considerably larger than in the previous book. This phenomenon may be connected with the different teaching methodology applied. As a consequence both the number of drawings and number of texts are much more abundant. It is characteristic that the book presents ideas and notions in a series of small pictures, very similar to children's cartoons.

However, the numbers and ratios found contradict the overall impression of better quality and content. The difference between the total number of males and females in the illustrations is significantly bigger than that of the previous book. Women and girls are represented in a smaller number. This reader duly reflects the upsurge of the traditional patriarchal value system in the present Hungarian culture.

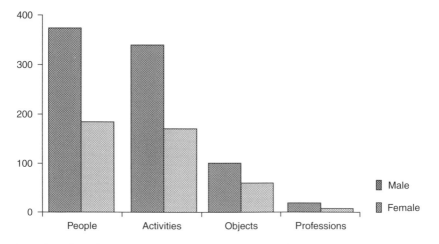

Figure 9.2 Distribution of Representation of People, Activities, Objects and Professions: Textbook 2

Characters depicted – adults–children ratio

The characters presented are most often children. The representation of adult characters does not differ much from the previous book and they are presented in their roles as parents and professionals. The professions depicted obey the characteristic stereotypical gender roles, for example, teachers are, without exception, women, and all doctors are men. In spite of the newness of the book it seems to promote traditional values. Without any doubt the woman's place is in the home. It is also noteworthy that the men's moustaches are strangely emphasised: probably the author did not want to leave children in doubt about the gender of the characters.

Elderly people are less important than the others in this reader as well. This phenomenon, however, seems to contradict the above-mentioned renewed interest and promotion of traditional conservative patriarchal values. According to those values elderly people were considered to be wise and respectable.

Environment

The scenes depicted are most often the most likely places where children would find themselves in their everyday lives: home, school, travelling, street, lake shores, picnic places and in the village scenes. There is a noticeable emphasis on the environments of leisure-time activities. Home scenes are depicted more frequently, in comparison with the Romankovics book. There seems to be an emphasis on the families spending time together in the home.

The work scenes for adults are even more limited than in the Romankovics book; for instance, the teaching profession is the only one significant women's profession represented. Although the number of scenes presented is higher, the variety of activities depicted are narrower and more restricted, and all of them are stereotypically-gendered activities.

Boys' and girls' spaces are very similar. They are also most often seen in their school environment. However, it is distinctly noticeable that the authors highlighted the importance of healthy living by the high number of outdoor scenes.

Activities

The activities described are, without any exception, stereotypically identified with male and female characters. Women do the housework and look after the children. Men, although they are more often found in the circle of the family in this reader, they are still engaged in solitary activities: they read the newspapers and smoke pipes, do woodwork, or do sports when outside the home. There are, however, several instances when we find men interacting with children, though strictly when the family is engaged in leisure-time activities.

Girls and boys do gendered activities all the time. Girls play with dolls, water flowers, make tea, blow bubbles, feed the cat, read books or draw, while boys play with toy aeroplanes and boats, build castles, and also read and draw. Boys tend to be naughty – they beat the teddy bear, or trip up other boys.

Interaction

The characters of this reader are friendlier to each other than the characters of the Romankovics book. It is especially important to point out that the family scenes and interactions are represented in the majority of pictures. Further, the characters touch each other a great deal more and look at each other. However, it is also noticeable that the mother's role is that of the person responsible for caring and attending to the needs of the family. In all the pictures in which a mother is looking after a child, the child is always a boy. We can conclude that male children have a more important place than female children in this book. There is no illustration in which the father would be the key actor who does the attending. Clearly, they are also attended to by women. However, we do not get to know what kind of activities they do outside the home which prevent them from taking part in the household activities. The picture is clearly biased and puts girls and women in a less important position than boys and men. (See Table 9.2.)

Values and expectations

This book is loaded with value expectations. There is a distinctly noticeable emphasis on the promotion of traditional family values. In the circle of the family the roles of men and women – fathers and mothers – are segregated. The suggested gendered behaviour is unquestionable and non-interchangeable.

Table 9.2 Representation of Interaction between Characters: Reader 2

Type of interaction	Number of occasions presented in reader
Children with mother	3
Children with father	0
Father and son	7
Mother and daughter	2
Father and daughter	0
Mother and son	9
Mother, father and children	16
Children with grandmother	1
Children with teacher	9

This reader provides a traditionally prescribed and idealised emotional world, recalling the good old days of the Hungarian past.

Reader 3 – *Az én ABC-m* (Földesi) (Figure 9.3)

Az én ABC-m is one of the more recent readers offered for elementary schools, published for the second time in 1995. This reader apparently attempts to fulfil the requirements of an altered school and social environment. In the case of this reader we cannot help noticing the great emphasis on national values, which are a great deal more visible than in the previous readers. This reader also offers a somewhat wider range of scenery and activities.

The illustrations and the drawings of this textbook are colourful, lively and playful, and would seem to be appealing to children. The illustrations are abundant and more communicative than the illustrations in the other two readers. The size of the book is significantly bigger than the other two, probably more appropriate for six-year-olds to handle and work with. The ratio of male and female characters is more balanced than in the Sélley book, but is similar to that found in the older reader.

Characters depicted – adults–children ratio

It is apparent that this is a child-centred book. The number of adults is even lower than in the other books. Children are seen in their own company rather than in adult company. They do most of their activities in the circle of friends or brothers and sisters.

Elderly people have disappeared from this book altogether. There is only one grandfather depicted, who is only an 'accessory' to the picture, in that he is not taking part in the activity presented. This phenomenon may strongly underline the social phenomenon that in real life respect for the importance and values of old people have diminished significantly in the

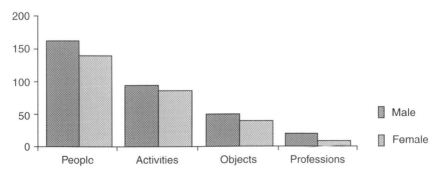

Figure 9.3 Distribution of Representation of People, Activities, Objects and Professions: Textbook 3

last few years. The few adults presented appear in gendered professions and activities without any exception.

Environment

The scenes in which the children are depicted are more varied than in the previous books, though they are still dominated by the home and school scenes. Apart from the home and school scenes, we can see children in the street and in public places a great deal (shops, gardens and parks). The representation of the environment is provided in meticulous detail, which was not the case in the other two readers. The scenes depicted seem to be the most realistic of the three books.

We do not see many of the adults' work settings. The adults are depicted in their environment only as related to one of the children who is watching them or using the services offered, for example, shopping for grocery or buying a newspaper. Many of the scenes are outdoor scenes. Farming, gardening and hunting scenes are depicted.

Activities

This book is not an exception to the anticipated patterns, in that the male and female characters are all represented in their gender stereotyped activities. Men work as postmen, dentists, newsagents, coaches; they are depicted when travelling in aircraft, giving a speech during a street demonstration, or working on the farm. Women work as shop assistants and teachers; they do the housework, cooking, serving meals, doing the washing, and so on. Women's scope of activities is extremely limited and tied to the home most of all.

The girls and boys we see in this book do the things children do most often: they are in school and study, or they play at home or go out to the zoo, circus, and to the garden. Boys do what they are expected to do most often: playing with toy aeroplanes, building castles, playing sports, or reading and drawing. Girls also do all the things which are usual for girls; they play with dolls, water the flowers, help mother with laying the table, do the ironing, play with the cat, and watch TV. There is not one exception to the stereotypical activities assigned to boys and girls. These children seem to have learned their lessons well already.

Interaction

In this respect, this reader is radically different from the other two. The first reader analysed did not show much in the way of interaction. The second emphasised interaction within the family. In this reader the family is neglected (see Table 9.3). The children are presented as having a great deal of independence and time for themselves alone or with friends. Most of the interaction occurs through children playing games or dancing. It is interesting to note that when children speak to adults in this book they do not speak to their parent but to 'strangers' (shop assistants, postmen, and dentists).

Table 9.3 Representation of Interaction between Characters: Reader 3

Type of interaction	Number of occasions presented in reader
Children with mother	3
Children with father	0
Father and son	1
Mother and daughter	3
Father and daughter	0
Mother and son	3
Mother, father and children	1
Children with grandmother	1
Children with teacher	5

Probably, it is of importance to speculate on the motives of this new phenomenon. Is this because family ties are not considered important or because of the value of the independence of children is appreciated by the authors of this book? In any case, it gives cause to worry that the children's social development and their chances for acquiring a sense of community is in danger when they are left alone to fend for themselves.

Values and expectations

It is almost impossible to identify any distinct and clearly identifiable set of values and expectations in this book. The images hardly ever convey values; they could be more easily described as 'pretty pictures' rather than representations which illicit behavioural expectations or morals. This book may be seen as a true reflection of the confusion and uncertainty that most Hungarians experience in the new social order of the transition period. Yet, it should be noted that the gender roles seem to be fixed and unquestionable in this setting as well.

Conclusion

Gender stereotypes are forcefully represented in these textbooks. All the details in the readers attest to the fact that social values regarding gender and expectations towards the characters belonging to the two genders are duly reflected in the illustrations and images of the schoolbooks. The fact that the authors of the readers examined – with only one exception, A. Romankovics – are women does not seem to affect this gendered view. It has become apparent, that although the number of women in the population of the nation is more than 50 per cent, their representation in the schoolbooks is less than this ratio. Women are depicted in a very restricted range of professions, slightly more often in household activities. In real life the ratio of working women is radically different from the schoolbooks' data. We may conclude that the schoolbooks create a world of their own, which differs significantly from the actual social world. This schoolbook world and their characters and activities follow the values and expectations of a traditional patriarchal society, in which women's positions are not regarded as significant as men's positions. Women's world is severely restricted in space and scope of activities. From an early age children are required to engage in gender specific activities, their choice of these gendered activities reinforced by the images of schoolbooks. Boys learn early on that their personalities are more important, they are carefully attended to, while girls get less attention from adults. Perhaps the most striking phenomenon in these schoolbook worlds is that fathers do not take part in any way in the household activities and they do not interact with their daughters at all. All the imagery of these schoolbooks maintain and further reinforce the gender division. There is a likelihood that women's lower social value and position will be taken for granted both by girls and boys who study from these educational materials.

The fact that the readers do not follow real-life patterns and the real-life environment – for example, computers and mobile phones are not present in the imagery of the schoolbooks – also supports our belief that these materials are designed to convey ideals and expectations rather than present and reflect reality. Another explanation for the choices of the authors may be that the values and events of the real life are so diverse, varied and fast-changing that it is impossible to picture it. The general social attitude of reviving traditional Hungarian values is in support of the first interpretation. The reality of the Hungarian elementary schools, however, seems to serve as proof for the second explanation. Hungarian society is in flux; Hungarians are in search of their individual, social and national identities.

References

Adamik, M. (1993). 'Feminism in Hungary' in N. Funk and M. Mueller (eds) *Gender Politics and Post-Communism. Reflections from Eastern Europe and the Former Soviet Union*. New York and London: Routledge, pp. 207–12.

Bollobás, E. (1993). ' "Totalitarian Lib": The Legacy of Communism for Hungarian Women' in N. Funk and M. Mueller (eds) *Gender Politics and Post-Communism. Reflections from Eastern Europe and the Former Soviet Union*. New York and London: Routledge, pp. 201–6.

Einhorn, B. (1993). *Cinderella Goes to Market. Citizenship, Gender and Women's Movements in East Central Europe*. New York and London: Verso.

Esztergályosné Földesi, K. (1995). *Az én ABC-m*. Celldömölk.

Ferge, Z. (1976). *Az iskolarendszer és az iskolai tudás társadalmi meghatározottsága*. Budapest: Akadémia Kiadó.

Gal, S. (1996). 'Feminism and Civic Society' *Replika, Hungarian Social Science Quarterly, Special Issue*, pp. 75–81.

Glenn, C.L. (1995). *Educational Freedom in Eastern Europe.* Washington DC: Cato Institute.

Golombok, S. and Fivush, R. (1994). *Gender Development.* Cambridge, UK: Cambridge University Press.

Háber, J. and Sas, H.J. (1980). *Tankönyvszagú világ.* Budapest: Akadémia Kiadó.

Horváth, Á. and Andor, M. (1980). 'Társadalomkép az általános iskolai olvasókönyvben' in J. Karlovicz (ed.) *Tankönyvekről – mindenkinek.* Budapest: Tankönyvkiadó, pp. 104–26.

Houston, B. (1996). 'Gender Freedom and the Subtleties of Sexist Education' in A. Diller, B. Houston, K.P. Morgan and M. Ayim (eds) *The Gender Question in Education.* Boulder, CO: Westview Press.

Ivánné Sélley, E. (1995). *Szótagoló ábécéskönyv.* Budapest: Tankönyvkiadó.

Kozma T. (1992). *Reformvitáink. Társadalom és oktatás.* Budapest: Oktatáskutató Intézet.

Lévai, K. and Tóth, I. Gy. (eds) (1997). *Szerepváltozások. Jelentés a nők helyzetéről 1997.* Budapest: TÁRKI, Munkaügyi Minisztérium.

Martin, J.R. (1994). *Changing the Educational Landscape. Philosophy, Women, and Curriculum.* New York, London: Routledge.

Neményi, M. (1996). 'The Social Construction of Women's Roles in Hungary' *Replika, Hungarian Social Science Quarterly, Special Issue,* pp. 83–9.

Romankovics, A., Romankovics, T.K. and Meixner, I. (1996). *Olvasni tanulok. ÁBÉCÉS-KÖNYV a szóképes előprogramra épülő elemző-összevető eljáráshoz.* 20. Kiadás. Mogyoród: Romi Suli.

Szabó, L.T. (1985). *A 'rejtett tanterv'.* Budapest: Oktatáskutató Intézet.

Thun, É. (1996). 'Hagyományos pedagódia – feminista pedagógia' *Educatio 5,* évf. 3, sz., pp. 404–16.

10
Gender Study and Civic Culture in Contemporary Russia

Anna Temkina

This chapter explores the influence of social movements on the agenda of scientific debates in contemporary Russia, with particular emphasis on the women's movement and gender and women's studies. It analyses trends in the field of gender study in contemporary Russia in relation to civic culture, including the question of the development of social movement networks.

The rise of social movements and the debate on civil society

The debate on civil society in post-Soviet Russia has included a considerable emphasis on the development of new social and political movements. As a result, we can attempt to conceptualise the women's movement and the question of women/gender study in terms of civic culture. Discussion on the subject of civil society in contemporary Russia has passed through two phases among Western and Russian scholars.

The first stage was heavily influenced by the interpretation of the processes of social and political transformation in the USSR and Eastern Europe, and several approaches can be distinguished in it. One approach, in the tradition of Juergen Habermas, connected civil society with the existence of independent associations, associational life, and open communication, that is, conceptualising civil society in terms of the public sphere (Arato 1991a; Arato and Cohen 1992). In another approach, drawing on the work of Hankiss, it is maintained that civil society differs both from the 'second' non-official society and 'first' official society (Hankiss 1988: 34–42). During the Soviet period the first, or official, society existed alongside a second, or non-official, society with its own economy, system of communication, subcultures and countercultures. Neither could be characterised as a civil society. However, in the intensive discussion on civil society in Russia/USSR that took place at the end of the 1980s, some researchers considered that the second society (or its analogies) could form the basis of civil society, while others considered it to be an alternative, or even an obstacle, to the formation of a civil society. In the first case, economic, social and demographic changes, together with modernisation (that is, urbanisation, education), and the development of an educated middle class were considered to be the roots of civil society. Various theories about the second economy, informal culture, informal and unofficial groups including dissidents, networking, and personal communications were widely discussed with regard to their significance in the development of civil society (Alapuro 1993; Lewin 1990; Shlapentokh 1988; Strubar 1994; Zdravomyslova and Heikkinen 1996). Gail Lapidus (Lapidus 1989) and Frederick Starr (Starr 1988) propose that it is possible to speak about a civil society as a consequence of modernisation and the development of a second economy. Vladimir Shlapentokh (Shlapentokh 1988) connects the roots of civil society with family and friendship.

In the second case, the notion of civil society is linked primarily with the presence of independent organisations and social movements. Andrew Arato (Arato 1991a and 1991b) considers that modernisation by itself provides an insufficient basis for the emergence of a civil society, and connects civil society primarily with free and independent (non-governmental) associations. According to Il'ia Strubar (Strubar 1994), modernisation and urbanisation led to the increasing role of 'social networks of distribution', rather than the creation of modern social relations.

In post-Soviet sociology and political science, new social movements were considered as elements of civil society This approach was applied to the labour movement, the ecological movement, the women's movement, and others (Temkina 1997). In the debate on the emergence of civil society that was held at the end of the 1980s and the beginning of the 1990s, transition was interpreted as meaning the destruction of totalitarianism and the communist state. In the early 1990s, however, the introduction of economic reforms led to a different analytical approach, which focused on the unfinished character of the transitional period in Russia. The emphasis on civil society disappeared, it seemed, for a time, subsequently to re-emerge in the mid-1990s. Now the focus was on the specific nature of Russian civic culture, in which networking was seen to play a key role. From this perspective, Anton Oleinik connects the development of the labour movement with friendship networks (Oleinik 1996). In Russia, there is a wide gulf between local communities and the state, and only actors from below, through networking, have an opportunity to overcome this discrepancy by establishing horizontal connections on the local level. It is through networking (that is, establishing close personal relations between members of groups) that movements can overcome a tendency towards an exclusively local focus, and also develop movement solidarity. This will help to avoid a situation where reforms are shaped by double standards, when everyday practices of behaviour do not correspond to official declarations, laws and norms (Oleinik 1996: 70). Il'ia Levin (Levin 1996) uses the concept of 'social capital,' adapted from Putnam (Putnam 1993). According to this view, the scope for the development of civil society depends on the extent of opportunities for self-organisation. Levin stresses the peculiarities of the contexts and the roles of informal groups and families in the development of a civil society. According to this approach, the fact that a large number of different associations, both formal and informal, exist in contemporary Russia, can serve as the basis for civil society.

I consider networking as an important element in the development of civic culture in Russia, and I therefore interpret gender study as a development of specific institutional structures, which have certain key characteristics of networking and social movements. (In a similar way, gender/feminist/women's study centres in the USA and Europe have also been considered by researchers as a new form of women's movement in the 1990s.) The women's movement, along with women's and gender studies centres in post-Soviet Russia, serve as fora in which open discourse is generated, with formerly excluded groups able to speak out publicly and bring silent issues into the public discourse. This does not mean that great numbers of women are engaging in this open discourse; rather, a relatively small milieu has begun to speak on behalf of women, sometimes prompted to do so because of very pragmatic reasons of survival, coping strategies, or self-help necessity. But through such activity they are creating a new public sphere, in which women's voices are heard, and they are opening up the public discussion of issues of discrimination, violence, abortion, reproduction, and sexuality. Gender discourse in contemporary Russia, therefore, while still relatively under-developed, has definitely become more open.

The development of gender and women's studies in the context of the rise of the women's movement

In Russia gender and women's studies first appeared in the mid-1990s. This was preceded by the development of the women's movement, which emerged as a social movement in Russia at the start of the 1990s (Aivazova 1998; Lipovskaia 1992; Zabadykina 1996). The reasons behind its late development are connected in part to the peculiarities of the nature of gender relations in Russia, where the 'working mother' gender contract (Temkina and Rotkirch 1997) has exerted a strong influence on the theoretical development of this field. Most Soviet women were supposed to combine wage working and looking after their children and family. The problems of the housewife who is excluded from public life, which played such a large part in the development of the feminist movement in the West, are thus not typical for Russian women. The position of the 'working mother', combined with contemporary problems of survival, restrain women from activity in the movement, thereby limiting the development of the movement itself.

Another reason is provided by the fact that the women's movement was slow to develop in comparison with other movements during the *perestroika* period. The development of the women's movement in the 1990s coincided with the decline of the mass protest mobilisation of democratic movements during the second part of the 1980s (Duka *et al.* 1995), and the growth of conservative movements, as well as the increasing role of institutions (parties and elections) in the political system. Gradually women's political organisations were created and the women's movement became a new collective actor (for political women's organisations see: Konstantinova 1994, 1996; Lipovskaia 1992; Zabadykina 1996). Although the organisations were relatively weak, they nevertheless influenced the opening-up of public discourse and highlighted the need for research and education in this field.

Women's organisations are strongest in Moscow and St Petersburg. In most cases, however, they have no mass support and they are not dominated by feminist ideology. Valentina Konstantinova identifies three types of women's political coalitions:

- nomenclature organisations (for example 'Women of Russia')
- grass-roots organisations
- spontaneously formed women's organisations, oriented towards one issue (for example, 'Committees of Soldiers' Mothers') (Konstantinova 1996: 238–40).

Ol'ga Lipovskaia distinguishes between formal/official and informal/unofficial women's groups (Lipovskaia 1992: 73–9). I perceive the women's movement in Russia as consisting of two branches: grass-roots activity and the activity of formal organisations. Both types of movement make use of networks: grass-root feminist organisations make great use of informal networks (Zdravomyslova 1996), while formal branches of the women's movement use the '*zhensovety*' (Women's Councils) networks, which were created in 1986 as a top-down initiative. (The networks of official trade unions, CPSU local organisations and the Komsomol were closely connected with '*zhensovety*' and women's networks.) Single-issue organisations were a combination of the two afore-mentioned organisational types. The women's movement represents various ideologies – democratic, communist, social-reformist – while their gender views range from traditionalist to feminist.

The women's movement, in common with other social movements, has attempted to take advantage of those institutional opportunities that exist to further their cause (mainly through fielding candidates at elections). Women's political organisations (for example, 'Women of Russia' and 'Women of St Petersburg') participated in the various national and local elections that took place in Russia in 1993, 1994 and 1995. In 1993, the coalition 'Women of Russia' won 22 parliamentary seats in the State Duma, although their success in the 1995 Duma elections was more limited. In 1994, the group 'Women of St Petersburg' nominated candidates for the City Assembly, but did not win any seats. These organisations held social 'protectionist' ideas in the political sense and a combination of traditional and egalitarian ideas with regard to gender. Female candidates from other political coalitions did not have any platform concerning women's issues, they did not articulate gender problems, and they distanced themselves from feminists. By the second half of the 1990s, a large number of networks of grass-roots and official women's organisations had been formed in Russia (39 organisations were officially registered in 1995, with half of these having emerged from former '*zhensovety*') (Zabadykina 1996: 256). In 1998, according to the data of the St Petersburg Gender Center, about 50 organisations were functioning in that city alone.

The women's movement organises collective actions, such as gatherings and demonstrations (for example, against the war in Chechnia), but such actions are relatively rare. More common are seminars and conferences, publishing, psychological training, cultural events, and especially various educational activities. The women's movement in Russia also possesses a wide range of international contacts.

I argue that gender study and women's study have their backgrounds in different types of women's movement. In the mid-1990s, two main tendencies in education, feminology (women's studies) and gender study, coincided with two main tendencies in the development of the women's movement, that is, the 'official' women's movement and the feminist movement. Later, towards the end of the 1990s, this rigid division became weaker.

Gender study at the crossroads

Under the influence of the women's movement, gender and women's issues became issues of public debate in Russia in the 1990s. Although their scope is narrower than was the case in the Western debates in the 1960s, research, education and publishing activities in women's and gender studies in Russia have the potential to exert an important influence on the gender debate in society as a whole. A focus on the gender dimension of social relations, for example, opens up new opportunities for the re-interpretation of women's position in Russia. Different approaches to the analysis of gender relations in society (for example, Kletsin 1998; Voronina 1997) have been developed since the beginning of the 1990s, drawing on different interpretations of gender relations. These stemmed from the practical needs of the women's movement (cognitive dimension), theoretical and methodological frameworks (epistemological dimension), and the everyday practices of gender relations (ontological dimension).

The first examples of educational activities emerged inside the grass-roots feminist movement (for example, the Moscow Gender Centre, the Gender Centre in St Petersburg) at the beginning of the 1990s. They were focused on the position of women in society, basing their approach on Western theories. In the epistemological sense, this approach emphasised the peculiarities of women's experience in terms of inequality, hierarchy, domination, and discrimination. The 'standpoint' of women became the basis for the analysis of women's position in a society, even without being specially articulated as such. The titles of such programmes and centres usually include the term 'gender' or feminism. In their treatment of theoretical approaches, gender studies courses are based on feminist approaches as well as on Western social theory. They include in their curricula issues of feminism, and theoretical frameworks of social constructivism and post-modernism (Zherebkina 1998).

Educational activities were also developing in the 'official' branch of the women's movement, with the first centres of 'feminology' (*feminologiia*) (women's studies) being set up (the largest is based at the university in the city of Ivanovo). They avoided, at least at the beginning, dealing with concepts of patriarchy, issues of inequality, and feminist approaches, and oriented themselves instead towards researching women's position in contemporary society, and in Russian history. This coincided in an epistemological sense with the stage of 'adding women' in Western theory. Approaches to educational programmes on such matters moved in the same direction. In the late 1990s, the first textbooks on 'feminology' appeared (see, for example, Khasbulatova 1998). Women's studies (feminology) are influenced by sex-role theory, and concentrate on women's position in a society (economic and political position, position in a family). They are based on an essentialist approach, tending to be much more neutral in comparison with women's study in the West.

Institutionally, educational activities are developing both inside and outside the formal education system, with both new and old institutions providing possibilities for such activities. Women's and gender studies were established in universities as new courses, or as elements of traditional courses in history, philosophy, psychology, sociology but they were based mostly on the movement's networks. In the mid-1990s, feminists became more active in education (see, for example, the textbooks by Tartakovskaia 1997; Zherebkina 1996, 1998).

One form of education that has become increasingly popular in recent years is that of summer schools for researchers, PhD students and lecturers. In the summer school that we held in 1998, it was clear that although the development of gender study is very weak, and progressing only slowly in Russia, new academic staff specialising in this field are emerging. Further, the number of students interested in taking courses on these subjects is also on the increase (sociology, psychology and philology seem to be the most common 'home' departments for gender issues in universities). Through such developments, the former rigid divisions between the two branches of the women's movement, and their corresponding educational orientations, appear to be growing weaker, as the two sides come increasingly into contact.

Conclusion

The traditions of women's and gender studies in contemporary Russia, therefore, have different backgrounds. The tradition of feminology is connected with the practical needs of the women's movement to foster recognition and understanding of the position of women within society as a whole (that is, this refers to the cognitive practices of the 'official' women's movement). Secondly, the theoretical and methodological approaches of feminology (the epistemological roots of theory) are influenced by the limited development of critical social theory during the Soviet time. For example, psychoanalysis and non-orthodox Marxism appeared on the Russian social science scene only during the *perestroika* period, a factor that continued to influence the development of theoretical approaches to gender relations in Russia throughout the 1990s. In this tradition sex-role theory and an essentialist approach are still widespread. Finally, in the feminological tradition the understanding of everyday practices of gender relations (that is, its ontological roots) are shaped by the notion of the 'working mother' contract.

The tradition of gender study is based on feminist interpretations of the position of women in society, and feminist perspectives on gender relations (that is, this refers to the cognitive practices of the feminist movement). Secondly, it is connected with traditions of Western critical social theory and Western feminist approaches (the epistemological basis of theory). With regard to its ontological roots, the emphasis is on the examination of the everyday practices of gender relations through comparison of the position of Russian women with that of women in the West (cf. studies on the position of white and non-white women in the West).

In this way the tradition of gender study questions the idea of a universal experience of women, and adopts a constructivist approach to the peculiarities of the experience of women in Soviet and post-Soviet culture. The construction of concrete (gender) experience allows the researchers to gain an understanding of the formation of gender culture in Russia, and thus to enliven debate and communication between different branches of the women's movement (Lorber 1994; West and Zimmerman 1991).

In general, in the development of gender and women's studies as subjects in Russia, the networking connections within the women's movement and between different branches of it have been crucial. The degree of solidarity between Russian and Western feminist scholars that has been achieved through personal involvement in networks and participation in seminars, conferences, summer schools and curricula development programmes are also of great importance. The development of this type of networking, and its gradual institutionalisation in educational centres, serves to create a new public arena in which discourse on gender issues can develop further.

References

Aivazova, S. (1998). *Russkie zhenshchiny v labirinte ravnopraviia*. Moscow: RIO Rusanova.

Alapuro, R. (1993). 'Civil Society in Russia?' in J. Iivonen (ed.) *The Future of the Nation State in Europe*. Aldershot: Edward Elgar, pp. 194–218.

Arato, A. (1991a). 'Social Movements and Civil Society in the Soviet Union' in J. Sedaitis and J. Butterfield (eds) *Perestroika from Below: Social Movements in the Soviet Union*. Boulder CO: Westview Press, pp. 197–214.

Arato, A. (1991b). 'Revolutions, Civil Society, and Democracy' in Z. Rau (ed.) *The Reemergence of Civil Society in Eastern Europe and the Soviet Union*. Boulder CO: Westview Press, pp. 161–82.

Arato, A. and Cohen, J. (1992). *Civil Society and Political Theory*. Cambridge MA: MIT Press.

Duka, A., Kornev, N., Voronkov, V. and Zdravomyslova, E. (1995). '"Round Table" on Russian Sociology: The Protest Cycle of *Perestroika*: The Case of Leningrad' *International Sociology*, vol. 10, no. 1, pp. 83–99.

Hankiss, E. (1988). 'The "Second Society:" Is There an Alternative Social Model Emerging in Contemporary Hungary?' *Social Research*, no. 55, pp. 13–42.

Khasbulatova, O. (1998). *Sotsial'naia feminologiia*. Ivanovo: Izdatel'skii tsentr Unona.

Kletsin, A. (1998). 'Dilemmy gendernoi sotsiologii' in I. Zherebkina (ed.) *Gendernye issledovaniia: Feministskaia metodologiia v sotsial'nykh naukakh*. Khar'kiv: HtsGI, pp. 187–92.

Konstantinova, V. (1994). 'No Longer Totalitarianism, but Not Yet Democracy: The Emergence of an Independent Women's Movement in Russia' in A. Posadskaia (ed.) *Women in Russia: A New Era in Russian Feminism*. London: Verso, pp. 57–73.

Konstantinova, V. (1996). 'Women's Political Coalitions in Russia, 1990–1994' in A. Rotkirch and E. Haavio-Mannila (eds) *Women's Voices in Russia Today*. Aldershot: Dartmouth, pp. 235–47.

Lapidus, G. (1989). 'State and Society: Toward the Emergence of Society in the Soviet Union' in S. Bialer (ed.) *Politics, Society, and Nationality Inside Gorbachev's Russia*. Boulder CO: Westview Press, pp. 121–48.

Levin, I. (1996). 'Grazhdanskoe obshchestvo na zapade i v Rossii' *Politicheskie issledovaniia*, no. 5, pp. 107–19.

Lewin, M. (1990). *The Gorbachev Phenomenon*. Berkeley: University of California Press.

Lipovskaia, O. (1992). 'New Women's Organisations' in M. Buckley (ed.) *Perestroika and Soviet Women*. Cambridge: Cambridge University Press, pp. 72–81.

Lorber, J. (1994). *Paradoxes of Gender*. New Haven: Yale University Press.

Oleinik, A. (1996). 'Est' li perspektiva u sotsial'nykh dvizhenii v Rossii: Analiz razvitiia shakhterskogo dvizheniia, 1989–1995' *Politicheskie issledovaniia*, no. 3, pp. 70–8.

Putnam, R. (1993). *Making Democracy Work*. New Jersey: Princeton University Press.

Shlapentokh, V. (1988). *Public and Private Life of the Soviet People*. Oxford: Oxford University Press, 1988.

Starr, S. (1988). 'Soviet Union: A Civil Society' *Foreign Policy*, no. 70, pp. 26–41.

Strubar, I. (1994). 'Variants of the Transformation Process in Central Europe. A Comparative Assessment' *Zeitschrift fur Soziologie*, vol. 23, no. 3, pp. 198–221.

Tartakovskaia, I. (1997). *Sotsiologiia pola i sem'i*. Samara: Institut 'Otkrytoe Obshchestvo'.

Temkina, A. (1997). *Russia in Transition: The Case of New Collective Actors and New Collective Actions*. Helsinki: Kikimora Publications.

Temkina, A. and Rotkirch, A. (1997) 'Soviet Gender Contracts and Their Shifts in Contemporary Russia' *Idantutkimus*, no. 4, pp. 6–24.

Voronina, O. (1997). 'Vvedenie v gendernye issledovaniia' in O. Voronina, Z. Khotkina and L. Luniakova (eds) *Materialy pervoi rossiiskoi letnei shkoly po zhenskim i gendernym issledovaniiam 'Valdai-96'*. Moscow: MCGS, pp. 29–34.

West, C. and Zimmerman, D. (1991). 'Doing Gender' in J. Lorber and S. Farrell (eds) *The Social Construction of Gender*. London: Sage, pp. 13–37.

Zabadykina, E. (1996). 'The Range of Women's Organisations in St. Petersburg' in A. Rotkirch and E. Haavio-Mannila (eds) *Women's Voices in Russia Today*. Aldershot: Dartmouth, pp. 255–66.

Zdravomyslova, E. (1996). 'Kollektivnaia biografiia sovremennykh rossiiskikh feministok' in E. Zdravomyslova and A. Temkina (eds) *Gendernoe izmerenie sotsial'noi i politicheskoi aktivnosti v perekhodnyi period*. St Petersburg: TsNSI, pp. 33–60.

Zdravomyslova, E. and Heikkinen, K. (eds) (1996). *Materialy mezhdunarodnogo simpoziuma 'Grazhdanskoe obshchestvo na evropeiskom severe'*. St Petersburg: CNSI.

Zherebkina, I. (1996). *Teoriia i istoriia feminizma*. Khar'kiv: F-Press.

Zherebkina, I. (ed.) (1998). *Gendernye issledovaniia: Feministskaia metodologiia v sotsial'nykh naukakh*. Khar'kiv: HtsGI.

11
Hypocritical Sexuality of the Late Soviet Period: Sexual Knowledge and Sexual Ignorance

Elena Zdravomyslova

In this chapter I discuss issues of sexual knowledge and sexual ignorance in relation to the social construction of sexual life. I see sexual ignorance as an essential feature of the hypocritical sexuality[1] of the late-Soviet period. I will demonstrate the linkages that exist between the private/public divide, notions of sexuality, sexual knowledge and ignorance and sex education. Hypocritical sexuality here is a metaphor used to describe a configuration of sexual life that combines liberalised sexual practices with a lack of institutional reflexivity towards these practices. This discrepancy of life practices and institutional arrangements in the sphere of sexuality resulted in the multiple deprivations of sexual life as experienced by Soviet people, contaminating it with discomfort, discontent, double standards, sanctimony, psychological and health risks, violence, and so on. The contemporary transformation of sexual life, though charged with commercialisation and politicisation, serves to destroy this configuration, while hypocritical sexuality is giving way to civilised sexuality, based on institutional reflexivity and sexual knowledge. The discussion on sex education is seen as an indicator of the conflict between a hypocritical and a civilized, or enlightened (*prosveshchennoe*) attitude towards sexuality.

I intend first to examine the ways in which the private/public distinction can be seen to be relevant in a discussion on the topic of sexuality in Soviet society. I then provide a periodisation of Soviet sexual discourse based on this distinction, which will help me to contextualise the subsequent discussion. I will then turn to the late Soviet period of 'Hypocritical Sexuality', and discuss the nature of sexual knowledge and sex education typical for this period. Finally, I focus on the recent discussion on sex education in secondary schools as an example of the conflict between hypocritical attitudes towards sexuality and new ideas of civilised sexuality.

The public/private distinction in Soviet society and issues of sexuality

I consider the concepts of public and private to be universal sociological and ethno-sociological categories, that are used by sociologists to understand the nature of modern societies, but which are also referred to in everyday life. The public/private distinction penetrates every social action, every human experience. According to this distinction, life experiences are formally regulated by procedural rules and critically debated in public but, on the other hand, certain aspects of the same experiences are silenced, tabooed, and excluded from public discussion, left to be considered in private. In the latter case, behaviour is regulated by traditional, religious and informal rules shared in the community. The boundaries between the private and public domains are ever changing, owing to legal reforms and collective action and media campaigns, which challenge hard distinctions and turn issues that were formerly private into matters of public concern. Thus, for example, in Western societies second-wave feminism brought issues of domestic violence, sexual minorities, child abuse, and so on, on to the agenda for public discussion. The slogan 'Private is Political' is but one example of such reformulation of the distinction (see, for example, Benhabib 1992, Elstein 1981, Gelb 1990).

The distinction of private and public in everyday life is mirrored in language. In the Russian language the words that are used to signify privacy are *'chastnoe'* or *'lichnoe'*. The latter is a derivative of the noun 'personality' – *'lichnost"* and *'litso'* (face, individual). It is used in such phraseological configurations as 'personal file' (*lichnoe delo*, that is, an official document), 'personal issue' (*lichnoe delo*, that is, an issue which a person considers and deals with privately), or 'personal property' (*lichnaia sobstvennost'*, that is, assets that belong to a person (not to be confused with private property as interpreted in Marxist thought to identify the assets of exploitation)) (*Bol'shaia sovetskaia . . . * 1978, pp. 577–80). In the Russian language, therefore, one set phrase – *lichnoe delo* – has different meanings in different contexts. In one sense *'lichnoe delo'* was (and still is) a personal issue that should be kept in secret, not discussed in public, and thus should not be either regulated or articulated by the authorities. The meanings of the personal – *lichnoe* – had to be learnt in the privacy of the family and/or friendship circle, disseminated by word of mouth through gossip and confession, with people sharing their thoughts and emotions in safety. The antonym for personal in this case is 'official', as interpreted by the general public.

In another context *lichnoe delo* was (is) a personal file, i.e. an official document containing information about the person that was kept in the personnel department of the person's place of work or in the KGB offices. This information could be used to promote or to hinder one's career. In this case, 'Personal' also meant secret, as bureaucratic personal files were considered to be secret information, available to party-state officials controlling one's career development. This public/personal division pervaded throughout the linguistic intercourse of Russians during the Soviet period (and beyond). Officially, the 'personal' was claimed to be subordinate to the 'public' (*obshchestvennoe vyshe lichnogo*). However, this border between personal and public was blurred, and changed in character quite significantly at various stages in the Soviet period (see, for example Chikadze and Voronkov 1997; Kharkhordin 1998).

All aspects of life experience belong to both private and public domains, and can be regulated by both sets of rules. This is valid for the sphere of sexuality as well. Sexuality has never belonged to the exclusively private sphere of Russian/ Soviet society. It has been structured directly or indirectly by different social institutions, such as legislation and regulations, healthcare system and its practices, system of education and its practices, housing conditions, and so on. Certain aspects of sexual life, however, escaped direct official regulations. The very fact that certain aspects of sexuality remained outside the scope of official politics is structurally important for understanding sexual practices. Sexual knowledge and patterns of its production provide a useful example of an arena in which the private and public aspects of sexuality meet, and thus lend themselves well to an analysis of sexual practices.

The public/private distinction in late Soviet society (from 1956 to the end of the 1980s) has its own distinctive features. Researchers identify an official public sphere – one controlled by the party-state – and a non-official public sphere that escaped the rigid control of the Soviet authorities. This latter realm of at least partly independent activities is labelled variously by different writers: the 'engendering milieux' of Oleg Ianitskii; the 'prerequisites of civil society' of Vladimir Shlapentokh; the 'spaces of freedom' of Leonid Ionin; the 'public–private sphere' of Viktor Voronkov[2] (Ianitskii 1996; Ionin 1997; Shlapentokh 1989; Voronkov 1997).

For late Soviet society it was characteristic that open public debates on sexuality were blocked, even though they were allowed, according to the law. Criticism, opposition and independent action took place in the so-called privatised or informal public sphere, that is, the sphere that escaped state control and that was instead based on rules established by the community. Soviet sexual practices were thus framed by tradition, official policy (official public discourse) and non-official public discourse. The contradictory messages of the official discourse on sexuality and sexual practices in the late Soviet period created the configuration that we can call 'hypocritical sexuality'. The discrepancy between what was ostensibly permitted by law, and the lack of institutional reflexivity or relevant provisions (including sex education and sexual knowledge) are characteristic features of hypocritical sexuality. When they are excluded from the official public domain, repressed human practices (including sexual practices) are forced into the illegal sphere. They become difficult to deal with in a frank and open manner.

They escape normative regulations and become risky, distorted, charged with fear, violence and uneasiness. This is exactly what happened to sexual practices in the late Soviet period.

Let us turn now to the periodisation of the official public discourse of sexuality as it is presented in the literature. This periodisation is just an example of the broader periodisation of the public–private distinction in Soviet society. Official discourses on body and sexuality were incorporated into the specific division of private–public domains in the Soviet period. Sexual practices were affected by the lack of privacy, which was relevant to the neglect in the official discourse of issues connected with the body, apart from when it was considered from the perspective of its mobilisation as a state-owned resource.

Three periods of Soviet sexual discourse

Researchers identify at least three periods of Soviet sexual and body official discourse (policy):

1 Sexual experiment and debate on sexuality after the Bolshevik revolution in 1917 and during the early 1920s.
2 A repressive mobilisation of sexuality and the body during Stalin's period in office.
3 A period of neglect of the body and sexophobia that started with the liberalisation of Soviet society at the end of the 1950s, and which lasted until the beginning of the societal transformations of the second half of the 1980s (Kon 1995).

The main borderlines for these public discourse periods were made by the legislation passed on abortion and homosexuality. Here I will refer only to the regulation of abortion and show how it structured sexuality and its meanings for common people.

I will not cover the first period here, for it has no apparent influence on the current debate. The policy of the repression of body and sexuality started with the prohibition of abortion in 1936: from that point, sex and the sexual body ceased to exist in the official public sphere. Sexuality was legally abandoned, this coinciding with the period of the policy of mobilisation of the body in general, that is, the purposeful construction of Soviet male and female bodies. To be precise, the onset of the administration of the body started in 1932, when restrictive passport and residency permit systems were introduced. In addition, mass physical training initiatives, mass studies in the use of arms, and campaigns for the cultivation of cleanliness in the household all took place in the early 1930s in the course of forced industrialisation and urbanisation (see Volkov 1998).

In accordance with these regulations, sex became officially limited to reproduction, and was not discussed in the mass media as a separate issue.

Sexual pleasure and hedonistic attitudes towards the body were labelled as decadent, and became illegal in the same way as old classes of the *ancien régime* (gentry and *kulaks*) and abortion. Sexuality was officially considered only in terms of reproduction and, in turn, reproduction (for biological reasons) was held to be the duty of female Soviet citizen-workers. Thus it was female sexuality that was seen only in terms of an exclusive reproductive asset, that had to be exploited (or mobilised) by the state. According to Dallin, 'Soviet officialdom...located women on their mental map somewhere between generators and milk cows' (Dallin 1977: 390), that should reproduce the necessary amount of labour resources demanded by the state for its purposes. Thus abortion prohibition can be interpreted as part of the exploitation of women's reproductive capacities: women gave birth not to children of their own, but to citizens of the Soviet state.

The socialist protection of women's reproductive capacities is thus seen not as liberalisation, but as a special type of enslavement grounded on their indoctrination. Women were provided with social security benefits in return for acting as a particular kind of labour force that should be used for a dual purpose: both as a resource of production and reproduction. Opportunities for individual liberal choice did not exist. Both work and maternity for fertile females were considered as social duties (as abortion was prohibited). The degree of sexual ignorance typical for this period very much fits the image of mobilised sexuality and body. Only professionals had training in these subjects – sexual enlightenment was a non-issue in education policy, as it might, if pursued, have led to the breakdown of the policy of personal body mobilisation being conducted by the party-state.

I should state, of course, that things were not completely as the policy makers would have liked them to be, for everyday life differed considerably from the aims set down in the official discourse. With the abolition of abortion, institutions of the regime thus declared that they would not concern themselves with issues relating to sexual practices (only to their consequences). Furthermore, there was lack of spatial arrangements to deal with personal matters. Sexuality, as a *personal issue*, was thus repressed. Literally speaking, there was no place for autonomous sexuality available for the Common Soviet Man under the totalitarian regime, as the communal flat and hostel were the most common form of accommodation for the urban household. This was only logical for the purposes of the official public discourse, which destroyed private property as the basis of personal–private–individual rights.

As autonomous sexuality was tabooed in official public discourse, it was forced into the private in the world of anecdotes. Further, popular traditions of contraception survived in privatised public discourse, helping to create niches for autonomous sexuality, and furthering its separation from reproduction. Family or peer-group sexual knowledge were enclaves of sexual enlightenment and sexual liberation.

The next stage of official sexual discourse – sexophobia and the neglect of the body – can be traced to the new abortion law that was adopted in 1955.[3] This period is the focus of my interest.

Hypocritical sexuality: liberalisation of practices combined with lack of institutional reflexivity and sexual ignorance

In the second half of the 1950s, certain bodily rights were restored and guaranteed. Mass housing construction policy was being implemented, allowing thousands of people to move into separate flats, and abortion ceased to be a purely illegal personal issue, with the introduction of a guarantee from the state with regard to the reproductive rights of women. The official regulation of reproduction was controversial (as was gender policy in general): its purpose was to promote dominant femininity based on the balance of work and motherhood. The granting of permission to have abortions, and the provision of separate apartments (though occupied often by the extended family), was the first step for institutional reflexivity on liberated sexuality.

Thus, we can argue, in comparison with the previous stage, this phase was much more liberal as far as sexuality was concerned. Structurally, the legalisation of abortion opened the window for sexual practices that would not be overshadowed by the anticipation or risk of pregnancy. Abortions were made available free of charge, they could be made in state gynaecological clinics, and medical certificates allowed three days full-paid leave after the operation. As a result, abortions were widespread, becoming a universal birth-control technique. As abortion was provided on the basis of medical expertise, women had a chance to get to know (better late than never) opportunities for birth-control through consultations with gynaecologists.

However, this is only one side of the coin. Legislature and statistics alone do not reveal the nature of the message that was being given in the official discourse on gender, body and sexuality in this period. The actual practices of legal abortion regulated by multiple local directions do give a picture of the meanings of abortions in the everyday life of masses of Soviet women. Although it had been legalised, the practice of abortion was inhumane, humiliating, and painful both physically and emotionally for women. Abortion in Soviet hospitals was administered without sufficient anaesthesia, and often it was the case that the medical staff were extremely rude towards the patients. This can be interpreted as a form of state-organised punishment for the sin of having sex without reproduction. Soviet Woman was punished by the state medical facilities for the decision not to be a mother, not to give birth for another Soviet citizen, and for the decision to separate sex from reproduction. Symbolic punishment in the form of physiological pain and psychological shame was considered to be the right price for autonomous sexual pleasure, making liberal sexuality very costly for women (see for example, Voznesenskaia 1991). The responsibilities of women for this sin were evident for both genders, as the punishment was executed on the female body exclusively. Thus, we see the contradiction in the Soviet gender policy: although by law bodily rights and reproductive rights had been declared and seemed to be guaranteed, in daily practice body politics handed out punishment for the privatisation of the female body.

The discrepancy between liberal legislature on sexuality and repressive provisions of this legislature via practices is only one of the aspects of hypocritical sexuality of the period. Another aspect of hypocrisy on the level of official regulations concerns the under-development of industrial production of contraceptive products, and the absence of officially trans-mitted knowledge on the body and sexuality. The absence of sex education is another indicator of the lack of institutional reflexivity towards sexual prac-tices, in which sexuality was neglected by official public institutions and was regulated by rules based on misinformation and misunderstanding, thus leading to the distorted (uncomfortable) sexuality that I call hypocritical.

In accordance with the general policy of bodily neglect, then, sex educa-tion was ignored, good quality contraceptives were not available and not used, and, as a result, sexual knowledge was obtained through folklore or through trial and error practices of learning by doing. The sexual discourse that circulated in the non-official public sphere was fragmentary and euphem-istic. It remained a private issue of a person. Thus, for example, under-ground abortions or abortions obtained through *blat* or bribes (see Ledeneva 1998) became the principal strategy of women in opposing the politics of the sexual body declared in official discourse. Private arrangements of abortion provided by the social networks of the shadow society worked as coping strategies in the sphere of gender relations.

One more aspect of hypocritical sexuality can be termed sexual privatisa-tion by default, part of a more general trend associated with the liberal-isation of Soviet society in the late 1950s, which was characterised by the practice of privatisation by default as a widespread coping strategy among Soviet citizens. People used state public arrangements (state-public places) for 'personal' matters: the shadow economy is one of the examples of this phenomenon. This privatisation project expanded also into the sphere of intimacy and sexuality, as sex in public places – sex in communal flats, in common dormitories, sex in pioneer (children's) camps, sex in the dormi-tories of student summer and work camps, sex in labour camps, sex in elevators, on the stairs of buildings, in the woods, at work, and so on – became widespread in Russia during the late Soviet period. These sexual practices were part and parcel of the appropriation and privatisation of official public places.

The liberalisation of sexuality and the 'sexualisation' of public places, however, coexisted with a lack of sexual knowledge and a lack of opportun-ities to put even this limited knowledge into practice. Uncomfortable sexuality in places that were not designed for sexual purposes was contaminated with violence and heavy drinking. The life stories of the older generation are full of narratives of sexual debuts perceived as rape, or intermingled with excessive alcohol consumption, by both male and female partners. As a result, the lack of institutional reflexivity of Soviet arrangements in relation to the body and sexuality made Russian Soviet sexual pleasures unsafe, difficult and risky (Rotkirch 1999, Temkina 2000).

This statement can be illustrated by the research of Mark Popovskii, who carried out interviews with 140 Soviet émigrés in the 1970s. In answer to the question: 'What hampered your sexual life in the USSR?', 126 informants mentioned the lack of an apartment, 122 the lack of a separate bedroom, and 93 the prying attention of neighbours (in Kon 1997b: 184). The question 'Where?' was always the most difficult one for the Soviet people, especially in the case of premarital and extramarital sex. As one architect told Popovskii: 'We are born in the hallway, we make love in the hallway and we die in the hallway' (in Kon 1995: 184).

There was neglect not only of sexual rights but also a huge cluster of other bodily rights in the official public discourse: the provision of insufficient and filthy, stinking public toilets is one striking and extreme example of this policy. In general, the whole service sector of the economy connected with the comfort of the human body was purposefully under-developed. However, the official and non-official understandings of sexuality differed. Two conceptions of justice (that is, of right and wrong) worked simultaneously in Russian society. If officially sexual rights were hypocritically neglected, unofficially, in the privatised public domain, sexual rights were acknowledged, and people developed strategies to assert them. In the non-official public sphere, people tried to give sexuality space, where and when this was possible. However, the discrepancy between official and informal understandings of sexuality resulted in hypocrisy and double standards on these issues.

In the everyday discourse on sexuality of this period, as we can see from biographical narratives and anecdotes, the focus was on distress and frustration, on the lack of sexual pleasure for women, on the affinity of sex with reproduction and violence, illegal or harmful abortions, and a lack of sexual knowledge (Rotkirch 2000; Zdravomyslova 2000). All these features of discourse can be embraced under the umbrella term of hypocrisy in sexual issues.

Sexual ignorance and first trials of sex education

The lack of institutional reflexivity towards sexuality in the Soviet society contains similarities with the situation in the Victorian era as analysed by Foucault. According to Foucault, in the Victorian era sexuality was silenced, tabooed and non-existent (Foucault 1990). However, such public neglect is interpreted by Foucault as plausible for the development of sexual practices, because they were not subjected to rigid discipline. In a certain sense, when sexuality became subject to public discussion it became distorted and oppressed by the discourse of power. According to this logic, the silencing of sexuality can be seen as a favourable precondition for the 'free' development of sexual practices. Although this partly fits the image of liberalised sexual behaviour in late Soviet society, I would argue that the sexual ignorance that follows from the silencing and neglect of sexuality narrows the horizon of tolerance, makes the stereotypes of normality very rigid, and results in discriminatory patterns of double standards and hypocrisy.

Ignorance is a complicated social phenomenon. Mass ignorance, that is, a gross lack of awareness among the public of a topic of major importance, results in rigid attitudes, a very narrow conception of the norms of healthy sex, and hypocritical attitudes towards the body in general. Hypocrisy is a central feature of late Soviet sexual culture. It reveals itself in the difficulties and unease that people in the late Soviet period found in expressing any kind of bodily desire, this discomfort in relation to the body being just part of a larger bodily ignorance syndrome. The contemporary revalorization of sexuality requires such hypocritical attitudes to be broken down, and for sex education to be developed.

Attitudes towards sex education and scientific research on sexuality underwent the same changes as sexuality itself. After the Bolshevik period of experimentation in the 1920s, the picture by the 1930s had changed radically, as if the door had slammed shut and the window been slapped closed.

Research on sexuality revived in Russia in the late 1960s and the beginning of the 1970s. In his comprehensive study of Russian sexual culture, Igor' Kon states that with liberalisation 'it became clear that both value orientations and the sexual conduct of Soviet youth were moving in the same direction as those of their counterparts in the West (Kon 1995: 85–106). Research conducted in the 1970s identified a number of trends in Russian sexual conduct. Sexual maturation and the awakening of erotic feelings among adolescents were occurring at an earlier age, as were the first sexual experiences of many. Meanwhile, there was greater social and moral acceptance of premarital sex and cohabitation, and a weakening of double standards in the assessment of the sexual conduct of men and women. Further, there was an enhancement of the significance of sexual satisfaction as a factor in sustainable happy marriage, and a re-sexualisation of women. The taboo nature of sexuality was decreased, and an increase in public interest in the erotic was observed. There was a rise in tolerance of diverse forms of sexuality, while a growing gap emerged between generations with regard to sexual principles, values and behaviour (Golod 1996; Kon 1995,).

The discursive institutionalisation of medical sexology (under the name of sexopathology) at that time claimed that normal sexuality was problem free, and that anyone who had a sexual problem was in need of professional help.

Normal sexuality was natural, which meant that it was learnt by doing and did not need education. Sexual knowledge should be practised and learned. This development was similar to the medicalisation of the discourse on sexuality in the late nineteenth century and in pre-revolutionary Russia (Engelstein 1992). The establishment of sexopathology as a discipline was an attempt to bring sexuality into the public domain and subject it to medical control. But the medicalisation of the discourse went ahead without the simultaneous establishment of a relevant pedagogical subject in the education system. Treatment was impossible without enlightenment and relevant research. The first Soviet opinion survey that covered this topic, conducted by Boris Grushin, showed that young people complained bitterly about sexual ignorance, and professed to a strong need for professional help.

The first wave of (albeit limited) discussion on sex education began in the late 1950s, and the Department of Ethical and Aesthetic Problems in Sex Education was set up in the USSR Academy of Pedagogical Sciences. At first, sex education was presented as a form of moral education (the subject introduced in the secondary school curriculum was called 'Ethics of family life'). In 1973 the first Consulting Office on Issues of Marriage and Family was established, and in 1983 a two-part course on preparation of marriage and family life was formally introduced in Russian schools. This course was studied by adolescents aged 15, within a course on human anatomy, while a 34-hour course on the Ethics and Psychology of Family life was studied by children aged 16–17. However, the introduction of this subject in the secondary school curriculum was not matched by appropriate training for school teachers. A generation gap between teachers and pupils resulted in the fact that attitudes and demands of teachers delivering these courses were often very different from those of school children. The fundamentals of contraception and safe sex were not taught in this course, drawbacks that made trials in sexual education ineffective, as they merely contributed to the imagery of hypocritical sexuality as described in this chapter. In the late 1980s, the USSR State Committee on Education announced that the course, which was deemed to have been a complete failure, would be replaced.

Evidence of sexual ignorance in biographical research

The lack of sexual and bodily knowledge, and the demand for proper sex education, is clearly demonstrated by biographical research on sexuality in Russia. The following analysis is based on the research on sexuality conducted in St Petersburg in 1996–98, as part of a project on 'Social Change and Cultural Inertia in Contemporary Russia' carried out by the Finnish Academy of Sciences and Helsinki University (Project co-ordinators in Helsinki: Elina Haavio-Mannilla and J.P. Roos). The guidelines of the interview covered the main landmarks in sexual life, reproduction, family, and so on. Additional topics included parallel relationships, abortion, birth, sexually transmitted diseases, contraception, sexual debut, violence and sexual abuse. In the course of the study we conducted 50 interviews with men and women belonging to three generations: those born before 1937, those born between 1937 and 1956, and those born between 1957 and 1973. Although there were a small number of homosexual stories, I focus here only on heterosexual relations.

The research revealed distinct generational and milieu differences in the way that people spoke about sexuality, and thus (I would argue) in sexual culture in contemporary Russia. In the third cohort (those born 1957–73), there is an obvious difference with the first two cohorts with regard to issues of institutional reflexivity towards the issues of sexuality: sexual knowledge, sex education, production and usage of contraception, separation of sex from reproduction, and so on. For the first two generations, the repressive mobilisation and neglect of body and sexuality were emphasised. This is expressed in complaints about uncomfortable sexual life in the communal apartments, the lack of contraceptive culture, poor treatment in the abortion and maternity hospitals, the lack of hedonistic orientations in sex. These violations of bodily rights are seen as harmful and depriving. Bodily knowledge for these generations was a privilege of certain professions: medical professions, biologists, dancers, sportsmen, that is, those for whom this knowledge (both practical and theoretical) was the main resource for status achievement in professional careers. Stories from all generations contain narratives of sexual violence and abuse, contamination of sex by alcohol consumption, a lack of body knowledge, and sometimes a feeling of hatred and shame of their own bodies as something insignificant and dirty. The stories give an impression of deprived sexuality and difficulties in expressing sexual desire, organising sexual life, fitting sexual practice into one's life. Elements of the Sex as a Sin script are much more vivid in the first two cohorts than in the younger one.

Public ignorance and a lack of open public discussion make everyday discourse on sexuality hypocritical. This hypocrisy shows itself in double standards in the sexual norms of men and women, a rigid understanding of the nature of 'normal' sex, as well as in risky unsafe and violence-charged sexual practices, and the reinforcement of the traditional mingling of sexuality with officially registered marriage and reproduction. I can illustrate such ignorance and hypocrisy on sexual issues by extracts from biographical narratives.

- Case one. A boy of 12 concluded that he had syphilis because he touched a girl with whom as he says 'everybody goes'. For him the clear symptom of the disease was his teenage pimples (1997).
- Case two. A young woman of 18 learnt from her mother that virginity is a highly valuable resource in her life strategy and that men have double standards with regard to the sexual conduct of men and women. She

started her sexual life when 15 and became a highly experienced sexual partner, yet never had actual sexual intercourse, managing to preserve her virginity (1997).

- Case three. A woman born in 1952 recollected that she had learnt from her mother that she should marry as a virgin, otherwise her husband would never treat her with proper respect. As she had had sexual experience before marriage, she had to simulate virginity on her wedding day, by undergoing vaginal surgery in 1972. Her husband never found out about this.
- Case four. In 1979 a woman of 19 consulted a gynaecologist as she was sure she was pregnant. When the doctor asked her when her last period had been, she answered that it had ended two days before. Her 26–year-old partner was not able to provide any further sexual knowledge.
- Case five. A woman born in the end of the 1920s was sure (in 1985) that her daughter's ectopic pregnancy had been caused by anal sex.

These are just amusing cases for the most part, but there are also dramatic and even tragic accounts. The lack of institutional reflexivity towards the ongoing changes of the liberalisation of sexual culture can be witnessed in the biographical reports on sexual debut, which was often accompanied by excessive drinking, unsafe sex, violence and abuse in an environment not conducive to the romanticisation of sexual practices. The official taboo around late Soviet sexuality was a subject of anecdote culture and children's folklore, that tells us much about the nature of the Russian Eros.

Discussion on sex education (end of 1990s)

A liberation of sexuality is taking place in the course of the current process of social transformation in Russia. One of the first symptoms is the problematisation of this sphere in public discourse. In common with many other post-communist societies, the developing discourse on sexuality has become a hot topic, with numerous TV programmes dealing with the subject, while pornographic films have become available for all ages with the spread of new media and information opportunities (video films and Internet sites are available without censorship). This reinvention of the sexual body – as a body of desire – and the manipulation that surrounds this desire should not be seen as a minor issue to be considered only from the pedagogical point of view. The manipulation of the sexual body is part of the marketisation of every item or aspect of life that is marketable, and part of the politicisation of every possible issue by different political forces. The mass media works as one of the main actors of such manipulation. The evidence of such tendency is the mass spread of pornography on the one hand, and moralising political discussions of conservatives on the other.

However, opinion polls show regularly that since the end of the 1980s, some 60–70 per cent of the population are in favour of sex education, while between three and 20 per cent are against it (Kon 1997a), thus demonstrating a clear social demand for sex education. In 1996 the Ministry of Education of Russia applied to the United Nations Foundation of Population and UNESCO for financial help for three years' support in developing a curriculum for a 30-hour course for the 7th to 9th grades (12–15 year old pupils) of 16 pilot Russian secondary schools. The pilot project started in summer 1996 and included research and trials in 16 secondary schools in the towns of Moscow, Krasnoiarsk, Novosibirsk, Kurgan, Samara, St Petersburg, Arkhangelsk, Izhevsk, Iaroslavl' and other large towns. The project was co-ordinated by the Russian Association for Family Planning, which has more than 200 regional offices all over Russia. New establishments were also set up, including medical pedagogical centres and youth centres.

Although the programme was not adopted, the research and trials that were made (which were not without their shortcomings) caused a discussion on this topic to take place in the mass media at the end of 1990s. The issue was debated not only in the media, but in the State Duma as well, which led the Ministry of Education to cancel the project on 'Sexual Education of Russian school Children' in April 1997.

Despite the fact that the population in general supported sexual enlightenment, a section of the pedagogical elite as well as parents, mostly from the older generation, rigidly opposed it. In the discussion on the issue of school-based sex education, national patriotic forces, as well as church authorities, started to moralise and criticise programmes of family planning and sex education, as well as the bill on the reproductive rights of women and commercial erotica. Certain voluntary associations of parents also expressed their negative attitude to the practices of the sexual education classes in primary schools (that is, Moscow NGO Parental Initiatives; the Iaroslavl' Committee for the Protection of Life and the Family). In their criticisms they used arguments similar to those of the Pro-life movement in the USA. Religious organisations also supported the anti-abortion attitudes, while a warning that sex education would provoke all of the social problems seen in Western societies was disseminated among the teaching force. This campaign was professionally launched by the Orthodox Church and the Foundation of Socio-Psychological Health of Family and Child. They argued that safe sex is the way to moral dissolution, and sex education in schools would provoke earlier sexual debuts.

The discussion was started by two psychologists, I. Medvedeva and T. Chikhova, opponents of the experiment on sex education, who published a paper that had been presented to the Duma Committee on Security in *Rossiiskaia gazeta* (15 March 1997). The opponents of the project claimed that it was the sexual revolution and the development of sex education in the USA that was responsible for the growth of the number of teenage abortions, and sexual deviance, including homosexuality and incest. They brought forward evidence that contraceptive pills resulted in the growth of the spread of breast cancer of women. Sex education, they argued:

> Should not be a school subject, but should be part of the enlightenment of one's soul . . . When a boy is taught to be brave and generous, and a girl is taught to be prim and proper and a good housewife – this is sex education which starts from the very first days of one's life.
>
> (Medvedeva and Chikhova 1997)

Similarly, Academician Baranov of the Research Centre for the Health Security of Children and Teenagers in Moscow believed that sexual education programmes would not prevent 'sexual dissolution (*raspushennost'*), which is a threat for the nation's health'. He noted that:

> It would be useful to return to the old traditions of the gender separate education in secondary schools where such educational programmes would be more efficient.
>
> (Baranov 1997)

Another argument against the introduction of sex education in secondary schools was based on the failure of the educational programme of the 1980s. This failure, as was explained above, was caused by the authoritarian pattern of education, as well as the psychologically naive material of the course. The Orthodox Church opposed the programme on the grounds that it was incompatible with Russian culture and had a destructive effect on morality. Church representatives collected more than 5000 signatures against the programme, and passed them to the Duma. The programmes were also opposed by conservative demographers, who argued that they promote a policy of national extinction, and would lead to the demographic decline of the Russian population. With regard to sexual knowledge, an Academician of the Russian Pedagogical Academy, D. Kolesov, even claimed that people have a right to be ignorant:

> A human being has a right not to know what he does not want to know. One should not impose the information that is not demanded.
>
> (quoted in Klimov 1997)

On the other side, experts and leaders of the research groups that were involved in the programme (I. Kon, A. Petrovskii, V. Cherviakov and B. Shapiro) emphasised the necessity of sex education for the development of civilised, responsible sexual behaviour. They claimed that opponents of the project misinterpreted statistics, and argued for a sexual puritanism that could not be achieved in the context of liberalised sexuality. It was agreed that the programmes should undergo accreditation, and that a commitment to collaboration among physicians, teachers, parents and the general public should be guaranteed before any programme was launched in the schools. The main issues to discuss are: who should teach such programmes, what forms of education on the topics of intimacy are relevant and effective, and the development of understanding of the cultural specificity of the programme of sex education in Russia.

In reaction to the campaign against sex education, Professor Igor' Kon, a famous expert on Russian sexual culture, claimed that the critique was part of a sexual counter-revolution, which he believed would not be successful. He saw the attack on sex education as a part of a broader campaign against sexual liberation, including opposition to the bill on the Reproductive Rights of Women that had been submitted to the Duma by the 'Women of Russia' faction (the head of which was then Ekaterina Lakhova – 1993–96). The issue of abortion was at the core of the bill. It was argued that the reproductive rights of women, including the right of abortion and the right for contraception, should be provided legally and institutionally (Kon 1997a). Kon claimed that the school is the only institution capable of dealing with the sexual enlightenment of the younger generation, as the family had proved to be inefficient in this sphere, and the mass media does not provide real education, but is full of cheap erotic material and semi-pornography.

In the end, the criticism aimed at the pilot project resulted in its suspension by the Ministry of Education in 1997, although this suspension may prove to be temporary.[4]

For civilised sexuality

Debates on sex education in school are symptomatic of debates on social change in post-Soviet Russia. In spite of the protests of conservatives, attempts to establish programmes of sexual enlightenment are being made here and there. For a sociologist it is important to see the reinvention of the body and sexuality as part of the general transformation process in Russia. The revival of sexuality in practice and discourse cannot be perceived separately from the major societal changes that are taking place.

The discussion of sexual knowledge and sex education is only one part of the discourse on sex and the reinvention of the body. When the body and sexuality have started to be public items – widely covered in marketised and politicised discourse – the education system can hardly remain untouched by such developments, for the realities of everyday life demand attention from the schools. It has to be seen, then, as an institutional reaction to the changes, and as part of the change itself. As part of the reinvention of sexuality and body, the discussion on sex education has come to the fore among the post-Soviet public. The problematisation of sexuality in the discussion on sexual knowledge and sex education revealed two main standpoints. The first – the conservative one – is articulated by the proponents of Soviet hypocritical sexuality. The second – the liberal one – is articulated by the supporters of civilised or enlightened sexuality. The main feature for hypocritical sexuality of the Soviet society is the combination of liberalised sexual practices with a lack of knowledge about, and acceptance of responsibility in, such practices. Hypocritical sexuality has harmful consequences for the quality of health and psychological development. The neglect of body and sexuality, and the absence of relevant knowledge has the serious effect of narrowing the definition of what constitutes normal sexuality, and results in sex becoming risky and unsafe. If the public demand for sex education is not provided by educational institutions, then such learning will take place through actual practice and through knowledge transmitted by peer groups. The social demand for sex education is evident, and the education system is being called upon to promote a civilised approach to sexuality, yet civilised sexuality will be difficult to achieve without a real attempt to develop efficient programmes of sex education. The results of the discussion on sex education are dubious. On the one hand, the project was cancelled, but, on the other, the issue was debated in the public domain. This means that there are prospects and hopes for the new developments of civilised sexuality.

Notes

1   Late Soviet sexuality is referred to as hypocritical by such researchers as I. Kon (Kon 1995) and A. Rotkirch (Rotkirch 2000).
2   In a similar fashion, the Hungarian sociologist Elmar Hankiss suggested the theory of 'second society'. He describes the split into first and second societies under Hungarian socialism, the latter including all actions that were not subject to party-state control.
3   Incidentally, this was also the time when gender division in schools was abolished.
4   The discussion on sex education formed just part of the process of problematisation of the issues of sexuality in the public sphere. In the discourse it is stated that the main feature for contemporary Russian sexuality is a combination of liberalised sexual practices with a lack of knowledge and responsibility of sexual practices. This discrepancy has harmful consequences for health and for psychological development. The level of venereal disease grew 51 times in the period 1994–99, for example, while the number of abortions per 100 deliveries in Russia is eight times more than in the USA, ten times greater than in France, and 20 times more than in Holland (Kon 1995)

References

Baranov, (1997). *Rossiiskaia gazeta*, 22 March.
Bol'shaia sovetskaia entsiklopedia, vol. 14. (1978). Moscow: Entsiklopedia.
Benhabib, S. (1992). 'Models of Public Space: Hanna Arendt, the Liberal Tradition, and Juergen Habermas' in C. Colhaun (ed.) *Habermas and the Public Sphere*. Cambridge: MIT Press, pp. 73–95.

Chikadse, E. and Voronkov, V. (1997). 'Leningrad Jews: Ethnicity and Context' in V. Voronkov and E. Zdravomyslova (eds) *Biographical Perspectives on Post-Soviet Societies*. CISR Working Papers, no. 5.

Dallin, A. (1977). 'Conclusions' in D. Atkinson, A. Dallin and G. Lapidus (eds) *Women in Russia*. Stanford: Stanford University Press.

Elstein, J.B. (1981). *Public Man, Private Women. Women in Social and Political Thought*. Princeton: Princeton University Press.

Engelstein, L. (1992). *The Keys to Happiness*. Ithaca NJ: Cornell University Press.

Foucault, M. (1990). *The History of Sexuality I: An Introduction*. London: Penguin Books.

Gelb, J. (1990). 'Feminism and Political Action' in R. Dalton and M. Kuechler (eds) *Challenging the Political Order*. London: Polity Press, pp. 137–55.

Golod S. (1996). *XX vek i tendentsii seksual'nykh otnoshenii v Rossii*. St. Petersburg: Aleteia.

Ianitskii, O. (1996). *Ekologicheskoe dvizhenie v Rossii*. Moscow: Nauka.

Ionin, L. (1997). *Svoboda v SSSR*. St Petersburg: Fond universitetskaia kniga.

Kharkhordin O. (1999). *The Collective and the Individual in Russia. A Study of Practices*. Berkeley: University of California Press.

Klimov, A. (1997). 'U vas ne ta poza' *Trud*, 11 July.

Kon, I. (1995). *The Sexual Revolution in Russia*. Free Press.

Kon, I. (1997a). 'Izmena! Kriknul malchish-kubalchish' *Chas pik*, 28 May.

Kon, I. (1997b). *Seksual'naia kul'tura v Rossii*. Moscow: O.G.I.

Ledeneva, A. (1998). *Russia's Economy of Changes: Blat, Networking and Informal Exchange*. Cambridge: Cambridge University Press.

Medvedeva, I. and Chikhova, T. (1997). *Rossiiskaia gazeta*, 15 March.

Rotkirch, A. (2000). 'The Man Question. Loves and Lives in the Late 20th Century Russia', University of Helsinki, Kikimora: Helsinki.

Shlapentokh, V. (1989). *Public and Private Life of the Soviet People: Changing Values in Post-Stalin Russia*. New York: Oxford University Press.

Temkina, A. (2000). 'Sexual Scripts in Women's biographies and the Construction of sexual pleasure' in M. Lijestrom, A. Rosenholm and I. Savkina (eds) *Models of Self. Russian Women's Autobiographical Texts*. Kikimora Publ. Series B: 18. Helsinki.

Volkov, V. (1998). 'The Concept of *Kul'turnost'*: Notes on the Stalinist Civilizing Process' in S. Fitzpatrick (ed.) *Stalinism: New Perspectives*, London: Routledge.

Voznesenskaia, I. (1991). *Zhenskii dekameron*. Tallin: Tomas s. m.

12
The Struggle for the Souls of Young People: Competing Approaches to 'Spiritual' and Religious Education in Russia Today

James Muckle

The Russian word *dukhovnyi*, usually translated as 'spiritual,' has a wider series of connotations than 'spiritual' in English or possibly even *'geistlich'* in German. One Russian educator defines *dukhovnost'* – 'spirituality', for want of a better word: it includes the development of the need for knowledge and self-knowledge, for reflection, beauty, intercourse with others, creativity, the autonomy of the inner world, the search for a meaning to life, for happiness, for an ideal (Bondarevskaia 1995: 30). In the Soviet Union this search for a meaning to life did not include exploration of religious faith; today it does. This paper investigates the widely differing ways in which Russian religious educators, lay and clerical, seek to impart knowledge and understanding of religion to young people. It seeks also to illuminate the standpoint and the motivation of those educators.

The purpose of this brief study is to introduce the fascinating and complex issues which surround the topic. There will be a cursory glance only at practical matters, such as organisation, materials, teacher education and the like. The reader is directed to John Dunstan's (1992) article which goes usefully into such points; his account must be updated sometime, but here discussion is confined to those who set the theoretical basis for religious education (RE), or who would do so if they could. There is no area of education in which Sir Michael Sadler's famous dictum – that 'in studying foreign systems of education . . . the things outside the schools matter even more than the things inside the schools, and govern and interpret the things inside' (Sadler 1900: 11–12) – is more important. None of the issues can possibly be understood without excursions into sociology and social history, theology and philosophy as well as education.

Real and apparent educational reform

A few years after the collapse of the Soviet Union, there has been little evidence of real 'inner', 'osmotic' change in educational attitudes, as opposed to outer, cosmetic reform. Communist thought is discredited, but when nothing can be found to replace it, the old tendencies creep back to fill the vacuum. For example, the tradition was always that a set of values was imposed from above. Many today are seeking a new set of values, but still to impose them from above – maybe after reaching consensus of a sort, but imposing them none the less.

Secondly, atheism was compulsory in the old days, and frequently atheist teachers would oppress believing children. One journalist (Polozhevets 1998) describes finding a teacher who had bullied children for having being seen in church, now begging on a street corner. That teacher was not very resourceful, for many of her fellow atheists have renamed their courses 'history of religion'; others have turned their coats in order to stay in work.

Thirdly, methods of imparting RE are often highly theoretical, and they require passive behaviour from the pupils. Some teachers in the Sunday schools that have sprung up all over the country place inordinate stress on authority, obedience and sin – and its dire consequences. Imposition of values, sharp reversals of the accepted ideology, and insistence that the approved line must be accepted – what could be more Soviet than this? Yet there are educators who are working to change the whole ethos. Let us not underestimate the task they face.

The historical legacy under Tsarism and communism in relation to religion in Russia

Religion and the Russian Orthodox Church (ROC) in particular must even today carry the weight of the national memory of their behaviour before the Revolution of 1917. The intelligentsia in the nineteenth century had a very low opinion of the intelligence, education and general culture of the clergy. There were exceptions to this, but even the devout had little respect for the priesthood in general. The role of the ROC in supporting the government and the Tsar and in hindering freedom of speech and religion was regarded with contempt. Nevertheless, the national religion was Orthodoxy. Dissenting denominations existed, but were persecuted by Church and bureaucracy alike. Prominent free thinkers were pilloried. Jews often suffered: anti-semitism was rife and there were notorious pogroms which drove many Jews from the country. Islam was strong, but mainly in fringe areas of the Empire. Even today, as we shall see, depressingly little is heard from religious educators about these faiths and their right to be considered.

Under communism the ROC found it very difficult even to survive. Attempts to forge an uneasy alliance with Stalin and other leaders caused a bitter schism in the Church, and to this day there are Orthodox abroad who see the present hierarchy as the 'Soviet Church' and even as Antichrist for having compromised with the communists. Anti-semitism continued and was especially encouraged by the government at certain times in Soviet history. It is hard to know how effective anti-religious propaganda really was, but faith was equated by many with superstition.

These factors are listed here merely to outline what may be termed the folk memory of the Russian people in regard to religion. They illustrate some of the difficulties which religious apologists and educators face in presenting the subject to the youth of today, whose parents may have passed on many of these views and prejudices to them. At the same time we need to remember that Orthodox Christianity has existed in Russia for over a thousand years, and its hold on the people's imagination should not be underestimated.

Individuals, society and the Church in Russia today

Mikhail Gorbachev began a rapprochement with the Church in 1988. This quickly gathered momentum and, by the time the Soviet Union ceased to be in 1991–92, a great deal of previously suppressed interest in things transcendental was liberated. The ROC, as we shall see, was not the only centre of this interest, but it did welcome many enquirers and indeed new converts. Existing believers and some reformist priests who had worked in obscurity now became prominent. One writer on the present situation (Nikol'skaia 1998) divides Church members into 'veterans' and 'proselytes'. It is not necessarily the 'proselytes' who look for reform in the Church's rituals and attitudes.

Speaking in another context, Vaclav Havel recently commented: 'Those of us who fought for freedom made a big mistake. [Democrats] failed to take account of the danger that freedom, suddenly gained, would awaken suppressed tendencies (of ethnic, religious and ideological intolerance)' (Havel 1997). Father Aleksandr Men' said in 1990, four days before he was murdered, 'When Gorbachev opened the floodgates, reaction as well as democracy poured in' (quoted in Roberts and Shukman 1996: 169).

Toleration and freedom of religion

Lack of religious freedom was not a phenomenon exclusively of Soviet Russian society. In the nineteenth century the ROC was largely incapable of coping with dissent, or even with mild difference of opinion. For instance, it was punishable by law for a Russian citizen to renounce Orthodoxy. Russian evangelicals were silenced and even banished from the country. Monasteries were used as prisons for turbulent priests. Tolstoi was anathematised for expressing unconventional religious views. At the same time, Price states that Orthodox Churches 'are traditionally tolerant of diversity' (Price 1998b: 1354). This view is doubtless based on the more progressive clergy of the nineteenth century; Ion Bria, writing in the *Ecumenical Review*, regards the ROC as 'not receptive to the insights of others' (Bria 1998: 162).

It is particularly distasteful to the liberal conscience when former victims of religious oppression become the oppressors after freedom is granted to them. It is hard to contemplate the state of mind of those who seek to preserve their own freedoms while restricting those of other believers, but such attitudes are not confined to Russia or to the present time: British history holds plenty of examples. As we shall see, some Russian believers have reverted to pre-1917 practices, by which Christians of all persuasions used legal and administrative methods to oppress fellow-believers, sometimes within their own denomination.

A further matter over which many Russians express disproportionate concern is that since the turnabout of 1991 Russia has been beset by evangelists, sects and cults of all sorts: no fewer than 14 000 groups were registered by 1997 (Bernbaum 1997). Some of these are of impeccable credentials; some may justly be considered to be harmless crackpots. Popular attitudes assume that these are all 'foreign' and therefore bad: very many are in fact innocuous Russian lunatics. Very few of these groups, with the possible exception of Jehovah's Witnesses and Scientologists, have established any sort of toe-hold in Russian society.

At the same time other religious denominations, long established in Russia but perhaps not all indigenous, have staked a claim for the same freedom as is enjoyed by the Orthodox Church. (These groups – Baptists, Evangelicals, Pentecostalists, Seventh-Day Adventists and other Protestant-type denominations predominantly of German or British origin – consist of many tens of thousands of members yet add up to a very small percentage indeed of the overall population.) The return of the Ukrainian Catholics to Rome, decades after they were forced by Stalin to accept the episcopal oversight of the Orthodox Patriarch, re-opened old wounds. All these facts and events may seem to some die-hard Orthodox Christians as a threat.

Because of the overwhelming dominance of the Orthodox Church, which far exceeds the power of the 'national' church in any other major West European or North American country, it is argued by some that Russia is not a multi-religious, pluralistic society. Consequently, this argument continues, what is required in schools is Orthodox education, not 'religious' or 'Christian' education. It is remembered that a similar attitude was adopted in England by the Anglican Church in the nineteenth century. In consequence many very respectable English citizens went to prison for non-payment of taxes in protest against the dominance of the Anglican Church in education: they were successful, in that this led to the 'agreed syllabuses' of non-sectarian Christian teaching in state schools. This fact is referred to here to demonstrate that the battle for denominational impartiality had to be fought in another European society; if it now has to be fought in Russia, one should not be too surprised.

Orthodox theology and its implications for religious 'freedom'

Myroslaw Tataryn declares that Western observers who urge Russian Orthodox to adopt the principle of religious liberty misunderstand Orthodoxy.

'Perhaps the problem lies in a discordance in ecclesiologies, definitions of person and community, and most importantly, differing understanding of the nature of the relationship between faith and culture' (Tataryn 1997: 56).

It is impossible to do full justice to Tataryn's analysis briefly here. A few points must suffice to illustrate the difficulties. What Tataryn calls the 'classical' standpoint represents the apparently 'hard-line' attitude in the Russian Church today. One problem is that individuality is not seen as good, rather does the 'individual' represent 'that manifestation of human nature...fundamentally defined by sin'. (Tataryn 1997: 58) The Church is 'the community of the loved and loving...the perfect embodiment of communion' (Tataryn 1997: 58). Most importantly, Orthodox Christians who hold the classical view regard the Church as 'the only true community for Christians in Eastern Europe. Rejecting that community in favour of another Church is not seen as an act of personal conscience, but rather as the act of an individual who is fragmenting the Una Sancta and rejecting the true communion of the Church' (Tataryn 1997: 59).

Tataryn further reminds the reader that Orthodoxy is closely linked with the culture from which it sprang originally – Byzantium – and consequently presents an Eastern (Hellenic) corrective to Western European culture and Christianity. 'Culture and Orthodoxy are thus inextricably linked... (and Serbian, Ukrainian and Russian Orthodoxy) all recognise an extensive responsibility for the cultural survival of their particular nations' (Tataryn 1997: 62). The anti-Western attitudes of the strongly traditionalist Orthodox educator are therefore not merely a question of a failure to embrace liberal democratic notions of religious freedom, but a manifestation of a fundamental theological and ecclesiological position. Nevertheless, this does not mean that an open and ecumenical attitude is impossible for the Orthodox. Such attitudes, as we shall see, exist among Russian religious educators, but these people have had to grapple with the traditional position.

Away from the theological academies, popular attitudes must be reckoned with. 'Ecumenism' is a word and a concept that is deplored by many. We are told by Fedorov (1998) that the ignorant mispronounce the word as 'ekommunizm' or 'ekonomizm', thus relating it to the hated former ideology or the detested economic situation of today. It was connected in the public mind with government policies in the 1960s, which encouraged the Church to develop links with churches abroad. The Soviet government had its own reasons for this, and the public consequently connected ecumenism with the KGB. Since 1988, anti-ecumenism has been embraced by some of the more fanatical converts to Orthodoxy, often, Fedorov says, ignorant of theology or the Church's teaching, and given to a crude fundamentalist approach to religious doctrines.

The sociological and political context of RE

What, then, are the attitudes to religion and the Church among the mass of the Russian people? Fewer people attend church in Russia than in any nominally Christian country. I make use here of two informative papers by Wallace Daniel (1996) and Boris Dubin (1997). The situation is diverse and volatile. Daniel reports conversations with the eminent Russian sociologist and historian Dmitrii Furman. Furman detects a strong falling-off in allegiance to the Russian Orthodox Church since the end of 1991; Dubin discovered a peak of support followed by decline rather later. Dubin establishes that there are fairly significant differences between young and old, men and women and town and country. Traditional believers (more likely to be rural inhabitants) have returned to the beliefs and practices before 1917. Younger urban believers (or perhaps it would be more accurate to term them 'seekers') combine sympathy for the ROC with an interest in astrology, the supernatural and 'non-traditional' beliefs. A high number of respondents to questionnaires declare that 'many people wish to be thought believers but do not actually believe'. And when the seriousness of people's religious allegiance is measured, it is discovered that half of those who declare themselves to be Orthodox (by Dubin's figures 48 per cent of the population in 1997) never, or hardly ever, go to church (Dubin 1997: 98). While 80 per cent of the population in 1997 said they 'celebrated Easter' (Dubin 1997: 95), the major Orthodox festival, only 7 per cent went to the midnight service (Dubin 1997: 103); the rest marked the occasion by painting eggs or holding a family reunion.

Furman declares himself decidedly worried by some of his findings (and they are in large part supported by Dubin). He found 'a surprisingly high correlation between people who attend religious services at least once a week and those who hold chauvinistic social or political values' (Daniel 1996: 371). Unlike the West, Christian allegiance in Russia seems to promote conservative attitudes. In stark contrast to the historic findings of Max Weber, Furman discovers that the work ethic among those who believe in capitalism has declined, and that it survives mainly among the remaining communists. (Perhaps this marks a triumph of Marxist–Leninist *vospitanie*!) A high proportion find such phenomena as prostitution and bribery to be acceptable. Daniel describes Furman's portrait of the ROC in relation to all of this as 'extremely pessimistic'. 'Rather than becoming an independent body... capable of exercising a critical voice the Church is steadily drifting back towards its traditional alliance with the government' (Daniel 1996: 373). Other writers confirm that the vast majority of church attenders is conservative, (for example, Veniamin 1998) and the pessimism of the sociologists was shared by Aleksandr Men' (Roberts and Shukman 1996).

The close relationship between politicians and Church has given rise to recent comment in the educational press. A commentator in *Uchitel'skaia gazeta* remarked that the sight of political figures holding candles (Zhirinovskii is said to have been televised igniting one in church with his cigarette lighter!) and appearing arm-in-arm with clerics does no service to religion and merely convinces a public sceptical of politicians that the aims of the appearance are political rather than spiritual (Borshchev 1998: 15). The complicity of the ROC with the communist government, even under Stalin, and its links with the KGB have come to light, and considerable anger has been expressed that the Church 'arrogantly' omits to express any regret. Men' likewise deplored the 'triumphalism and self-congratulation' of the Church during the millennium celebrations of Russian Christianity in 1988 (Men' 1996: 167).

While the hierarchy of the ROC holds to relatively hard-line attitudes, there are clergy who seek reform. Father Georgii Kochetkov was first transferred from his parish for celebrating the liturgy in modern Russian and later suspended from all exercise of his priesthood (Daniel 1996: 367; Price 1998a: 165). The Patriarch has condemned by name four leading priests for 'heresy' simply for raising the Church's complicity with communism in the course of broadcasts on the independent Orthodox radio station. Even the infamous excommunication by the Holy Synod in 1901 of Lev Tolstoi, apparently, cannot be discussed without the discussants being charged with heresy. There have, it is said, been cases of book-burning by Orthodox bishops: the works even of such nineteenth-century luminaries as Solov'ev, Leont'ev and Khomiakov have been publicly burned by some extremists. Aleksandr Men' was murdered. One may well ask what contribution some of the actors in these events could conceivably make to open discussion of educational matters. In any case, the sociologists have discovered that the public, even the believing public, has little more respect for the Orthodox clergy as a class than their great-grandparents had before the Revolution.

Relevant legislation

The Constitution of the Russian Federation affirms the separation of the Church from educational institutions. A law of 1990 on freedom of conscience reasserts the constitutional freedom of citizens to disseminate their own religious conviction, provided they act within the law of the land. Nevertheless, a former education minister, Eduard Dneprov – himself no stranger to controversy – has said that his advocacy of maintaining such religious neutrality in schools earned him more unanimity of support than any other of the policies he espoused while in office. Even some of the faithful, it would seem, prefer schools to be free of ecclesiastical influence (Borshchev 1998). The Russian Ministry of Education has been wary about allowing priests to visit schools, fearing the subjection of children to indoctrination (Sutton 1996: 59). The Duma passed a law in 1997 restricting the freedom of religious organisations. It is a truly objectionable measure, which would appear to have been drawn up in such a way as to deprive as many religious groups as possible of their legal existence, including several which have been active in Russia since the nineteenth century: the Molokans, the Quakers, the Salvation Army, the Pentecostalists and the Seventh-Day Adventists among them. However, private educational institutions registered with the Ministry of Education are apparently excepted from the provisions of this Law (Bernbaum 1997; Bodrov 1998; 'Duma Passes "Crudely" Discriminatory Religion Law' 1997). Bodrov reports that, while the preamble to the Law is liberal in spirit, it is subject to a wide variation of interpretations by local officials, some of whom enforce outdated Soviet attitudes to religious freedom.

Trends in 'spiritual' education today

So far little has been said about schooling. Discussion has of necessity centred on the context in which education is carried on. We now turn to an account of the main competing philosophies in RE.

The survival of atheism

Once it was suggested that religion should be taught in schools, the objection was raised that this would be difficult, 'since all teachers were atheists'. Naive though this assumption is – that everyone was convinced by the antireligious propaganda of the previous age – there is something of a problem here. Particularly in higher education, some former experts in atheism have moved over to a 'religious studies' approach (Sutton 1996: 42–3). This enables atheist and agnostic teachers to keep a job in the new circumstances. While a neutral attitude has a certain amount to recommend it, and while it may be found preferable to an openly or even aggressively proselytising manner, many educators doubt the value of a 'clinical' approach avoiding the spiritual and contemplative side of religion.

Orthodox approaches

RO Christians approach RE in a wide variety of ways. First, in sharp contrast with the clinical religious studies attitude of the residual atheists is one type of Russian Orthodox approach, which one may go so far as to term 'evangelistic'. 'What is the fundamental task of our upbringing?' says the theologian A. I. Osipov. 'It is to help a person to see the damaged state (*povrezhdennost'*) of the condition in which he finds himself' (Osipov 1998: 9). Based on the Orthodox Doctrine of Man, Professor Osipov and those like him would set out to convince people of their need for salvation and help them rediscover the potential for beauty within the human soul. It is a noble cause, but scarcely feasible, many will think, within a secular and dispassionate education system.

A second Orthodox approach may be taken as an 'official' view of education held by many in the hierarchy of the ROC. It is stated by the present

Patriarch, Alexius II (1996). He makes a strong plea for Orthodox (not merely 'religious') education in state schools. He expresses misgivings about the separation of state and church. A particular concern of his is the rootlessness of Russian society – a recurrent theme of traditionalists, nationalists and neo-Slavophils of all sorts: it is the Russian roots they are most concerned with. Another concern is with 'neo-paganism', the fact that so many young people are seeking satisfaction in cults, sects and astrology; Orthodox education would be a bulwark against this phenomenon.

The Patriarch's tone is not exclusive, and does not appear to be hostile to other religions. The best of Protestantism and Catholicism is said to be present in Orthodoxy; the ROC can work with the other great monotheistic religions, Judaism and Islam. It is odd, none the less, that the same Patriarch can suspend Father Georgii, rebuke those who would discuss the Church's past mistakes and support oppressive legislation against other groups – to the extent of trying to oblige parishes to submit petitions in support of the new law. He is further quoted as saying recently to the assembled priests of Moscow: 'Whoever of the clergy dares to think (other) than I do will be subjected to ecclesiastical censure and canonical suspension' (Price 1998b: 1355, English corrected).

The need to return to Russian roots is a concern of populist extremists, intellectual neo-Slavophils and of many in between. Klarin and Petrov (1996) typify a moderate Orthodox intellectual approach, which we shall contrast with the nationalist position described below. It is a handbook for students and teachers outlining the religious and educational thought of certain nineteenth-century Russian philosophers, exploring how Solov'ev, Leont'ev and Khomiakov and others sought to reconcile Orthodox thought with modern enlightenment. (It will be remembered that some Orthodox have burned the books of these very thinkers!) The authors omit to note that it was not only Russian traditional ways of thought that were challenged by eighteenth-century 'enlightenment'; one virtue of their book is the way it illustrates that the neo-Slavophil approach can be moderate and non-exclusive.

The ethical and moral standpoint

Spiritual values play an important role in other approaches to moral education which are based principally on an ethical foundation. Orthodox educational attitudes are not excluded from this section of our discussion, since it is argued that RE would combat the moral breakdown in society: drugs, prostitution, promiscuity, abortion, crime. While secularists assert that ethics can be free of religion, it is the view of the ROC that faith alone provides the basis for truly moral behaviour. Atheists and faithful have long agreed, however, on the need for a clean-up (Dunstan 1992: 91).

Professor Nikolai Nikandrov expresses this view. In 1995 he wrote that people were concerned about the commercialisation of all spheres of activity, the growth of criminality and the fact that the worth of education itself was even called into question. He refers to two changes in values: one as *perestroika* came in and the second at its demise (Nikandrov 1995). He touches on several issues: the feeling of the teaching profession against 'inculcation' of morality as being against personal freedom, the unhelpful notion of 'universal human values', the need to encourage students to question what they are taught, and – important for our theme – the recognition of religious pluralism. In a later article, 'The Moral Lessons of Orthodoxy', Nikandrov praises the Bible as 'a great store of treasure for man and for the business of Russian education' (Nikandrov 1997: 3). While Orthodoxy is praised, the main stress is on Christianity, the Bible and its ethical teaching. The ten commandments contain as many 'universal human values' as they do religion. Despite atheistic ideology, socialism and communism shared many Christian precepts.

Some of these ideas would appear to be incorporated into a new syllabus for Ethics and Psychology of Family Life, produced for state schools by the Psychological Institute of the Russian Academy of Education (Etika i psikhologiia ... 1997). A course with this title was compulsory in schools until 1992 (Muckle 1988: 29–31). The feeling is that children need such teaching, and the new syllabus is intended as guidance to teachers who wish to deliver such a course. Its ideological standpoint stresses the patriarchal family, lacks methodological guidance, and deplores sex education (as 'provocative' and likely to encourage sexual experimentation by children. This is a common theme of Orthodox educators (Smirnov 1998)). Of the ten lessons planned on 'The family in the light of spiritual–moral and cultural traditions of society', four are concerned with 'the family in various cultures', while six are entitled: 'Moral norms of marriage in Christian culture'. The family as 'the little Church, the head of which is the husband' and the section on 'folk traditions of the Russian Orthodox family' strengthen the influence of the Church on this course. The style in which this syllabus is framed has a strongly Soviet ring about it, with a clearly tendentious and didactic attitude. The more one considers it, the more it begins to look like Russian religious nationalism in neo-Soviet dress.

The 'Russian school' and the nationalist 'temptation'

We have moved away from approaches from within the Orthodox Church to attitudes which make use of Orthodoxy for their own purposes – ethical teaching on the one hand and the purveying of the Russian heritage on the other. There is a much stronger variety of this second view.

The breakdown of the former Soviet Union and its dispersal into component parts invigorated an already existing feeling that the Russian nation needed to return to its roots. There is much talk of 'the Russian school', and curricular discussion turns on ways of reinforcing pupils' national identity. One Russian educator, contributing to a conference held in 1998, was of the opinion that, while this strand in Russian education consisted of little more than 'decorative folkloristics' and sometimes contained a deal of minor idiocy, the notion was not unsound in itself, and could lead to a constructive curricular approach (Belkanov 1998).

We have seen already that Orthodox nations tend strongly to identify faith and culture. The 'Russian school' movement is in that way typical. It does not have to be – and in fact is not by any means always – nationalistic, but the spectre of nationalism, even jingoism, lurks in the background. The danger comes when children are taught too close an identity of Russianness with Russian Orthodoxy. Not without reason do progressive Orthodox educators write of the 'temptation' of nationalism (Levina 1997). In no major Western country is there a monocultural society in which one church is related so closely to the cultural identity of the nation. Roman Catholicism is by its very nature international; Protestant churches, while often centred more obviously on one country, do not dominate society as do the Orthodox churches; in no other society is there so much talk of the national church encapsulating the age-old folk wisdom of the people. Some of the proponents of this view would not deny being considerably less concerned with the teaching of the Church than with Orthodoxy as priceless heritage.

Other propagandists of the national strain in education are concerned with diatribes against the Western trash that has invaded youth culture. Many Western teachers will sympathise. It is a matter for concern when people young or old choose rubbish in preference to something better, or when they cannot distinguish between a genuine work of art and a fraud. The answer is not to engage in xenophobic outrage. It is surely an educational issue to be met by good teaching rather than chauvinistic fulminations.

One may feel similar sympathy with those who would combat the influence of the more extreme and lunatic-fringe cults and sects among the 14 000 referred to above. Again, this is a matter for education: the arousal of a critical attitude to apparently plausible persuaders. Unfortunately, many nationalistic educators simply reject 'all Western preachers and sects' as bad: an insufficient response, if only because very many of those objected to are not of Western origin. It is less easy to deal with statements that allegiance to Orthodoxy is an indispensable part of being Russian and that the ROC has always preserved the essence of the Russian people (Mal'tseva 1995). Goncharov writes: 'Orthodoxy is the decisive foundation of Russian life, the ground from which it springs, its nerve-centre and its pivot.' He argues for a change in the content of all school subjects 'which relate to the formation of national character'. (Goncharov 1997: 9). The concluding remarks of the article by Mal'tseva read: 'One would like to hope and believe that the foundation-stone of a renewed education[al philosophy] will be the timeless wisdom of the Russian people and its basis – Orthodoxy' (Mal'tseva 1995: 38).

The ecumenical approach

Under this heading we return to Orthodoxy and to an attitude to RE which acts upon some of the more liberal remarks of the Patriarch quoted above. One aim of RE in state schools in England today includes 'to develop a positive attitude towards other people, respecting their right to hold beliefs different from their own, and towards living in a society of diverse religions', and to develop 'the ability to see the world through the eyes of others, and to see issues from their point of view' (Schools Curriculum and Assessment Authority 1994). Would this liberal ecumenical and non-proselytising position be conceivable in Russia?

There is indeed an open, interdenominational spirit shown by certain Orthodox clergy in their educational work, despite a church hierarchy which seems determined to establish Orthodox RE and to stifle discussion of dissident opinion. Archpriest Vladimir Fedorov, a leading theologian and church official, writes: 'Religious education...is not restricted to the study of Christianity' (Fedorov 1997: 71) and 'The only way...is above any single religious tradition, that is, multi-traditional' (Fedorov 1997: 73). Also: 'There is the objective of instilling the idea of tolerance toward other traditions and cultures...which is a necessity when one lives in a pluralistic society such as our own' (Fedorov 1997: 72). In higher education Jonathan Sutton has described in his book institutions such as Open Christianity and the Open Orthodox University, which adopt a similar stance (Sutton 1996).

Dina Levina describes a RE syllabus for state schools which at first glance appears to incorporate this attitude. She is a research fellow in the Orthodox Institute of Missiology, Ecumenism and New Religious Movements. She advocates the fostering of tolerance and co-operation between religions and resistance to indoctrination, whether that comes from an authoritarian teacher or from the proponents in society of some disreputable cult. The syllabus she outlines, and the textbook intended for using with it, disappoint her when closely examined: they 'seem to be less democratic than the rationale' (Levina 1997: 87). It is a frequent problem in Russian history. Twenty lessons are devoted to theory of religion before the child is taught anything specific about any one faith; interpretation (the teacher's and the textbook's interpretation, of course) comes before factual knowledge. Religion is studied 'in terms of perception, but not in terms of relation'; in other words, the believer's views are neglected. The theory of religion, Levina states, is exactly the same as used to figure in the atheists' handbooks, with the adjective 'false' omitted. She further attacks the course for religious exclusivity and its notions of Orthodox superiority. It reduces religion to 'something much less than it is' by concentrating on the description of religious practices rather than the religious person's life and way of thinking (Levina 1997: 91).

Levina writes of social demands for new approaches to RE; to avoid intolerance on the one hand and becoming a prey to indoctrination on the other,
she recommends child-centred learning, an empathetic approach to religion
and the experiential approach which has entered the English RE curriculum,
based on research done at the University of Nottingham. These are not
uncomplicated matters; Levina writes of the possible danger of relativism.
She seems, however, to lean towards the experiential approach as a way of
developing 'an understanding of the sphere with which religion deals, of the
emotions, feelings, senses and relations involved in religious experience'
(Levina 1997: 95).

It is reassuring to discover this open approach in Orthodox pedagogues
who have in effect an official relationship with the ROC. They form a
refreshing counterbalance to the views of such as the 'Orthodox educator'
whose drivelling 'notes' sullied the illustrious pages of Pedagogika in 1995
(Mal'tseva 1995 – but she is not alone!).

Conclusions

The situation of RE in Russia at present may be described as complex.
Whether it ought to be allowed at all in the schools is a matter for dispute.
Traditional attitudes and Russian educational culture ensure that many
educators adopt a prescriptive, maybe even dogmatic, manner in teaching.
Atheistic opinions and a reluctance to end the separation of Church and
state survive; religion is sometimes taught as an aspect of thought or culture.
Some see RE mainly as a means to fight delinquency and low ethical stand-
ards.

We have seen that there are many who adopt the view that Russian
Orthodox Christianity is a worthwhile part of the national heritage. More
sinister are the attempts of extreme nationalists to recruit religious educators
to their cause. They are not without allies in the Church.

The ROC is concerned with RE at more than one level: it seeks converts on
the one hand and strives to strengthen the faith of those already within the
fold on the other. Other Orthodox lay people and clergy adopt an open,
ecumenical and intelligently critical approach to religious teaching, which
appears more acceptable to the Western mind. We have seen that Orthodox
theology predisposes some believers to exclusivist attitudes, and that certain
political views are closely related to assiduous church attendance. Finally, it
has become obvious that the Duma and individual officials are apt to work
against religious freedom and to reinforce traditionalist views. The next few
years will show whether Russia becomes or remains democratic enough to be
pluralist and multi-religious, or whether pre-revolutionary attitudes to the
exercise of religion will return and pervade education after 80 and more
years.

Acknowledgements

The earliest variant of this paper was prepared in a brief German version for a conference of the Centre for Comparative Education Research of the Ruhr University, Bochum, and the German Association for East European Studies at Vlotho an der Weser in July 1998. Its development owes more than a little to the discussion which took place there. I am also grateful to Dr John Dunstan, who kindly commented on a later version, which was then re-written and presented at the joint conference of the Study Group on Education in Russia, the Independent States and Eastern Europe and of the Civic Culture Forum in November 1998. Further amendments were made in the light of responses on that occasion. I am extremely grateful to all who expressed their opinions and who provided information.

References

Alexius II, Patriarch of Moscow and All Russia (1996). 'The Foundations of Orthodox Education in Russia' *Russian Education and Society*, vol. 38, no. 9, pp. 6–24, (translated from *Pedagogika*. no. 3, 1995, pp. 74–81).

Alexius II, Patriarch of Moscow and All Russia (1998). 'Slovo Sviateishego Patriarkha Moskovskogo i vseia Rusi Aleksiia Vtorogo na otkrytii chteniia' *Vospitanie shkol'nikov*, no. 3, pp. 2–6.

Belkanov, N. (1998). 'Neue Entwicklungen und Theorieansätze in der russischen pädagogischen Wissenschaft' (Oral presentation, conference at Vlotho, Germany, 5 June).

Bernbaum, J. (1997). Privately circulated newsletter of the Russian-American Christian University, dated 25 October.

Bodrov, A. (ed.) (1998). 'Some Developments in Higher Religious Education in the Former Soviet Union' *Education in Russia, the Independent States and Eastern Europe*, vol. 16, no. 2, pp. 77–84.

Bondarevskaia, E. (1995). 'Tsennostnye osnovaniia lichnostno orientirovannogo vospitaniia' *Pedagogika*, nos. 3–4, pp. 29–36.

Borshchev, V. (1998). 'Iz religii nel'zia delat' shou' *Uchitel'skaia gazeta*, no. 9, p. 15.

Bria, I. (1998). 'The Orthodox Church in Post-Communist Eastern Europe.' *Ecumenical Review*, vol. 50, no. 2, pp. 157–63.

Daniel, W. (1996). 'Religion and the Struggle for Russia's Future' *Religion, State and Society*, vol. 24, no. 4, pp. 367–83.

Dubin, B. (1997). 'Religiia, tserkov', obshchestvennoe mnenie' *Svobodnaia mysl'*, vol. 11, 1468, pp. 94–103.

'Duma Passes "Crudely" Discriminatory Religion Law' (1997). *Current Digest of the Post-Soviet Press*, vol. 49, no. 26, pp. 9–10 and 19.

Dunstan, J. (1992). 'Soviet Upbringing Under *Perestroika*: From Atheism to Religious Education?' in J. Dunstan (ed.) *Soviet Education under Perestroika*. London: Routledge, pp. 81–105.

'Etika i psikhologiia semeinoi zhizni' (1997). *Vospitanie shkol'nikov*, no. 6, pp. 11–18.

Fedorov, V. (1997). 'Perspektivy razvitiia religioznogo obrazovaniia v Rossii segodnia: opyt mezhkonfessional'nogo sotrudnichestva' in S. Trokhachev (ed.) *Problemy religioznogo obrazovaniia v Rossii: traditsiia i novyi opyt/Problems of Religious Education in*

Russia: Traditions and Innovations/Probleme christlicher Erziehung in Russland: Tradition und Erneuerung. St Petersburg: Russian Christian Institute Press, pp. 11–15 (in Russian), pp. 71–85 (in English), pp. 121–39 (in German).

Fedorov, V. (1998). 'Barriers to Ecumenism: An Orthodox View from Russia' *Religion, State and Society,* vol. 26, no. 2, pp. 129–43.

Goncharov, I. (1997). 'Novaia shkola Rossii: kakoi ei byt'?' *Vospitanie shkol'nikov,* no.1, pp. 2–5 and no, 2, pp. 7–19.

Havel, V. (1997). Quoted by V. Rich, *Times Higher Education Supplement,* 5 December, p. 12.

Hilarion (Alfeyev), Hieromonk (1998). 'The problems facing Orthodox theological education in Russia' *Sourozh,* August, pp. 5–29.

Isakova, E. (1997). 'Religioznaia situatsiia v Sankt-Peterburge: novye religioznye dvizheniia v shkole' in S. Trokhachev (ed.) *Problemy religioznogo obrazovaniia v Rossii: traditsiia i novyi opyt/Problems of Religious Education in Russia: Traditions and Innovations/Probleme christlicher Erziehung in Russland: Tradition und Erneuerung.* St Petersburg: Russian Christian Institute Press, pp. 52–60 (in Russian), pp. 102–9 (in English), pp. 159–67 (in German).

Klarin, V. and Petrov, V. (1996). 'Idealy i puti vospitaniia v tvoreniiakh russkikh religioznykh filosofov XIX–XX vv.' Moscow: publisher not stated.

Kulakov, P. (1996). 'Religion and Young People in School' *Russian Education and Society,* vol. 38, no. 9, pp. 50–68.

Levina, D. (1997). 'Religioznoe obrazovanie v Rossiiskoi srednei shkole: novye podkhody i metody' in S. Trokhachev (ed.) *Problemy religioznogo obrazovaniia v Rossii: traditsiia i novyi opyt/Problems of Religious Education in Russia: Traditions and Innovations/Probleme christlicher Erziehung in Russland: Tradition und Erneuerung.* St Petersburg: Russian Christian Institute Press, pp. 33–47 (in Russian), pp. 86–97 (in English), pp. 140–53 (in German).

Mal'tseva, V. (1995). 'Zametki pravoslavnogo pedagoga' *Pedagogika,* no. 4, pp. 55–9.

Men', A. (1996). 'The Russian Orthodox Church today' in E. Roberts and A. Shukman (eds) *Christianity for the Twenty-First Century.* London: SCM Press, pp. 164–70.

Muckle, J. (1988). *A Guide to the Soviet Curriculum.* Beckenham: Croom Helm.

Nikandrov, N. (1995). 'Russian Education after Perestroika: The Search for New Values' *International Review of Education,* vol. 41, nos. 1–2, pp. 47–57.

Nikandrov, N. (1997). 'Nravstvennye uroki pravoslaviia' *Pedagogika,* no. 3, pp. 3–9.

Nikol'skaia, T. (1998). 'O nashei religioznosti' *Posev,* nos. 5–6, pp. 41–2 (response to Veniamin 1998 – see below).

Osipov, A. (1998). Untitled report of a speech. *Vospitanie shkol'nikov,* no. 3, pp. 8–10.

Polozhevets, P. (1998). In *Uchitel'skaia gazeta,* no. 12, p. 2.

Price, R. (1998a). 'Moscow Clips the Liberals' Wings' *The Tablet,* 7 February, p. 165.

Price, R. (1998b). 'Moscow's New Persecutors' *The Tablet,* 17 October, pp. 1354–5.

Roberts, E. and Shukman, A. (1996). *Christianity for the Twenty-First Century,* London: SCM Press.

Sadler, M. (1900), 'How far can we learn anything of practical value from the study of foreign education?' Guildford: Surrey Advertiser Office.

Schools Curriculum and Assessment Authority (1994). *Model Syllabuses for Religious Education. Model 2. Questions and Teachings.* London: SCAA.

Shemshurina, A. (1997). 'Eticheskaia grammatika v VIII klasse' *Vospitanie shkol'nikov,* no. 1, pp. 6–9.

Smirnov, D. (1998). Untitled report of a speech. *Vospitanie shkol'nikov,* no. 3, pp. 10–11.

Sutton, J. (1996). *Traditions in New Freedom. Christianity and Higher Education in Russia and Ukraine Today.* Nottingham: Bramcote Press.

Tataryn, M. (1997). 'Orthodox Ecclesiology and Cultural Pluralism' *Sobornost,* vol. 19, no. 1, pp. 56–67.

Trokhachev, S. (ed.) (1997). *Problemy religioznogo obrazovaniia v Rossii: traditsiia i novyi opyt/Problems of Religious Education in Russia: Traditions and Innovations/Probleme christlicher Erziehung in Russland: Tradition und Erneuerung.* St Petersburg: Russian Christian Institute Press.

Veniamin, I. (1998). 'Iz razmyshlenii o nashei religioznosti' *Posev,* nos. 1–2, pp. 45–6.

Zinchenko, V. (1997). 'O tseliakh i tsennostiakh obrazovaniia' *Pedagogika,* no. 5, pp. 3–16.

Part IV
Towards a Brighter Future?

13
The Abandoned Children of Russia – from 'Privileged Class' to 'Underclass'[1]

Svetlana Stephenson

> A child, living in summer and in winter on underground water-pipes, a child collapsing out of hunger, a child in alcoholic intoxication, a child sniffing toxic substances with a plastic bag over its head, a child who instead of being at school or in after-school classes is working for commercial shop owners, a child sold to work as a beggar, and finally, a child, killing its parents!

This array of images is a part of the Declaration of the Movement 'In Defence of Childhood', which had its founding Congress in Moscow in spring 1998. The movement was organised by the Duma Committee on women, family and children. Much of the rhetoric of this document seems to be aimed against the 'democrats' in government, who are to blame for the current crisis. However, the anxieties expressed in it capture the universal feelings about the fate of children in Russian society. Children, who were always declared to be the only 'privileged class' in Soviet society, are now perceived as victims of poverty and exploitation, as out of control, a threat to adults. And finally, children are seen as an embodiment of a frightening future. In its Declaration the Congress expressed this fear quite clearly, appealing to society to 'clean the dirty streets of impoverished Russia of its homeless future'.[2]

The Russian street and homeless children have recently become a matter of a serious national and international concern. In Russia it is possible, it seems, to speak about the emergence of a *moral panic* about this problem (Cohen 1972; Goode and Ben-Yehuda 1994). This moral panic is based on the perception of homeless children as 'a threat to well-being, basic values and interests of society' (Goode and Ben-Yehuda 1994: 31). The shocks and uncertainties of transition prepared fertile ground for public anxiety about the very foundations of society. Children – one of the primary victims of transition – became a focus of this anxiety. Thus the problem of street children was constructed as a social problem requiring urgent measures, and this process of construction involved public officials, state law-enforcement bodies and NGOs.

The policies and agendas of various actors in the area of child protection are very different. Most of the official efforts are connected with attempts to reconstitute social control, in the shape of the establishment of provisions for putting the children into publicly run state homes, boarding schools, detention centres or after-school classes. The problem is also constructed as a 'juvenile delinquency issue' rather than an issue of poverty and associated family breakup, violence and neglect to children. Little attention is paid to the actual social processes that result in children's homelessness and neglect, and their implications for social policy. These processes, as I will argue, are connected with the social and economic situation of the ex-Soviet working class, whose lowest, unqualified and often already marginalised section, has become the primary victim of the collapse of the Soviet social structure. The end of state paternalism, on which this group was highly dependent, erosion of welfare provisions, poverty and exclusion from the organised labour force hit it very hard. As a result serious social disorganisation has occurred: broken families, antisocial behaviour, violence in the family and a lack of formal and informal controls over the behaviour of adults and children.[3] The key issue here is how to prevent the development of social exclusion and ghettoisation in the long run, and establish a system of detection and prevention of child abuse in the short run.[4]

Street children as a new social problem

Dislocated children have not been seen in Russia as a 'problem' since the 1920s and 1930s – since the disappearance of *besprizorniki* ('homeless waifs'). The small amount of research conducted on 'problem' children in the period from the 1960s to the end of the 1980s was mainly focused on children in children's homes and special schools for young delinquents. Some publications touched upon flawed socialisation as a cause of delinquency, in particular the upbringing of children by single mothers (Kharchev 1979, 1983). Also, parental alcohol abuse was often evoked as a predominant correlate of deprivation of parental rights (see Beliakova 1983). Some research concerned runaway children, especially those who were put into special schools for young delinquents (Selitskii and Taratukhin 1981). Most publications tended to explain such behaviour in terms of individual psychopathology (see, for example, Bochkareva 1967; Boldyrev 1964). Problems of poverty, dysfunctional families, family violence or abuse were virtually never discussed.

In the *perestroika* period the situation of the so-called 'social orphans' (children lacking parental care rather than actual orphans) started to attract the attention of sociologists and social policy experts. The main objects of research were children in children's homes. The authors of some of the studies undertook to show that 'deviations' in children's behaviour and values were a result of unsatisfactory conditions in the institutions (Aristova 1992). This was in line with the massive criticism of Soviet institutions generally and a part of the movement of the early *perestroika* years to decentralise child care, substitute notorious children's homes with smaller, family-type homes and develop foster families (Harwin 1996). This movement led to the adoption of progressive legislation that created a legal basis for adoptive and foster families, and family-type children's homes. The Family Code of 1995 included many of the provisions from the International Convention on the Right of the Child and is considered to be very progressive by the human rights community. The Family Code, for example, contains article 34 that allows for a child suffering from abuse to be taken from the family on the basis of a decision of the court. According to article 131 of the Family Code, only if the child cannot remain in the natural family or cannot be put into an adoptive family, should he or she be put into a state institution. Using these provisions, some of the Russian regions have started developing foster care at their territories. Samara is the most active of them: in January 1999, Samara had 500 of the 876 foster families in Russia. A similar project, sponsored by UNICEF, is currently under way in Kaliningrad. These efforts are, however, very localised.

The onset of major public concern about the street children as opposed to children in the institutions can be traced to 1992–93, to the increased visibility of poorly dressed, dirty and hungry children in public places. Soon these concerns were picked up by numerous agencies (militia, NGOs, state departments) which started to come up with their own assessments of the situation. A true 'inflation of numbers' occurred, with the numbers of street children currently estimated between one and three million. These figures, given that the total number of children in Russia is 37 million, even at first glance look out of proportion. We have not managed to find any description of the methodology by which these figures were obtained.

Figures named for the numbers of street children in Moscow are in the order of dozens of thousands. Evgenii Balashov from the Moscow city Duma quoted in 1999 a figure of 28 000 homeless children in Moscow.[5] However, our survey in Moscow in June 1998 showed that at any given point in time there were not more than 800 children living in the streets (and about 4000 spending most of their time in the streets, but occasionally coming home), as opposed to the figures of 30–80 thousand quoted by some NGOs and media sources for the city. Our figure is based on counting children in the streets and in lofts/cellars in two districts of Moscow – Central and South-Western – and then extrapolating the results to the whole of the city territory. Our figure is similar to those presented in surveys of street children in other countries where they constitute a visible problem. For example, a survey conducted in Peru in 1989 showed that there were fewer than 500 street children in a capital of seven million inhabitants (Ordonez 1995). NGO representatives in St Petersburg, who work directly with homeless children, say that there are about 600 of them in the city, although the city authorities claim that the numbers are not less than 10 000.

From 1991, but particularly in the period 1996–99, Russian newspapers have regularly published alarmist articles dedicated to the problems of children. Trading in dismay about children deprived of the care of adults, they also portray them as irresponsible, uncontrollable and deviant. Teenage crime is made to look particularly alarming – although the rate of juvenile criminal offence has actually decreased in the last three years. According to Professor Zabrianskii, a leading Russian criminologist, the so-called 'hooliganism', unmotivated violence and harassment of passers-by that had been a major problem before *perestroika*, has decreased significantly. The energies of teenagers are now increasingly channelled into the world of work – mostly in informal markets (or organised rackets – but this is a different problem than that of hooliganism as far as social order is concerned).

The dominant discourse about street children in Russia concentrates for the most part around two interconnected themes: the erosion of the Soviet system of social control, and the increase in juvenile delinquency. In its turn, the later theme in some cases tends to rely on medical or 'genetic' explanations.

The Ministry of Education and the Ministry of Labour and Social Development – the two state departments responsible for child education and care, have the difficult task of reforming the system of state homes and special boarding schools for 'social orphans'. This has proceeded only extremely slowly, with most state funding still directed towards increasing the number of state institutions. Children's homes continue to be the main agency in the system of child protection: from 1996–98 the total number of children's homes increased by almost 50 per cent. By 1999 there were about 1000 of them across Russia, in comparison to the figure of 560 in 1995. The network now also includes 170 homes for disabled children (administered by the social security system), 250 homes for small babies under the Ministry of Health and more than 500 various institutions of the Ministry of Social Protection: shelters, rehabilitation centres, and so on.[6] In fact, it would be much cheaper for the state to give money to foster families rather than to state-run homes. In the first half of 1998, the total cost of one child's upkeep in a state home, at least according to the official rate, was about 7.5 thousand roubles (about $1250). Foster families were entitled to receive about $250.[7] Conditions in the closed state-run institutions are very severe: more than 200 000 children run away each year from the state homes, from schools for delinquent children and homes for children with mental and nervous conditions (*Istoriia voprosa*... 1996). In a December 1998 special report, 'Abandoned to the State: Cruelty and Neglect in Russian Orphanages', the human rights non-governmental organisation (NGO)

Human Rights Watch exposed the severe lack of facilities for rehabilitation or socialisation of children in such institutions (*Abandoned to the state . . . 1998*). In the absence of effective public control, psychological and physical abuse is very common.

In the speeches and writings of state officials, children who leave home and live on the streets are often presented as deviants who were allowed to become 'disaffiliated' because of the collapse of social control over young people exercised under the Soviet regime through school, after school classes, Pioneer and Komsomol organisations and summer camps. According to the Russian Ministry of Education, the rising tide of criminal behaviour by young people on the streets reflects the collapse of Soviet-era arrangements for structuring leisure time activity and the rise of alternative and largely Western role models in the media.[8] Under the impression that the lack of control is the main cause of *besprizornost'*, the Moscow city authorities have designed a programme called 'Children of the Street'. A major feature of the programme is the creation of special centres where children can spend time after school engaged in various 'classes' and activities. The most needy children – those who are homeless and who come from problem homes – would hardly benefit from the huge investments made into this programme.

The medical profession, and child psychiatrists in particular, often sees the problems of street children in medical terms. Much of the research conducted in this area is centred on the mental deficiencies of 'unadapted' children, although the authors admit that these deficiencies are aggravated by the conditions at home or in institutions.[9]

This 'medicalisation' of social problems, which was an intrinsic part of the Soviet discourse, has suddenly been reinforced with the advent of new 'genetic' explanations. Our interviews with public officials and the personnel of institutions during this project, and also previous research into adult homelessness in Moscow, showed that, in the vocabulary of many public administrators, genetic predisposition had become a common way of explaining the causes of homelessness. Sergei Smirnov, Deputy Head of the Ministry of Interior's Department for Prevention of Crime Among Minors said in an interview with a journalist in 1998: 'Street children must be an object of attention primarily of psychologists and not of the militia personnel. A child should be tested and a decision taken – what is he? Is he a person who got into a difficult situation? Or a criminal at the genetic level?'(quoted in Paniushkin 1998).

The Militia (police) remains the main agency dealing with street children in Russia. Its main function is to detain children suspected of being homeless or runaways and put them for a 30-day period into special detention centres for under-age criminals. Such a situation obviously violates the human rights of children and has no legal justification. In September 1993, Russian president Boris Yeltsin signed a Decree 'On the Prevention of Child Neglect [*beznadzornosti*] and Violation of Law among the Minors and Protection of their Rights'. According to the Decree, the Ministry of Social Protection was to become responsible for the prevention of child neglect and for child care. The militia's role was to be confined to dealing with crime. Militia reception centres for children were renamed as 'Centres for Temporary Isolation of Under-age Criminals'. A 1999 Law 'On the Prevention of Child Neglect and Juvenile Crime' confirmed this development. However, the militia continues to be the main agency dealing with street children. In 1999, there were about 80 reception centres in Russia. The militia has to investigate, within a 30-day period, whether a child committed a crime or ran away from an institution. If none of this happened, and he or she has a home, they should be sent back home regardless of the circumstances. There are numerous cases when the same child is escorted home several times, on each occasion ending up back in the militia's care shortly afterwards. If there are no parents, or the parents are deprived of parental rights, the children are put into state homes.

As the number of street children increases and long-term *'besprizornost'* (that is, adaptation to a 'street' way of life) – inevitably associated with crime and disassociation from mainstream society – emerges on a large scale, attitudes to street children can become more harsh, and penal solutions more welcome.[10] Already the criminal justice system has progressively come to treat juvenile offenders more harshly. The rate of convictions of juveniles exceeds the rate of new criminal investigations; the rate of juveniles receiving prison sentences exceeds the rate of those convicted. The sentences are extremely harsh: in 1996, of those juvenile offenders who received prison sentences (these are 27 per cent of all sentences), 6.1 per cent were sentenced to less than one year, 22.2 per cent to one to two years, 31.6 per cent to three to five years, and 10.6 per cent to five to ten years (Zabrianskii 1997).

The Russian human rights community and emerging NGOs are trying to reorient the agenda towards the issues of children's rights. The efforts of the NGOs are mainly directed towards reforming the system of child care (including developing foster cares), establishing public control over the state institutions and introducing new juvenile justice legislation. Some NGOs have established shelters for homeless children (in Moscow the most well known are the shelters run by the NAN Foundation (Net alkogolismu i narkomanii [No to Alcohol and Drug Abuse]) and Mariia Ternovskaia's 'Our Family' Project). However, they come across many obstacles, not least the fact that by a rule established by the city authorities, these shelters can only accept children who have a Moscow residence permit. Other children have to be sent to the militia detention centre.

The survey of street children in Moscow

Our survey was aimed at identifying the main causes of *besprizornost'*. One of the key questions we had to answer was whether the children ending up in the streets are really uncontrollable delinquents, looking for trouble, or whether they are the product of a particular social milieu, which has experienced the stresses of poverty and social dislocation. The social policy implications in these two cases can obviously be very different.

The fieldwork of our survey took place in May–July 1998. The total sample in Moscow comprised 123 street children. We limited the age bracket to 7–17 years (we did not interview children under seven, as it would not be possible to use with them the standard questionnaire that we designed). The questionnaire included closed questions, but also many open-ended questions. The age distribution in our survey is presented in Table 13.1.

A limitation of our survey was that we only interviewed children who could understand and speak Russian, thus excluding non-Russian migrants from Central Asia, the Caucasus or Moldova. Some indication of the national composition of street children can be derived from the records of the militia reception centre, which show that, in the second half of 1997, 52 per cent of all the children there were from Russia. 17 per cent came to Moscow from Ukraine, 10 per cent from Tajikistan, 8 per cent from Moldova, 3 per cent from Azerbaijan and 3 per cent from Uzbekistan. Belarus', Georgia, Turkmenistan, Kazakhstan, Latvia, Lithuania, Kyrgizstan were places of origin for 7 per cent of children – about 1 per cent from each of these former USSR states.

Most of the interviews took place in agencies – in the militia receptions centre (67) and shelters (24), while 32 interviews were taken in the streets. For interviews that were conducted in organisations we used age and sex quotas, based on the registration of all the children who passed through the

Table 13.1 Age Distribution of the Respondents

Age in years	Percentage
7	1.6
8	0.8
9	2.4
10	4.9
11	9.8
12	12.2
13	19.5
14	10.6
15	17.1
16	12.2
17	8.9
Total	100.0
Total N	123

militia reception centre in 1997. In the streets we used a random sample. The majority of the interviewees (72 per cent) were boys. This survey also included in-depth interviews with street children (we conducted ten interviews, each about three hours long) and focus-groups with children selected by sex and age (four groups).

The current crisis is often compared to the *besprizornost'* in the 1920s and 1930s. Then, as a result of the 1917 October Revolution, seven years of wars (the First World War and the civil war), economic devastation, starvation, and a high level of population migration, the complete collapse of the social structure occurred. One of the consequences was the presence of masses of children in the streets. In one of the worst years of the crisis, in 1922, there were an estimated 7.5 million 'starving and dying children in Russia', many of whom, having lost one or both parents, had come to the towns in search of food (Goldman 1993: 60).

The fact that *besprizornost'* emerged in Russia both at the birth of the Soviet state and at its collapse, suggests comparable degrees of social disintegration. One important difference between the 1920s and 1930s and today, though (which accounts for the much smaller number of street children now), is that direct population losses in recent years are on a significantly smaller scale. Hence the share of orphans among the street children is much lower. A survey conducted in Moscow in 1924 among the children passing through Children's Commissions (*Detkomissii*), bodies that determined the future fate of *besprizorniki*, showed that 40 per cent of street children were orphans (Goldman 1993: 80). Our survey in 1998 suggested that only four per cent of Moscow street children are orphans.

However, in some ways the composition of the families from which the street children come is similar, which seems to suggest similar processes in play. In the 1920s, single-parent families produced a high share of *besprizorniki*. These families found it very difficult to care for their children in a period of high unemployment and low wages, especially for women. Twenty-eight per cent of the *besprizorniki* in Moscow in 1924 had only a mother, seven per cent only a father. Only 24 per cent came from homes with both parents (Goldman 1993: 80).

Our data show striking similarities with 1924 data as far as single parents are concerned: 28 per cent of the children come from families with single mothers, and seven per cent from families with single fathers. While a significant number of children in the 1998 survey come from families with two parents, households with two natural parents were a minority (see Table 13.2). Most of the children came from reconstituted families. Monoparental and reconstituted families should not automatically be equated with domestic problems and ineffective upbringing of children. However, when these are families with low socioeconomic status and when they are also experiencing significant deterioration of their life chances, the results for the children can be quite dramatic. Our survey showed that the

Table 13.2 Types of Families (in per cent)

Single mother	27.6
Single father	7.3
Mother and father	18.7
Mother and stepfather	22.8
Father and stepmother	3.3
Grandmother	7.3
Others	8.9
Orphan, lived on his/her own	4.1
N	123

parents of street children as a rule occupy the lowest positions on the social scale. These are predominantly low-qualified manual workers, both urban and rural. Urban dwellers are a majority – about 85 per cent in the sample. The answers of the children to the questions about the occupations of their parents are not, of course, totally reliable. About six per cent of the children could not answer these questions at all. Some of the children had relatively vague ideas about what their parents were doing. However, the data can be regarded, it seems, as an indication of the specific characteristics in the parental occupations and job situations. The rate of unemployment, particularly among the mothers, is quite high (see Table 13.3). Many of the parents have casual jobs (see Table 13.4).

The conditions of employment of most of the families are very insecure. 68.4 per cent of the children said that their parent(s) had previously experienced periods of unemployment. Fathers experienced unemployment in 37 per cent of the cases, mothers in 52.8 per cent. The situation of single parents seems especially precarious. Half of single fathers and 75 per cent of single mothers had experienced unemployment.

A significant number of the children stated that their families had acute or very acute financial problems (see Table 13.5). About 30 per cent reported that they did not eat enough. Poverty and exclusion from the labour force are compounded in many cases by alcohol abuse. In answering to the question, 'Does either of your parents consume alcohol often and in large quantities?', 71.7 per cent of those interviewed answered positively. According to

Table 13.3 Employment Status of Parents/ Step-Parents (in per cent)

	Works	Unemployed	Retired (disabled)	In prison	N
Father (stepfather)	75.6	15.4	6.4	2.6	78
Mother (stepmother)	55.1	39.9	6.0	–	98

Table 13.4   Types of Employment of Parents/Step-parents (in per cent)

	State organisation	Employed in a private company	Kolkhoz, sovkhoz, private farm	Service sector	Industrial enterprise	Casual jobs, self-employed, begging	N
Father (stepfather)	13.3	16.7	6.7	11.6	25.0	25.7	60
Mother (stepmother)	27.5	2.4	3.3	17.6	21.6	28.8	51

the children, most alcohol abuse takes place in single parent and reconstituted families, with maternal alcohol abuse almost as frequent as paternal. Half of the single mothers are drinkers, while in families with a stepfather, half of the mothers and 82 per cent of the stepfathers drink. In families with fathers and stepmothers, the incidence of alcohol abuse is equal between men and women (one third).

The picture of social disorganisation becomes even more convincing when we look at the incidence of problems with the law among family members.

Table 13.5   'Are There Financial Problems in Your Family? If Yes, How Acute are They?' (in per cent)

Very acute	32.7
More or less acute	20.3
Arise from time to time	31.2
No financial problems	15.8
N	121

Table 13.6   Incidence of Family Members Having Trouble with Militia (in per cent)

In the total sample	69.1
Of them:	
mother (stepmother)	36.1
Father (stepfather)	45.8
Brother(s)/sisters(s)	9.6
Other family member	8.4
N	83

Note: the sum exceeds 100 per cent as in some cases there was more than one family member named. 39.8 per cent reported that one or more family members had been convicted in the past.

Table 13.7 'What are Your Feelings About Your Step-Parent(s)? (in per cent to the total number of children with step-parents)

Indifference	31.9
Hatred	30.1
Fear	7.8
Love, attachment	30.2
N	50

Some 69.1 per cent of children reparted that members of their family had been in trouble with the militia (See Table 13.6) while 39.8 per cent reported that one or more family members had been convicted in the past. Many children had experienced emotional traumas, such as the death of one or both of their parents: in 24.7 per cent of cases the father had died, in 13.9 per cent of cases the mother. Many had lived through a family breakdown. The households in most of the cases are conflictive (see Tables 13.7 and 13.8).

Eighty per cent of the children were punished at home. Of them, 59.6 per cent were punished several times a week. About 80 per cent experienced beatings, and, of these, 44.4 per cent reported injuries and wounds from beatings. In 56.1 per cent cases a mother was being beaten too. The atmosphere of conflict in the family, together with the violent behaviour of adults, constitutes the most frequent reason for a child's wish to leave home. The need to have more freedom, to escape from boredom, to travel and have fun, or to become independent are, in most cases, secondary reasons. In our sample, 64.5 per cent of children ended up on the streets because they left home (the rest of the sample, as will be discussed below, came to Moscow with their parents, left children's institutions or had homeless parents).

A decision to leave home, it seems, can best be described as a result of 'push' and 'pull' processes. Among the conditions that 'push' the children into the streets are a lack of parental care, abuse at home, lack of emotional

Table 13.8 Conflicts Between Family Members (in per cent)

	yes, often	*yes, not often*	*no*
Mother and father	47.8	28.5	23.7
Stepfather and mother	53.5	25.6	20.9
Father and stepmother	40.0	40.0	20.0
Adoptive parents	33.3	33.3	33.3
Parents and brothers (sisters)	24.4	37.2	38.4
Parents and grandparents	19.7	32.8	47.5
Respondent and brothers (sisters)	24.1	29.9	46.0

attachments to the family members. These family problems are closely correlated to overall poverty and are exacerbated by it. The 'pull' is created by the real or imaginary opportunities provided by life on the streets and by the big city.

The 'pull' of the streets is in many cases connected with the opportunity to make money there. Some 70.6 per cent of all the respondents used to work when they still lived at home. Among the most frequent occupations were casual work for money or food, that is, looking after cars near shops, working at petrol stations, unloading goods, small trade, begging, and helping their relatives or family. Other children used to earn money regularly by collecting and selling empty bottles, regular stealing and working as prostitutes (see Table 13.9). Although 19.5 per cent of the children started working because they were asked to by their parents, the majority claimed to have made the decision to work themselves. Involvement in deregulated markets showed many of them that they could earn and thus be independent from their parents.

Work was not their only way to survive. About 40 per cent of the children admitted that they used to steal sometimes before they came to the streets (slightly more then a half admitted that they often stole during their life on the streets). Alcohol and drug abuse, glue sniffing and smoking all took place in street groups to which the children belonged before making the decision to leave home.

Most of the children (68.4 per cent) left home more than once (two thirds of these left home three times or more).[11] Their dissociation from home, however, is not complete. Of those children who came from Moscow and the Moscow region, 71.2 per cent periodically visited home to sleep, wash, and to get (or, on the contrary, give) money.

As some evidence shows, children from dysfunctional families who spend their time on the streets, but who also preserve at least some connections with their homes, are a reality in many Russian towns and cities. About half of the street children in Moscow are like this. However, the other half, on

Table 13.9 'How Did You Earn Your Living Before Leaving Home?' (in per cent to the total number of those who used to earn)

Casual work for money or food	53.8
Helping relatives or family members	14.2
Stealing	13.0
Begging	2.3
Playing a musical instrument	8.7
Collecting bottles	5.2
Prostitution	2.8
N	84

their own or with their parents, migrated to Moscow. They can be divided into several categories:

- There are 'tourists' – children who run away from home to have fun, see Moscow, visit old friends. Sooner or later they go back or are sent home by the militia. Some of them come from 'normal' families, others from problem homes.
- Another category – 'vagrants' – are children who are travelling on their own and who are very often connected to the organised criminal world. Many of them ran away from children's homes. They move through Moscow on their way to other destinations (to the south of Russia or to other big cities, such as St Petersburg). Sometimes they come to Moscow for a period of time, in order to earn money by crime.
- Some of the migrants come to Moscow with their parents (or other people) to earn money and go back home. The children are used for begging, selling small items, singing and, in some cases, prostitution. Most of them come from Ukraine, Moldova and Central Asia. This category is the most visible in Moscow, but they are not the most under-privileged.
- A substantial number of children come to the city with their homeless parents.

The children from the last category seem to be on the way to joining the ranks of the most destitute and marginalised groups of the urban population. As in-depth interviews with the homeless children and their parents have shown, on their arrival to the city they and their families often try to find work. Initially they can have some money and can rent accommodation. There is a whole infrastructure in Moscow, where homeless families live with their children. These are cheap hotels where those migrants who have not yet descended into utter poverty can live together with refugees, small traders and petty criminals, or flats, rented from the local impoverished pensioners or alcoholics. Eventually some of the parents, unable to find a stable and decently paid job, sink into utter poverty. A train station or the street becomes the next stop.

Children can be the main providers for such families, as they are often more successful in begging or trading in small merchandise like stationery or books. As schools will not accept children who have no residence permit, they have no chance of getting education unless their mothers take them to a shelter or a state home. However, many of our interviewees spent several years without setting foot in school.

These children call themselves (and are called by other street children) 'small *bomzhi*' (a word which is closer to the pejorative term 'bum' than to 'the homeless'), as opposed to the 'big (adult) *bomzhi*'.[12] They identify with the stigmatised social group of adults and share the fate of the latter. The

1920s term *'besprizorniki'*, which referred to homeless *children* as a special social group, is not used at all. Those children who left their homes perman-ently and live on the streets (in cellars, lofts, underground pipes and so on), surviving by petty stealing, occasional work in a market and other odd jobs, join the ranks of the small *bomzhi* as well.

Sinking down: the process of marginalisation

Our research made it possible to look at the changes in the everyday realities and strategies adopted by families in crisis situations, and to see how the collapse of the Soviet system influenced those who depended on it most. Many of them were made to look for 'innovative' ways of adaptation[13] in the market, which often led to utter failure.

'Olesia', a seventeen-year old prostitute, comes from such a family. 'We were a decent family. I finished nine years at school, trained as a cook, everything was normal, my future was programmed... While we lived in Ukraine, in Kirovsk, my father worked in the mine, we lived very well, nobody was hungry, everything was clean and neat. We were a wonderful family. My mother worked at first at the meat factory, and later she started working in a restaurant as a night guard. And, as all the people do, she would bring something from the restaurant. I do not mean food, she would bring like a hundred plates, and the next day she would sell them and that is all. In the Soviet Union we even had special privileges [*l'goty*] as a family with many children. We often used to go to shops to collect lots of *l'goty* [goods, which were otherwise in shortage, that families with many children could buy]. We had a TV in each room, everything was normal.' Three years ago, Olesia's parents, faced with the need to find new ways of earning a living, decided to start their own business. In order to get initial capital, they borrowed money from several people they knew in town. But their business was not success-ful, and angry lenders started demanding money back. In what has become a typical scenario, the family escaped and started moving from town to town trying to earn money. All the roads to prosperity led to Moscow, and the family eventually settled in a Moscow suburb, where the parents found jobs with a Turkish construction company. But old habits die hard, and the parents were fired from the company after it emerged that they were stealing from it (for example, all the furniture in the rented flat was stolen from the employer). The family would then try to earn money selling fruit and vegetables at the market. But they soon discovered that casual employment at the market, contrary to the assumptions of many Russians who do not trade in the market themselves, is not a source of super-profits. On the contrary, hoards of migrants who come to the cities to look for work, are ruthlessly exploited by their employers – a natural outcome of a huge surplus of labour. As Olesia and many other of our respondents experienced, the earnings she and her parents were getting were quite meagre and barely enough to feed themselves, not to mention the other six younger children in the family. In the meantime, relations in the family deteriorated. The parents, especially the father, started to drink heavily. He began to beat the mother – this, as Olesia claims, never happened in their previous life. There were constant quarrels. The younger children were hungry and neglected. Finally, the parents started to force Olesia to engage in prostitution with the Turkish workers from the company where they used to work. She decided to leave home and went to live at the train station. Like many of the homeless girls, she at first tried to find young men with whom she could stay for some time. But this was a precarious existence. Many times she had to sleep at train-stations. So, when she was approached by a woman in the metro who asked whether she would like to work as a prostitute, Olesia agreed. Now she lives in a flat with several other under-age girls like her and works for a '*mamochka*' – something between a 'madam' and a 'pimp'. She feels that this is the only way for her to survive.

Olesia's family became visibly a 'problem' family recently, under the strain of poverty and misfortune. Some street children come from homes that would have been considered as problem families in the Soviet days as well. But many come from the families of low-skilled industrial and service sector workers who were well integrated by the Soviet system. Such families suddenly found themselves redundant in the new conditions. In Soviet days too, families could be nests of problems, such as alcohol abuse, family conflict and violence. However they were not necessarily marginalised and left to their own devices. First, a system of full employment, child support, welfare provisions for families with many children, cheap food and basic commodities meant that there was quite a substantial safety net, and total destitution was rare. Even when the wages were not enough, there were widespread possibilities of supplementing them by stealing something from work (which was largely tolerated). Secondly, the absence of private property meant that parents could not sell their housing and be left in the streets. Thirdly, the absence of uncontrolled migration meant that families were within easy reach of social control bodies. However inefficient these controls were, school, the militia, and municipal commissions on minors did monitor the situations in the families. In cases of neglect parents would be deprived of parental rights, while the children would be placed with relatives or in children's homes.

Formal controls over families like this have been relaxed significantly since the end of the Soviet system. Informal controls are also lacking because of the destruction of work-related affiliations as a result of direct unemployment or forced leave, frequent changes of jobs and, in some cases, migration.

The current crisis needs urgent solutions, as well as the development of long-term strategies for child protection. At the moment the vested interests of state institutions, the restrictions on social benefits for migrants (imposed by the city authorities), together with a situation of a severe budget deficit prevent these solutions from being developed. Hysteria about the plight of Russian children, and a search for penal solutions for those who become a threat to adults, can do little to help in these circumstances. The only way forward can be in a profound reform of the system of child care, including the monitoring of 'problem families', an expanded role for the system of education, the development of foster care and assistance to the voluntary organisations that work with the street children and their families. But above all, the serious effects on families and children of poverty and marginalisation have to be recognised and brought into the public agenda.

Notes

1   In this chapter I will be discussing some of the results of my research project, 'Street Children in Russia', which took place in 1997–98. I am very grateful to the Ford Foundation, which sponsored the project, and also to Alexey Levinson, Nigel South, Richard Sakwa, Alastair McAuley, Robert Dingwall, Jane Lewis and Judith Harwin for their comments.

2   'VChK – v zaschitu detstva' (1998). *Tverskaia*, 13, 9–15 April.

3   The notion of social disorganisation was put forward by the Chicago school. See, for example, Shaw and McKay (1931).

4   By ghettoisation I mean not the ethnic spatial exclusion, common, for example, in the United States, but spatial isolation of the marginal unemployed population, with ensuing problems of reproduction of poverty and crime. This term was suggested in this sense by Paul Wiles (1993).

5   ITAR-TASS, 27 May 1999.

6   Interview with Nadezhda Ivanova, senior researcher, Institute of Childhood, October 1997.

7   *Ibid.*

8   RFE/RL, 14 June 1999.

9   As seen, for example, in most of the articles in *Sotsial'naia dessadaptatsiia* (1996).

10   Such a trend was described by Margaret Stolee for the 1930s. Then it coincided with a general shift for repressive solutions to social problems (Stolee 1988).

11   Clearly, not all the children were sincere when answering the questions about socially (and sometimes legally) unacceptable practices. That is why such data should be treated as having insufficient reliability.

12   The word '*bomzh*', an abbreviation for '*bez opredelennogo mesta zhitelstva*' (without fixed abode), was born in militia protocols in the 1970s, and is now widely used to refer to homeless street people.

13   On innovative adaptation see Merton (1957).

References

Abandoned to the State: Cruelty and Neglect in Russian Orphanages (1998). Human Rights Watch.

Aristova, N.G. (1992). 'Sotsial'nye prichiny i mekhanizmi formirovaniia sirotstva v rannem detstve' in N. Aristova (ed.) *Problemy sirotstva i deiatelnost' uchrezhdenii, zameshchaiushchikh semeinoe vospitanie*. Moscow: Institut sotsiologii RAN, vol. 2, pp. 5–24.

Beliakova, A. (1983). *Okhrana prav nesovershennoletnikh.* Moscow: Znanie.

Bochkareva, G. (1967). 'Psikhologiia podrostkov-pravonarushitelei' *Sovetskaia iustitsiia,* no. 22, pp. 30–45.

Boldyrev, E. (1964). *Mery preduprezhdeniia pravonarushenii nesovershennoletnikh v SSSR.* Moscow: Iuridicheskaia literatura.

Cohen, S. (1972). *Folk Devils and Moral Panics: the Creation of the Mods and Rockers.* London: McGibbon & Kee.

Goldman, W.Z. (1993). *Women, the State and the Revolution. Soviet Family Policy and Social Life, 1917–1933.* Cambridge: Cambridge University Press.

Goode, E. and Ben-Yehuda, N. (1994). *Moral Panics: The Social Construction of Deviance.* Oxford: Blackwell.

Harwin, J. (1996). *Children of the Russian State: 1971–95.* Avebury: Aldershot.

Istoriia voprosa i aktual'nost' problemy desadaptatsii podrostkov i molodezhi v moskovskom regione. Moscow: NAN.

Kharchev, A.G (1979). *Brak i sem'ia v SSSR.* Moscow: Mysl'.

Kharchev, A.G. (1983). 'Sem'ia kak ob"ekt demograficheskoi politiki' in V. Varshis *et al.* (eds). *Aktual'nye voprosy sem'i i vospitaniia.* Vilnius: Institut filosofii, sotsiologii i prava, pp.4–16.

Merton, R. (1957). *Social Theory and Social Structure.* New York: Glencoe.

Ordonez, D. (1995). *Ninos de la Calle y sus Familias en Lima: Yna Realidad en 852 Variables.* Lima: Tetis Graf.

Paniushkin, V. (1998). 'Nam nuzhen zakon o pravakh rebenka' *Kommersant-Daily,* 5 May.

Selitskii A. and Taratukhin, S. (1981). *Nesovershennoletnie s otkloniaiushchimisia povedeniem.* Kiev: Vischa shkola.

Shaw, C. and McKay, H. (1931). *Social Factors in Juvenile Delinquency.* Washington, DC: Government Printing Office.

Sotsial'naia desadaptatsiia: narusheniia povedeniia u detei i podrostkov. Materialy rossiiskoi nauchno-prakticheskoi konferentsii. (1996). Moscow: Graal.

Stolee, M. (1988). 'Homeless Children in the USSR. 1917–1957' *Soviet Studies,* no. 1, pp. 64–83.

Wiles P. (1993). 'Ghettoisation in Europe?' *European Journal on Criminal Policy and Research,* vol. 1, no. 1, pp. 52–69.

Zabrianskii, G. (1997). *Sotsiologiia prestupnosti nesovershennoletnikh.* Minsk: Minsktipproekt.

14
Psychological Development Programmes for Civil Society Building

Darejan Javakhishvili and Natalie Sarjveladze

The post-Soviet period in Georgia, as in all post-communist societies to a greater or lesser extent, is characterised by social, economic and political crises. In common with the experience of all of these countries, the transformation process is proving extremely painful for the population. The transition to a market economy, democratisation and civil society building demands changes in the ways of thinking and the stereotypes of accustomed behaviour, and adaptation to a constantly changing environment. The situation in Georgia has been aggravated by protracted ethno-political conflicts, in the regions of Abkhazia and Ossetia, as a result of which there are some 300 000 Internally Displaced Persons (IDPs) in the country. These people have been left, for all intents and purposes, without adequate social protection. The majority of IDPs have to cope not only with the everyday problems associated with the transition, but also with a feeling of isolation from society. Latent tensions with the locals have become increasingly serious, thus making the question of the IDPs' integration into the local community quite acute, and a crucial issue not just for the IDPs themselves, but, we could argue, for the entire process of democratisation in Georgia (Chervonnaia 1994).

The Georgian non-governmental organisation 'The Foundation for the Development of Human Resources' (FDHR), with the financial support of the Norwegian Refugee Council (NRC), is involved in the psycho-social rehabilitation of IDPs (*Annual Report of the Foundation for the Development of Human Resources* 1996 and 1998). One of the most important aspects of its work concerns the problems of children and adolescents, and is focused on educational and developmental programmes. In this chapter, we will describe the approach that has been taken to the design and implementation of these programmes, and provide an evaluation of their performance.

The psycho-social rehabilitation of IDP children in Georgia

The most important concern to address when designing the programme was the fact that the development of IDP children takes place in the context of post-traumatic experience and an ambiguous, stressful reality (Charkviani and Sarjveladze 1997). The aim of the programme was to help them to: discover and develop their own resources; overcome the label of 'refugee', and the feelings of estrangement and isolation typical among IDPs; overcome a sense of victimisation (see Beberashvili *et al.* 1998: 448); understand the meaning of the legends and folklore that circulate about 'refugees'; overcome tendencies towards a revengeful disposition and aggression; be able to think independently and adjust creatively to the environment.

In accordance with these goals, the emphasis was on development-focused programmes. The objective was to help children and adolescents to acquire the skills necessary for the development of constructive behavioural potential, to broaden their outlook, to help them to develop relations on a non-conflict basis within the group, in the wider community, and of course, inside themselves. The programme was divided into seven stages:

1 Development of communication skills
2 Training in conflict management and resolution
3 Work on the notion of the 'enemy image' (see Javakhishvili *et al.* 1998: 456)
4 Creative work
5 Cultural activities (concerts, exhibitions, and so on)
6 Ecology and the environment
7 Encounter activities for Ossetian and Georgian children to stimulate peace-building activities (with the aim of building a bridge of folk diplomacy between adolescents who had been on opposing sides during the military conflict).

These development-focused activities were run on a continuous basis, with the same target sample engaged in them over the course of a year. The emphasis was on creative self-expression and psychological training in order to provide a suitable atmosphere, as 'problematic' children, that is, children experiencing communication difficulties because of their psychological problems (shyness, low self-esteem, and so on) are usually able to engage in the activities only gradually. Thus the two objectives of development and correction were mutually supportive.

1 Development of communication skills[1]

The aim of this stage was to facilitate the acquisition of effective interpersonal communication skills, through: the development of 'non-verbal' language; improvement of abilities in congruent communication; the development of skills in stimulating communication; improvement of listening ability; the development of empathy; the development of the ability to lead persuasive communication; awareness of the stages of effective communication.

The activities included staging non-verbal sketches, various verbal and non-verbal games, problem-solving with subsequent discussions, group decision-making, training in setting open and closed questions, and exercises to stimulate non-standard ways of thinking.[2] From the very beginning, the enthusiasm of group members towards such activities manifested itself in almost 100 per cent attendance, although the children were, despite this willingness to participate, very cautious at first, finding it difficult to express their own thoughts and feelings. Something said by one child, for instance, would be repeated by everyone, and the children would react in a sarcastic way to new, unusual ideas. A competitive relationship was observed in everything, showing itself most strikingly when working materials (paper, pens) were being distributed. In one case, a little boy hid the felt tip pens that had been laid out for everyone in his clothes, so that no one else could use them. In response to such cases, a good deal of time was devoted to fun games for building trust and creating a secure atmosphere within the group, the main principle of these games resting on the idea that members of the group should refrain from evaluating the work of the others.

In the transition to non-verbal activities, the children's difficulties in understanding and conveying their emotions were clearly visible, with incongruence the most striking feature (for instance, non-verbal conveyance of love to the partner through hitting them). For this reason, we had to deliver additional sessions in order to improve their abilities in congruent communication and the use of non-verbal language. The same was the case with persuasive communication, with children who were either too shy or too aggressive encountering difficulties in acquiring the relevant skills. As the workload increased, another problem with 7–12-year-old children was noted, that is, concentration. To correct this it was necessary to deliver several unplanned sessions promoting the development of mental abilities, with group exercises focused on attention and memory. Another problem arose with the introduction of planned sessions for the development of non-standard thinking, particularly with adolescents, and, accordingly, additional sessions were delivered to foster this skill, an essential foundation for conflict management training.

We can conclude that at the end of the communication training stage children were better able to understand their feelings, had successfully learned 'body language' skills and had acquired self-congruence and self-confidence. The atmosphere within the group was that of a team, with a prevalence of trust. The children were enthusiastically involved in the work, and showed that they were prepared to cope with the difficult tasks related to conflict management training.

2   Conflict management and resolution[3]

The objectives of this stage were: the development of understanding of the essence of conflict by children and adolescents; raising awareness of the reasons of conflict; familiarisation with conflict resolution approaches; acquisition of management and prevention skills; learning skills of mediation in conflict; tolerance building.

The activities included drawing, staging sketches, analysis, role playing and exercises for active listening. Although the children were already 'flexible' and open, thanks to the previous group work, the introduction of the conflict theme made it clear that they were trying to avoid it because of its traumatic influence. This appears somewhat paradoxical, indeed, as the children had manifested conflict behaviour quite often in real life situations. To give some examples: when they were asked to produce drawings on conflict-related themes in the initial sessions of the stage, some children manifested a total avoidance of the theme and drew a landscape or still life, while the majority depicted conflict between things or natural phenomena. For example, they might draw a quarrel between a pen and an eraser, a 'quarrel between a cloud and thunder', or a 'quarrel between a dog and a wolf'. For this reason it was necessary for the trainers to be extremely tactful in creating a constructive framework for role-playing conflict situations. Sometimes proposals were unnecessary, as the conflict tendencies that spontaneously emerged among group members were used as a resource for the explanation of this or that aspect of conflict. Through the exchange of roles in role-playing situations the children were able to view the event from the perspective of the 'confronting' party. They were encouraged to try to understand the other person's position, to learn to be impartial, accept other people's interests and subjective reality. This included coaching them in the skills of mediation as well as constructive patterns of communication through the 'I-message'.

By the end of the stage, the children's mutual aggression and conflict behaviour had visibly decreased. When conflict tendencies did emerge, the children, without intervention, tried to settle the relationships through self-management, reminding each other about 'non-evaluation' and co-operation principles, using humour, re-evaluating the event that triggered the conflict, and employing I-messages (frequently for fun). Each group followed the programme from stages 1–6, while in the seventh stage only eight Georgian and eight Ossetian adolescents participated. This last-mentioned group is a special case: these children did not participate in the programme from the beginning, as this refugee settlement was not originally included in our plans.

3 The 'enemy image'

The 'heritage' of a refugee child is very difficult, from its very birth. Even the words 'persecuted person', which Georgian IDPs prefer to the word 'refugee', reinforce the sense of being a victim, as well as the existence of a 'persecutor'. It is through this that a feeling of victimisation and the enemy image are formed. Since the child's intellect is in the process of formation, and the ability of generalisation is not yet well-enough developed, the enemy image, transmitted through 'inheritance' to the child, is projected on to people who are unfamiliar to, or different from, the child in some way. This could explain certain problems that were observed during the initial stages: a high level of mutual aggression; rejection of new or alternative ideas, values or opinions; and the presence of victim-aggression types of relationship. It proved necessary to work on the overcoming/prevention of the enemy image throughout the year and within the framework of every stage. A great deal of attention was devoted, for instance, to the development of tolerant attitudes towards 'other', different persons. The objectives of this stage, then, were: the revelation of the enemy image; once it had been revealed, the elimination of generalisations, omissions, and distortions;[4] awareness of the aggressor–victim stereotype and the means to be used for its correction; acquisition of parity-based relationship styles; recognition of other people's subjective reality; tolerance building; development of the ability to consider another person's point of view; awareness of personal responsibility stemming from ethical choice; development of a sense of responsibility for one's own behaviour. The activities used included: story-telling; group interviewing; exercises for emotional discharge and reframing[5] of negative experience; meditation techniques; and thematic drawing.

It is interesting to note that when the children were asked to draw an 'Enemy', some children avoided the theme (drawing landscapes or still life instead), some drew parts of the national costume, others painted a colour spot, and so on. Such symbols (patterns) point to the existence of an enemy image at the embryonic stage. It needs to be worked on tactfully, gently and carefully, and it is desirable to carry out this kind of work with the youth of the confronting party.

The results of this work were positive: before the children embarked on the programme, 'victimisation' was used as a means of achieving desirable results (for example, members of the 7–12-year-olds' group tried to attract American guests' attraction by crying), and victimisation and competition in victimisation were the prevailing behaviour patterns. Following their participation in the programme, the trend was towards achievement orientation, achievement of results through one's own efforts and an emphasis on co-operation.

The work carried out in one school should be also mentioned in this context. In the first year of the programme, there was a conflict in the school between local and IDP teenagers. The programme staff facilitated the resolution of this conflict through working with the entire school. While no obvious conflict was discerned at the beginning of the programme's work, for preventative purposes a joint group, comprising local and refugee teenagers, was formed, and operated over the course of a year. The children got so close to each other that they ended up working jointly on the setting-up of a youth club. The co-operative relationships established among the group members extended to pupils in the senior grades, and created an atmosphere of mutual respect and trust.

4   Creative self-expression and creative labour

This stage was aimed at the development of creative potential in adolescents and children, with a focus on the development of basic working skills, and on building greater confidence and self-respect through creating things that have aesthetic value. The teacher planned ten sessions, involving diverse themes and arranged according to increased complexity. The frequency of these sessions was one per week. From this experience, it was clearly visible right at the start of the stage that 7–12-year-old children were very enthusiastic about participation in these sessions, while the teenagers were more attracted by psycho-training. According to the initial plan, sessions on creative work were supposed to be held separately from psycho-training programmes, but this was amended to facilitate joint sessions, in which the combined work of the teacher and the psychologist-facilitator turned out to be very fruitful. Consequently, except for those sessions where the children required all the time available to make the items, the articles they made were used as a means for psychological correction. For instance, in the first half of the session the children learned to make a 'goldfish' and a rod, while the second half was devoted to acting: the children role-played the part of the fisherman and uttered three wishes on his behalf, which served as material for the correction work.

As the work got underway, the activities included in the original plan were also modified. This happened for two reasons. First, the working environment at the locations (lifts, corridors, small size of rooms, insufficient number of tables and chairs in the room) made it impossible to do more subtle work, such as making more complex toys. Secondly, it gradually became clear that the children's general and working skills did not meet the demands of school programmes. Children of 9–10 years found it difficult to do the homework provided for 6–7-year-old children. It seems that in the schools that these children had previously attended creative work had not been given sufficient attention. Consequently, they were not confident in their abilities and would often say 'I can't do this' or 'This is too difficult', frequently asking the teacher to do part or all of the work on their behalf. If they had enough courage to start the work themselves, they often asked for feedback: 'Is that correct?' or 'Is that OK?'. Sometimes, even if their work was as good as the model they had been shown, they expressed dissatisfaction: 'Your work is good, mine is not.' They became aggressive when members of their team deviated from the expected standard ('What have you done, you fool!').

The purpose of the programme's work is to overcome such problems. The work started with simple assignments (to make objects from paper), so that the children would believe that they were able to do something. The complexity of assignments gradually increased in the direction of more subtle work that required patience. At this point natural materials were introduced (for example, cones, branches, leaves). In order to create a team-work atmosphere the children made items together. The final sessions were devoted to moulding and making objects from clay.

On the whole, in spite of the difficulties described above, the creative activities sessions saw visible results by the end of the stage. The children became more independent and less attached to the things that they had produced. They tried to make up different designs using the same material, developed a positive attitude towards innovation, and even encouraged one another to make something new. As the stage developed, some other needs also emerged, such as a desire to hold an exhibition: indeed, several small exhibitions were staged. This fact shows that the children liked their own creations. They expected something new from every meeting. They also expected to use and develop the knowledge and experience that they had acquired, showing a desire to engage in ever more complex and subtle work.

5   The protection of nature and ecological education

This stage involved excursions to Tbilisi (the capital of Georgia) and the surrounding countryside, so that the children could overcome the feeling of estrangement from their present living environment. Until the conflict flared up, this population had lived in their home towns or villages, they had their own houses, gardens, yards and so on. After displacement they were now living in a densely populated environment in hostels in another part of the country. It was felt that this stage would also help them to become more familiar with the national culture, in order to strengthen national identity and overcome an identity crisis. They were also given the opportunity to acquire skills related to survival (the idea being that the acquisition of such skills would increase self-confidence). Finally, they were able to familiarise themselves with the bases of eco-culture, to foster a caring attitude towards the environment.

6   Cultural activities

This stage was aimed at the promotion of self-expression and self-actualisation among the children and adolescents. Throughout the year, 'mini concerts' and 'mini exhibitions' of working groups were encouraged and arranged on a regular basis. The programme was enriched with the ideas generated by the children and staff. For example, apart from the concerts, the children arranged (on their own initiative) a quiz on 'Guess the tune' and quizzes for 'Happy and Smart people'. Adolescents from various schools, who had made friends with each other during the joint trips, expressed a desire to arrange a joint quiz. This meeting visibly increased the participants' achieve-ment motivation and creative activity. IDP adolescents prepared and arranged a school concert in the autumn, in which local adolescents also participated, and which somehow reflected the results of the work.

In the final stage of the rehabilitation work, the aim was to look for ways of fostering further this self-organising principle. At one of the weekly brainstorming sessions, devoted to the solution of the above problem, an idea was generated to set up so-called 'children's clubs' at the working locations. The idea was felt to be appropriate also for another reason: during the year's work the importance of reinforcing team-like and co-operative relationships through some common aim or activity had become apparent. The children were very enthusiastic about the idea of setting up a club, and soon came up with the idea of publishing a club newspaper. Each club established its own newspaper, and the children willingly provided material for publication (for example, pieces of their own poetry, drawings, stories, puzzles), which was then printed and returned to the children in the form of 'home-made' newspapers. The children enjoyed reading the newspapers of the other clubs, and this activity soon became one of the most important components of the rehabilitation work. Through their involvement in the production of the newspapers the children satisfied their needs of recognition, self-expression and communication.

The IDP adolescent group decided to set up their own club, and, with our help, they wrote an application and submitted it to the OSGF (Open Society Georgian Foundation) to set up a 'Club for local and IDP adolescents'. Thus by the end of the implementation of the action programme, the children were full of creative ideas and the enthusiasm to accomplish them.

7 Encounter activities for Georgian and South Ossetian children

As is well known, a protracted ethno-political conflict has been in progress between Georgia and South Ossetia since 1991. If reconciliation is to be achieved, much depends on the current generation of children and adolescents: will they be revengeful, or will they show a readiness for constructive dialogue? This is why it is so important to build folk-diplomacy bridges between adolescents, to help them to overcome the 'enemy image', and develop a mutually tolerant attitude that can make a positive contribution to the dynamics of the relations between the confronting parties. This last stage was duly designed to work towards these objectives. It provided for a meeting of eight Georgian IDP adolescents from South Ossetia and eight Ossetian adolescents, in the setting of a five-day training seminar. Preliminary work was carried out for six months. During this period, Foundation staff periodically visited South Ossetia to hold negotiations with the management of a local 'Youth Palace'. The meeting of the adolescents was held on 17-23 June, with the participation of 16 adolescents, two Georgian refugee teachers and two Ossetian teachers. The age of the adolescents ranged from 12 to 17. The five days were devoted to the training of communication skills and conflict management training, sessions on creative thinking and creative work, and courses in ecological education. The activities and methods used comprised story-telling, staging of sketches and role playing, brainstorming, creative labour, art therapy, mediation exercises, and excursions. In their free time, the children communicated with each other, talked and amused themselves with dances and sports.

At the beginning the children were very cautious and tense when communicating with each other, and remained in their separate groups. We managed to overcome this through a joint group activity and training. In particular, a story-telling session held on 18 June was very important as an icebreaker. The children and their teachers had an opportunity to 'voice what they had not voiced before' and to react emotionally. The training work involved not only children, but also teachers. The wide age range proved to be something of a problem, as did the question of language, as there was no common language. The Ossetians spoke Russian, but the Georgians could not speak in Russian, even though they understood it. But neither the first, nor the second difficulty impeded the effective implementation of the stage, as the aim of the meeting was achieved: the children became very close to each other, and were very eager to communicate, and felt that they didn't have enough time together. In the last three days of the meeting, they gathered in the room of one of the children and could not stop talking in spite of tiredness or the teachers' instructions to go to bed (not even the language barrier proved to be an obstacle here). When they were leaving at the end of the seminar, many of them had tears in their eyes. Subsequently, so their teachers reported, the adolescents kept in touch with one another.

Outcomes and conclusions

The results of the work were studied by the FDHR's work activities monitoring group, which measured the programme's effectiveness in developing the children's and adolescents' self-confidence, their communicative competence, their ability to behave in constructive ways in conflict situations, creativity, and the degree of awareness of their own skills and abilities. In all areas, the study found positive dynamics. In addition, useful information was gained from feedback given by the children and their parents, in which a universally high level of satisfaction was expressed. In the words of one fourteen-year-old boy: 'Now I know much more about myself and about the world, and I also know that I'm not alone.' The results of our work were also highly praised by the evaluation group from the Norwegian Ministry of Foreign Affairs whose report included the phrase:

> A Norwegian assessment of NRC activities and local co-operation on conflict resolution in particular rates the FDHR programmes for children and youth positively. The shared activities for children and youth from

Georgia and Ossetia are especially emphasised.

(Evaluation of Norwegian Support . . . 1999)

Apart from its work with IDP children, the FDHR has also developed programmes for use in the school system. The initial work in this area has focused on training for head teachers, administrators, teachers and psychologists, which includes the use of experiential teaching methods, conflict management and mediation skills, team-orientated and multi-ethnic approaches to learning.

Tackling the problems of IDP children represents just part of a broader set of problems that seem to exist in general in the education system. In the post-Soviet environment, the principles of the old system do not appear to be compatible with the aims of democratisation and civil-society building. The dominance of the teacher that was accepted in Soviet times, when pupils were expected to confirm to norms of behaviour, and when only one way of 'correct' thinking was expected, are not acceptable now. The transition to democracy demands co-operative relations between teachers and pupils, the encouragement of individuality, and the awareness of alternative realities. A great deal of work will be required to deal with such needs, over many years.

Notes

1 On the development of communication skills, see Beebe and Masterson (1989).
2 On these issues, see De Bono, E. (1997).
3 See Rubin, J. and Prutt, S. (1994).
4 See Grinder, J. and Bandler, R. (1996).
5 Reframing is a psychotherapeutic method aimed at helping people to change ways of thinking about a particular problem. For example, it can focus on important personal experiences that have caused trauma, the lessons one has learned from the problem, and so on.

References

Annual report of the 'Foundation for the Development of Human Resources' (1996) and (1998). http://www.welcome.to/fdhr

Beberashvili, Z., Makhashvili, N., Sarjveladze, N., and Javakhishvili, D. (1998). 'Rehabilitation Work on the Victimization Phenomenon' Sixth European Congress on Research in Rehabilitation: Congress Proceedings, Berlin, p. 448.

Beebe, S. and Masterson, J. (1989). *Communication in Small Groups – Principles and Practices.* New York: Addison Wesley.

Charkviani, D. and Sarjveladze, N. (1997). 'Multifactoral Study of the Attitudes of Internally Displaced Persons (IDPs) in Georgia' Abstracts, Fifth European Congress of Psychology, Dublin, p. 223.

Chervonnaia, S. (1994). *Conflict in the Caucasus – Georgia, Abkhazia and the Russian Shadow.* Glastonbury: Gothic Image Publications.

De Bono, E. (1977). *Lateral Thinking – A Textbook of Creativity.* Harmondsworth: Penguin.

Evaluation of Norwegian Support to Psycho-Social Projects in Bosnia-Herzegovina and the Caucasus (1999). Oslo: Norwegian Ministry of Foreign Affairs.

Grinder, J. and Bandler, R. (1975) *The Structure of Magic.* Palo Alto CA: Science and Behavior Books.

Javakhishvili, D., Sarjveladze, N., Makhashvili, N., and Beberashvili, Z. (1998). 'Overcoming of the "Enemy Image" as a Form of Psycho-Social Rehabilitation' Sixth European Congress on Research in Rehabilitation, Congress Proceedings, Berlin, p. 456.

Rubin, J. and Prutt, S. (1994). *Social Conflict: Escalation, Stalemate, and Settlement.* New York: McGraw Hill.

15

The Culture of the Russian School and the Teaching Profession: Prospects for Change

Stephen Webber

In the 1990s, the Russian school system has been tasked with implementing a wide-ranging and ambitious reform programme, building on a momentum that had begun in the mid-1980s. It has had to respond to the demands of change against the backdrop of the ongoing political, economic and social crises that have afflicted the country as a whole over this period. For the most part, there seems to be relatively little that the schools and the teaching force can do, in the short term at least, to ensure that the education sector receives greater support (moral and material) from society, and thus the long-term fate of the school system will continue to rest in the balance for some time to come. However, within the system itself, there has been far greater scope to change the ways in which the schools are run, and thus facilitate reform. In this chapter,[1] I will examine the nature of the 'culture' of the Russian school, to assess the extent to which the conditions that prevail in the schools can be said to be conducive to the implementation of change. I will also highlight a number of ways in which this school culture is shaped by developments in broader society.

The subject of school culture has attracted a great deal of attention in the West, with research demonstrating the important role that such factors as professional relations within the school play in the process of reform (Dalin and Rolff 1993; Sarason 1971). An ideal type of establishment to have emerged from the debate in the West on the culture of the school and the quest for school improvement is that of the 'learning organisation', in which, as Dalin and Rolff explain:

> Initiatives for change may come from within the school, as well as from the environment. The school is *open* to improvement [original emphasis], clear about strengths and weaknesses, and has motivation and capacities to cope with improvement processes.
>
> (Dalin and Rolff 1993: 18)

In other words, change has become part of the culture of the school, the evolutionary approach coming to replace the stop-go, reactionary model common in most systems. However, as yet most schools in most systems across the world are, in fact, a long way from this goal: 'The school is not now a learning organisation. Irregular waves of change, episodic projects, fragmentation of effort, and grinding overload is the lot of most schools' (Fullan 1993: 42).

We should not, therefore, be tempted to judge the Russian school too severely against such paradigms. Nevertheless, it does serve as an example of what can be achieved, if the factors that have been shown to exert a strong influence on change patterns are all afforded the attention they require, and the school approaches change as an evolutionary matter that is integral to the life of the school as a whole. Given such criteria, to what extent can the Soviet school model be said to have been a learning organisation? An examination of aspects of the culture of both the Russian school, and the teaching profession, allow us to understand better the course that reform has taken in the Russian system.

The Soviet tradition of reform

The top-down approach to reform engrained in the Soviet system reflects a drawback common in many systems, where the potential significance of the teacher's participation in the change process has tended to be overlooked. As Hord notes: 'In school change, teachers tend to be recipients rather than initiators of change' (Hord 1987: 15). In the case of the USSR, however, the possibilities for open and active participation seemed to be especially restricted; the application of individual initiative in curricular matters was not encouraged, indeed, it was actively discouraged, and the teacher was supposed to act as a 'teacher-fulfiller' (*uchitel'-ispolnitel'*), who would ensure that the centrally-imposed timetable was delivered according to plan. Failure to do so could result in sanctions of various kinds being imposed on that teacher and her or his headteacher by the authorities.

This does not mean that initiative was stifled completely; some teachers were able to introduce an element of individuality and diversity into the curriculum through employing approaches and materials that differed in some way from the official norm. (In the city of Iaroslavl' I interviewed one such 'innovator', a retired primary-class teacher, who told me of the text-book which she had prepared in secret in the 1960s and had retained without showing it to the authorities ever since, but the contents of which she had used in her teaching.) Nevertheless, the lack of attention paid in the Soviet system to the potential input that teachers might make to reform has undoubtedly handicapped Russian teachers in adapting to the new expectation that they participate actively in change, and become, to employ the current Western terminology, 'change agents'. As systems across the world have found, the complex nature of change requires staff to become adept at understanding the processes of change as they operate at the classroom level. It was important, therefore, that the educational authorities in Russia appreciate the need for teachers to be given the opportunity to acquire those skills, before embarking on the ambitious programme for change. As I have argued elsewhere, the question of introducing change in the teacher-education system – a crucial element in any major reform effort – was, at least until the mid-1990s, somewhat neglected, and lagged behind the momentum for change being promoted in the schools (Webber and Webber 1994a; Webber 1996). Would the existing school culture be able to offset the shortcomings of the teacher-education system and provide a suitable environment for the implementation of reform?

The hierarchy of power in the school

Research findings in the West demonstrate the key part played by head-teachers in those schools which are seen to be successfully implementing change, and the handicap caused by inadequate leadership in other schools suffering setback or failure in change (Rosenholtz 1989). Much depends on the headteacher's ability to manage the staff, guide them through the problems of reform, and set the agenda for the broader tasks that the school faces in adjusting to new educational and social conditions. Such patterns hold true in the case of Russian headteachers as well, for they face challenges which are very similar in their nature to those experienced by principals in the USA or headteachers in the UK. Indeed, the conservative tendencies observed among some American headteachers (Lortie 1987: 80–90) might be seen to be even more firmly engrained into the culture of the headship in Russia, given the amount of control imposed on heads by the authorities in the Soviet era, an experience which still shapes the attitudes of many head-teachers in Russia today.

Now this control has been significantly reduced, as a result of the devolution of educational administration and curriculum management, leaving headteachers both to take advantage of the opportunities that this brings to assume greater control over their school, and to face the greater responsibilities that have come with devolution and the general nature of change in society as a whole. Headteachers whom I interviewed complained that they had been given insufficient support in coming to terms with the increased administrative load that they now bear, problems which have inevitably contributed to delays in implementation and confusion in schools' approach to reform.

Nevertheless, despite the considerable pressures that they have to contend with, Russian headteachers now enjoy substantially increased influence over the running of their own schools. While they may still be constrained by the nature of the system as far as recruitment of staff is concerned, and while they must devote considerable energy and time to addressing the school's material problems, many heads appear to have welcomed their new found freedom in the sphere of the curriculum. It may well be that the power thus enjoyed by a headteacher will provide the most effective means of moving a school towards the adoption and implementation of change, as the head is able to 'persuade' the staff of the need for such developments.

Empowerment brings with it much responsibility, for choosing a suitable course of development for the school, and for creating the right conditions for her or his staff to work towards that goal. In some schools, there will be a conservative core of more experienced teachers who may be reluctant to engage in change, at least to the extent proposed by the head; at times, even an energetic and skilful headteacher may find that such teachers can foil attempts to introduce change. The problem is exacerbated in the Russian case by the low level of mobility of teachers, and the difficulty of recruiting younger staff who might be more able to adjust to the demands of reform. In some cases, therefore, the difficulties of persuading what are seen as 'conservative' teachers to follow the head's views on change have been used by some headteachers as a motive for setting up an alternative school, where they will be able to recruit a new team of staff and, they hope, thereby ensure a greater degree of cohesion and ambition for change.

With regard to the teaching staff, the potential for 'bottom-driven' change, that is, the ability of individual classroom teachers to influence the course of development in their own school, is still somewhat limited. This is not to say that teachers are not heavily involved in change activities; indeed, many of the teachers interviewed during this research appeared to be taking advantage of the new freedoms brought by empowerment to engage in innovation to varying degrees. Further, in some schools visited for this study a more balanced relationship seemed to have been fostered between the headteacher and senior staff and the other teachers. Nevertheless, the fact that the headteacher wields such a large influence can mean that a teacher whose views on change do not coincide with those of their headteacher may find the possibilities to develop their own agenda are limited.

This situation can be ascribed in large part to the 'flat' structure of management traditionally found in the Soviet school (to some extent paralleled in Soviet society itself), in which power was concentrated in the hands of a small number of people at the top of the organisation. Beneath the headteacher the levels of responsibility comprised only that of deputy headteacher (*zaveduiushchii uchebnoi chast'iu* or *zavuch*), with two deputies responsible for the curriculum and 'upbringing work' (*vospitatel'naia rabota*) respectively; senior teacher (adviser) (*metodist*); form tutor (*klassnyi rukovoditel'*) and classroom teacher. If we compare this with the English system, we find that in the latter the hierarchical structure of the school is 'tall', based on a varied and complex network of posts and responsibilities, and in which junior members of staff are expected to assume responsibility for certain issues of school life from an early stage in their career.

While some would contest that a flat structure can be more conducive to the emergence of a more 'democratic' workplace, in which collective decision-making is facilitated, in practice the organisation of the Soviet school served to deny the ordinary class teachers, and in particular the younger members of staff, the opportunity to have a real say in the running of the school. In recent years new posts have emerged, including heads of department in a growing number of schools, and additional deputy head positions with responsibility, for instance, for innovative work. Nevertheless, the pattern of responsibility remains orientated towards the senior members of staff; ordinary classroom teachers, and in particular the younger staff, can be given comparatively little opportunity to make an input.

Teacher overload and stress?

Russian teachers have come increasingly in recent years to talk of being overloaded, and of the new stresses that they have begun to encounter in their work (Rybakova, Moroz and Panova 1993: 59–63). In one 1994 survey of 500 teachers, for instance, some 30 per cent reported that they were experiencing increased stress in their work (Orlov 1995: 64). Such problems will obviously affect their capacity to introduce change, and therefore represent an area of concern for the reform planners; yet further investigation of these claims allows us to place the extent of these problems in perspective. There is no doubt that the work of Russian schoolteachers has become more difficult, as they have to contend with the pressures that empowerment brings, attempt to implement reform, deal with growing social problems among their pupils, and contend with the material conditions of the teaching profession. Clearly, problems of non-payment of salaries (which are, in any case, miserly), compounded with the relatively low level of job-related material benefits, must have a significant detrimental effect on the work of the teaching force, and must be taken into consideration when assessing the system's capacity for change (see Postavalova 1997: 7).

If one compares the experience of Russian teachers with that of teachers in England, however, one can see that the difficulties of the former are very similar to those of the latter; indeed, in some areas the English teachers, perhaps, could have greater grounds for complaint. The problems faced by Russian teachers may not be as bad as they perceive them to be; it is the speed with which such changes have occurred, and the confusion and anxiety that they have caused in a teaching force which is relatively inexperienced in dealing with such problems, that have caused them to express dissatisfaction.

Take, for instance, the matter of teacher overload ('A poutru oni prosnulis'...' 1998: 7). Many Russian teachers decide to assume responsibility for additional teaching hours, on top of the standard load (*stavka*) of 18 hours per week, with some taking on two full loads for a 36-hour timetable (Tumova 1998: 6). The motivation is financial: extra salary payments are given for each additional hour, an attractive proposition for staff whose material position, always comparatively weak in the Soviet system, has declined further still in recent years. Naturally, the acquisition of extra hours reduces the amount of time available for staff to engage in preparation, professional development, and reflection on their professional activities, and thus affects their capacity to implement reform. Many interviewees also complained of the physical demands placed on them by such a heavy workload. One can sympathise with the teachers' predicament, and if one were a teacher in the French or German systems, perhaps such sympathy would be stronger, yet for an English teacher, such conditions may appear much more familiar.

Of course, an 18-hour timetable (similar to the norm in France or Germany) does allow more scope for out-of-class activities, including professional development, and can help to raise the level of teaching quality. In addition, they are given the privilege of one day per week free as a 'methodology day' (*metodicheskii den'*), which, in theory, is to be spent on developing materials or for in-service training (INSET), but which in practice is left to the teacher's discretion, and is often seen by teachers as a 'free' day that compensates for having to work on Saturdays. Furthermore, apart from the *klassnye rukovoditeli* (class tutor), the pastoral duties of Russian teachers are relatively limited; they are required only to be present for the lessons they teach, and for staff meetings, and are free to leave the premises of the school at other times.

One suspects that many teachers in the English system would dearly like to have an 18-hour timetable; instead, the average is considerably higher (sometimes over 30 hours per week), and additional contact time (including extracurricular work) brings, for the most part, no additional payment. (In the English system, pastoral duties are obligatory, for instance, and do not bring the entitlement to extra income that is enjoyed by the Russian *klassnye rukovoditeli*.) When not teaching, English teachers are expected to remain in the school, and are often liable to be called to 'cover' for absent colleagues. Finally, while the professional demands on Russian teachers have increased with empowerment and curricular reform, taking a double teaching load may not prove as difficult as the 30+ hour timetable of the English teacher, which, combined with their various other responsibilities and activities, make an intensive, demanding workload for the average teacher (Lawton 1995: 45–51). Russian teachers still do not face such extensive demands in their work. Traditionally there has been less marking for teachers to do (with less written work in general practised in the school), for instance, and this largely remains the case today; the requirements of the new educational standards are far less comprehensive in terms of teacher administration than the English National Curriculum; and to a large degree, while they may well be trying to implement curricular change, many Russian teachers can still rely on the framework provided by Soviet-era curricula and materials in their work. These traditions of the Soviet system have tended to reduce, therefore, the likelihood of stress-related problems among Russian teachers, as far as the specific issue of teaching the curriculum is concerned. While many teachers are committed to their work and to their pupils, the lower level of freedom that they had under the Soviet curriculum with regard to content and methodology, and the consequent sense of at least partial detachment from responsibility for what was taught, has helped Russian teachers to avoid falling victim to the phenomenon of 'burnout' that has been so widely documented among the teaching forces of, for example, the UK and the USA (Dworkin 1986). This may change now, as teachers take advantage of empowerment and some feel an ever-growing sense of commitment to curricular changes that they, perhaps, feel direct ownership of. For the time being, however, the legacy of the old system acts as a buffer against such problems.

With regard to matters of discipline and stress-related problems, many of the Russian teachers interviewed during my research remarked on what they see as the rapidly declining standards of discipline among pupils and the lack of interest that many pupils show towards their studies. Furthermore, teachers complain that they have to contend with the social problems that have worsened in society in recent years, ranging from drug and alcohol abuse, to hooliganism and criminal activities. It is clear that such problems have indeed increased, and that Russian teachers have struggled to deal with these issues, owing both to the speed and intensity with which such problems have grown, and to the lack of training and advice given to the profession on how to face such new challenges. Yet if we compare objectively the problems of Russian teachers with those which many of their colleagues in England have to face, some of the more desperate conclusions made on the Russian situation are tempered somewhat. During a visit to the University of Pedagogical Mastery (*Universitet pedagogicheskogo masterstva*) in St Petersburg, an in-service training centre, I was asked to talk to groups of teachers about the English school system. Many professed to being surprised, even shocked, to hear of the discipline problems that English teachers encounter, the stress that pupils and parents can place teachers under, and the potential threat of dismissal, even prosecution, that can, occasionally arise in extreme cases of teacher–pupil conflict. However, such problems are now becoming more prevalent and more serious in Russia, fuelled by the worsening social problems seen in that country, a situation that demands urgent measures to be taken to equip teachers with the skills needed to deal with these issues.

Professional communication: the macro-level

Communication between those working in the same field is, of course, an essential prerequisite of a healthy, developing profession. In the case of

Russian teachers, however, there are a number of weaknesses in the nature of the communication that exists, at least at the macro-level, problems that stem to a considerable degree from the legacy of the Soviet era. As Johnson notes, the Soviet authorities were able to restrict the ability of teachers to develop a separate professional identity, controlling the degree to which teachers could influence the nature of such issues as teacher education, educational research, and the type of professional associations in which teachers could participate (Johnson 1996: 37; see also Jones 1991: 152–66). Soviet teachers could feel a sense of unity with their colleagues across the country by virtue of the fact that they all worked within a highly-centralised and controlled system, in which the experience of teachers was remarkably common from one end of the USSR to the other. Despite such close ties, however, there was relatively very little communication between teachers on a national basis; indeed, even at the regional level, communication was not that extensive. For most teachers the circle of professional communication comprised colleagues in their own school and district, along with staff from their town whom they would meet during in-service training. Apart from this, there were few channels for teachers to engage in a dialogue with their counterparts in other regions and republics. The pedagogical press and the Union of Educational Workers (*Profsoiuz rabotnikov narodnogo obrazovaniia i nauki*) did provide a link between the centre and the grass roots, but these were under the control of the authorities, and offered inadequate scope for the discussion of, say, methodology, not to mention problems of discipline or teachers' complaints about their salary. While the work of teachers across the USSR may have contained much that was similar, the lack of effective means of communication meant that the teaching profession was rather fragmented, and teachers' sense of professional identity somewhat fragile.

From the mid-1980s onwards this situation changed somewhat, as the work of the so-called teacher innovators (Suddaby 1989) gained recognition and the momentum of change at the grass roots gathered pace. Apart from the increasingly lively and informative debate taking place in *Uchitel'skaia gazeta* (the Teachers' Gazette) and other sources in the mass media, together with the popular publications produced by the leading innovators, a large number of teachers from across the USSR began to travel to attend seminars and workshops in various locations. Further, the newly-formed Creative Union of Teachers of the USSR (*Tvorcheskii soiuz uchitelei SSSR*) promised to lend a sense of professional cohesion to the debate on school reform, and provide greater access for educationalists to these processes. The Creative Union did not live up to expectations, however, and its demise left the field of trade union activity to the traditional Union of Educational Workers, which, while it does participate in the debate on educational policy, tends to concentrate on issues concerning the material position of teachers, and does not provide that much support or advice to members, it would seem, on issues directly relating to curricular matters. This might be seen as an obstacle to the professionalisation of the teaching force, but Johnson's criticism of those responsible for leading the Russian reforms at the Ministry of Education in the 1990s may be too harsh:

> This [a set of strategic policy errors identified by Johnson] was compounded by the failure to use state or ministerial power to help forge new professional associations and a new, democratically-elected teachers' union, instruments that were absolutely necessary to guide decentralization and democratization...
>
> (Johnson 1996: 44)

While one can sympathise with such sentiments, it is perhaps too much too expect of a federal ministry to initiate and oversee the development of, presumably not so independent, professional associations. The fact that the teaching profession has been slow to break free from the legacy of the Soviet practices reflects rather a broader pattern of inertia in Russian society as a whole.

In other areas of communication, however, as the Soviet reforms became the Russian reforms, so the potential for the development of professional communication has seemed to grow further still. The pedagogical press is now much more varied than before, and information is also available on the Internet through the RedLine (Russian education on-line) site. A number of professional associations have been set up, catering, for instance, for teachers of particular subjects, thus providing a forum for focused discussion of issues of particular concern and interest (Shchedrovitskii 1994: 1), although their membership appears still to be relatively small. There have also been improvements in the amount and quality of in-service training provision, opening up additional opportunities for exchange of experience, and the level of support available from district advisers has, in certain towns, been extended.

Despite the greater availability of opportunities for professional dialogue which now exist, however, in interviews conducted by the author in 1995, 36 of 47 teachers questioned stated that they engage in such activity relatively infrequently, a figure which reflects the results given in a small questionnaire survey of 132 teachers that the author conducted in 1995 (see Table 15.1).

The problem for many teachers lies not in the lack of availability of sources of professional information and support, but in material limitations on their access to and participation in such discourse: the school may well have cut down its expenditure on professional literature in favour of more essential purchases, while the fees demanded by INSET providers (and the cost of travelling to attend a course) can act as a further disincentive.

Such are the difficulties facing teachers in their attempts to communicate with colleagues not just across the country, but in their own region. Add to

Table 15.1   Teacher Questionnaire q. 10. 'How Often Do You Engage in the Following Forms of Professional Communication?' (N = 132)

Form	Never	Rarely	Monthly	Weekly	Daily	No response
1 Read pedagogical literature	23.5% (31)	21.2% (28)	12.8% (17)	9.1% (12)	2.3% (3)	31.1% (41)
2 Discussion with colleagues	2.3% (3)	8.3% (11)	23.5% (31)	40.2% (53)	14.4% (19)	11.3% (15)
3 Read educational press	9.8% (13)	14.4% (19)	34.8% (46)	28.0% (37)	5.2% (7)	7.8% (10)
4 Participation in teachers' association	65.2% (86)	15.9% (21)	5.2% (7)	0.9% (1)	–	12.8% (17)
5 Read official documents	35.6% (47)	43.3% (57)	8.3% (11)	5.2% (7)	3.8% (5)	3.8% (5)
6 Attend lectures / courses	6.8% (9)	47% (62)	21.2% (28)	6.8% (9)	–	18.2% (24)
7 Research work	52.3% (69)	23.5% (31)	6.1% (8)	9.8% (13)	4.5% (6)	3.8% (5)

these problems the fact that many teachers complain that the strains of daily life leave them often with no great desire to devote their energy to reading pedagogical literature or attending workshops, even if they are committed to their job and wish to engage in such activities. To gain the benefits of professional dialogue, teachers must have the time to do so, a luxury that is not always available. In addition, apparently minor practical problems can prove a major obstacle. In one teachers' centre (*metodicheskii tsentr*) which I visited in St Petersburg, for instance, periodicals were taken and subscriptions made to associations, thus allowing access for all staff in that district, while local teachers themselves deposited their own work in the centre for the benefit of their colleagues. However, in order to use this extensive range of materials teachers had no option but to copy texts laboriously by hand, since photocopying facilities were not available.

A further barrier to professional dialogue is caused by the relatively low level of staff mobility, owing to the difficulties of obtaining housing and a host of other problems that moving entails. Thus, while Tumalev can state that there is a relatively (for Russia) high level of mobility within the profession, with 68 per cent of teachers in his sample of 1587 St Petersburg educationalists (Tumalev 1997: 41–2)[2] having moved job at least once in their career, it is far more likely that teachers will find posts in another school in the same town, rather than move to a job outside of their town. While this does hold certain benefits stemming from staff continuity, it also restricts considerably the opportunities for the 'cross-fertilisation' of pedagogical experience gained in other parts of the country.

Teachers' professional identity: a 'geological' survey

The limitations of professional communication at the macro-level are offset by the fact that the teaching force shares a common heritage, which means that geographical and generational distance will not prevent teachers from, say Petrozavodsk and Sakhalin, or a 25-year-old and 55-year-old teacher, from being able to identify quite closely with one another's experience. The levels of commonality and continuity that characterise the Russian teaching profession stand in some contrast to the pattern of development found in the English system. A British teacher educator once remarked to me that observing British teachers is rather like conducting a geological survey – one could tell exactly during which period a particular teacher had been trained, since the effects of that initial experience almost invariably left their mark, influencing that generation of recruits' approach to teaching for the rest of their careers.[3] Given the frequency with which change occurs in teacher education in the UK, the 'geological pattern' of British teachers can be seen to comprise a series of rather thin layers, indicating the manner in which each wave of innovation has given way to the next, with certain concepts re-emerging perhaps decades after their previous period of domination. To some extent this might be seen to weaken the bonds that tie each generation with its predecessor and successor, and to cause a degree of diversity in the attitudes that teachers of different generations will take towards educational matters, including the question of change. The effects of this fragmented development may have both negative and positive effects. On the one hand, one might argue that it reduces the amount of cohesion and continuity in the profession, with constant changes in approaches and policies causing disruption in the pattern of professional identity of the teaching force; on the other hand, one might see this diversity as a positive influence, allowing greater flexibility and increased scope for progress, as teachers are not bound by tradition.

A 'geological survey' of the Soviet, and now Russian, teaching profession would show a very different pattern, with very little variation discernible across the decades, a reflection of the comparatively far greater degree of continuity and far lower amount of change that characterised the Soviet teacher-education system. Indeed, the basic structure of the system changed little from the 1930s to the 1980s and beyond (Webber and Webber 1994b: 4–5). Thus teachers trained in the 1970s and 1980s would have followed programmes that differed relatively little from those followed by their predecessors in the 1940s, 1950s and 1960s. This degree of homogeneity and continuity in the profession can be said to have a strong influence on the professional outlook of Russian teachers, whose views on teaching will have been influenced not only by their training and subsequent classroom experience as professionals, but also by their memories of their own school years as pupils – quite literally, they grew up in this system, with the childhood experience of teachers in their twenties remarkably similar to that of staff aged over sixty. An additional factor contributing to the continuity found in the Russian system, stems from the fact that one discovers, in the central schools of major cities as well as in small rural communities, that a good number of teachers are actually former pupils of that school themselves, something which, again, must hold significant implications for the trans-mission of values between generations of teachers.[4]

To some degree, therefore, the long-standing traditions of the Soviet teaching force act as a unifying bond between the generations. The extent of the influence this has on teachers' attitudes and approaches to various aspects of their professional activities requires further research (a topic, perhaps, for comparative studies), and one should be cautious about drawing too many conclusions on the basis of these hypotheses. Yet these factors do have a bearing on the course of reform in the Russian school, affecting the nature of teachers' attitudes to change, and the general perception that teachers hold of the attributes of a 'good teacher', the purpose of education and the position of the school in contemporary Russia.

Professional communication: the micro-level

The issue of co-operation among staff has been investigated extensively in the West, and highlighted frequently as an area of concern. A common theme is that of isolation (Goodlad 1984), that is, teachers tend to perform their professional activities as individuals, without a great deal of collabor-ation with their colleagues, an issue that has been addressed in many systems, but not always successfully (Dalin and Rolff 1993: 101).

To some extent, the culture of the Russian teaching profession possesses the potential to overcome these problems, for there is a greater tradition of peer evaluation and peer observation in the Russian system, with teachers expected to visit and be visited by other teachers on a frequent basis. As a result, the school culture is much more one of 'open' rather than 'shut' doors, and teachers often seem to be more prepared to listen to advice and criticism (and praise) from their peers than would teachers in an English school. Yet this apparent collegiality does not necessarily imply that Russian staff engage in constructive dialogue and provide active support to their colleagues as a matter of course. Indeed, in the Soviet system peer observa-tion and support were often seen by the authorities as a means of control by which senior staff would 'guide' younger teachers into the 'right' way of behaving moulding them into the patterns expected of a Soviet teacher, and 'correcting' deviations from the accepted norm.

Whereas student teachers and newly-qualified teachers in England are encouraged to develop their own personality as a teacher, and bring their own strengths as an individual to bear upon their teaching, the approach in Soviet schools was often to reduce this element of individuality, which was sacrificed in order to satisfy the system's desire for commonality. Although a good number were able, despite these restrictions, to allow their personality to shine through none the less, this practice clearly restricted the ability of Soviet teachers to develop styles that suited their own particular needs; it is taking the Russian school some time to change this deeply embedded tradition.

School–society relations and the status of the teaching profession

In the previous sections, a necessarily brief overview has been given of some of the factors associated with the culture of the Russian school, and the effect of this culture on the prospects for reform have been noted. I should state that this evidence was gathered over a period form 1990 to 1997, a substantial time-frame in the context of post-Soviet Russian society. By the later stages of my research, the teachers whom I interviewed were certain that a culture change was underway in the schools, albeit progressing relatively slowly in many cases, but nevertheless perceptibly. Towards the end of the 1990s, there was a sense that the reform agenda, which had appeared to be so radical (and in some ways more remedial than constructive) when it was introduced in the 1991 Law on Education, had reached a stage of institutionalisation in the schools (its content having been adapted by the teaching force to render it more workable) (Webber 2000: 163–6). While certain restrictive characteristics of the school culture still needed to be addressed, then, it seemed that they had not acted as a sufficiently strong obstacle to prevent real change from taking root in the schools.

However, while a settling down of reforms may have taken place within the school system, it was the nature of the school's relations with society that held most concern not only for the fate of the reforms, but, one might argue, of the system as a whole. A 'shallow' societal debate on education, resulting from a relative lack of interest among the population, politicians, business leaders and others to engage in an informed dialogue on the needs of the schools, along with a breakdown in the safety net functions that are afforded to such social institutions in a stable society (Webber 2000: 169–80), rendered the school system vulnerable to a crippling funding crisis, and even to what I describe as 'attempts' on the life of the school (Webber 2000: 180–93). Apart from the material damage inflicted on the schools by such neglect, a price has also been paid by the children, of course, especially by those who became victims of the trend to remove some pupils (principally those deemed academically 'below average' pupils) from certain schools (and restrict the entrance of new pupils), a trend that reached its height in the mid-1990s.

In such conditions, trying to persuade a demoralised and underpaid teaching staff to implement reform and carry on teaching is a tall challenge, a problem compounded by a feeling that the status of the profession has sunk lower than ever. Despite propaganda to the contrary, the Soviet teaching profession never enjoyed a high level of status in material terms, with teachers' salaries and other benefits (such as housing, access to kindergartens, and so on) set at a lower level than the norm in the industrial sector (Jones 1991; Panina 1995: 10–16). Nevertheless, in terms of professional status, Soviet teachers fared somewhat better, as they were afforded a good deal of respect by parents and citizens in general (Shturman 1988). The teacher's views on pupils' progress and behaviour were comparatively rarely challenged openly by parents, who were often passive recipients of praise or admonishments delivered by form tutors at parents' evenings. This amount of reverence shown towards teachers stemmed in part from the general culture of Soviet society, in which education, upbringing, the virtues of a good citizen and the acquisition of knowledge were portrayed as noble matters which transcended the perspective of the individual, and were related directly to the development of the State and the progress towards communism.

For many teachers, therefore, belonging to this profession was a matter of pride, notwithstanding the poor material rewards. This perception still continues: in Tumalev's study of St Petersburg teachers, 76 per cent of respondents stated that they valued their profession highly (Tumalev 1997: 27). Indeed, this apparently strong sense of confidence in their profession may have been increased in the case of some teachers, who feel that the greater pedagogical freedom they now enjoy has heightened their status as professionals. The changes in the social structure of the 'new' Russia, however, and the worsening state of the teachers' material position cannot but detract from the greater sense of professional autonomy that empowerment may have brought: in stark contrast to the high level of self-belief shown in the survey referred to above, a mere 2 per cent of teachers stated that they felt their profession was highly valued by both the State and by society at large (Tumalev 1997: 27).

Across the country, teachers' experiences of the non-payment of salaries, perhaps for as much as four months at a time, have been all too common, as regional administrations, with their own budgets severely limited, seek to impose control over their expenditure (Iakovlev 1996: 4). Russian teachers did not have a tradition of taking political action, and for many the strike option is still viewed with unease, yet the severity of their financial problems, along with concern for the schools and the pupils, has given rise to a feeling of deep dismay and considerable anger among a growing number of teachers, expressed in an ongoing round of local and national strikes which have grown in scale during the 1990s. Indeed, educationalists have consistently been the most active participants in strike action among employees of all sectors in Russia: strikes in the education sector accounted for some 92 per cent of all strikes conducted in the Russian Federation in 1997 (Rodionova 1998: 2).

While one could argue that one positive result of such strike action may be the development of a greater sense of professional identity and cohesion among Russia's teachers, the negative factors which also accompany participation in action must surely counteract any such gains, at least to a large degree. With regard to the achievement of the aims of strikes, the weakness of the teaching profession's bargaining power, in comparison with, for example, miners, who can exert economic pressure on the government, has meant that it has only achieved partial victories, which have often been overturned or rendered ineffective by subsequent actions on the part of the central and regional authorities (Buniakina 1996: 4; Rodionova 1998: 2).

Given such pressures, it is not surprising that the problems of the recruitment and retention of teaching staff have intensified, with staff shortages the inevitable result (Levitskii and Goriunova 1996: 3; Molodtsova 1995: 19). Indeed, given the severity of the problems faced by the schools, it is remarkable that so many teachers not only retain a commitment to a job for which they are often not paid for weeks and months, but that many of them are even trying to introduce change in the schools. How much longer such resilience can last, however, remains to be seen.

Notes

1 This chapter has been adapted from material in Webber 2000, principally from Chapter 5 (pp. 79–98). It appears here with the kind permission of Palgrave and editors of the CREES–Palgrave series (based at the Centre for Russian and East European Studies, University of Birmingham).
2 One can also note that St Petersburg may not be a typical example here, as the large size of the city, and the relatively prosperous living standards enjoyed by its inhabitants, may well make it easier for teachers living in this city to move jobs.
3 The credit for this analogy (and the chain of thoughts it set off in my research) is due to Dr Edward Neather of the School of Education, University of Exeter.
4 I am grateful to Professor Arfon Rees of the European University Institute, Florence, for reminding me of this point.

References

'A poutru oni prosnulis' kontorskimi krysami'' (1998). *Uchitel'skaia gazeta*, nos. 14–15, 14 April, p. 7.
Buniakina, N. (1996). 'Tak skol'ko zhe vse-taki deneg vydelili uchiteliam?' *Uchitel'skaia gazeta*, no. 25, 18 June, p. 4.
Dalin, P. and Rolff, H.-G. (1993). *Changing the School Culture*. London: Cassell.
Dworkin, A. (1986). *Teacher Burnout in the Public Schools: Structural Causes and the Consequences for Children*. Albany NY: State University of New York Press.
Fullan, M. (1993). *Change Forces*. London: Falmer Press.
Goodlad, J. (1984). *A Place Called School: Prospects for the Future*. New York: McGraw-Hill.
Hord, S. (1987). *Evaluating Educational Innovation*. London: Croom Helm.

Iakovlev, V. (1996). 'Tak zhit' nel'zia!' *Uchitel'skaia gazeta*, no. 38, 24 September, p. 4.

Johnson, M. (1996). 'Russian Education Reform in the 1990s' *The Harriman Review*, vol. 9, no. 4 pp. 36–45.

Jones, A. (1991). 'Teachers in the Soviet Union' in A. Jones (ed.) *Professions and the State: Expertise and Autonomy in the Soviet Union and Eastern Europe*. Philadelphia: Temple University Press, pp. 152–66.

Lawton, D. (1995). 'The National Curriculum in England Since 1988' in D. Carter and M. O'Neill (eds) *International Perspectives on Educational Reform and Policy Implementation*. London: Falmer Press, pp. 44–51.

Levitskii, M. and Goriunova, T. (1996). 'Uchitelem stat' legko. Trudnee im ostat'sia' *Uchitel'skaia gazeta*, no. 31, 30 June, p. 3 (supplement 'Iz pervykh ruk').

Lortie, D. (1987). 'Built-in Tendencies Toward Stabilizing the Principal's Role' *Journal of Research and Development in Education*, vol. 22, no.1, pp. 80–90.

Molodtsova, V. (1995) 'Kto daet sovety Prezidentu?' *Uchitel'skaia gazeta*, no. 15, 18 April, p. 19.

Orlov, A. (1995). 'Professional'noe myshlenie uchitelia kak tsennost'' *Pedagogika*, no. 6, p. 64.

Panina, L. (1995). 'Gosudarstvo ravnodushno k uchiteliu' *Narodnoe obrazovanie*, no. 1, pp. 10–16.

Postavalova, V. (1997). 'Avtoritet uchitelia vysok, no polozhenie ego uzhasno' *Uchitel'skaia gazeta*, no. 35, 2 September, p. 7.

Rodionova, O. (1998). 'Plany ministerstva – nashi plany?' *Uchitel'skaia gazeta*, no. 13, 7 April 1998, p. 2.

Rosenholtz, S. (1989). *Teacher's Workplace: The Social Organization of Schools*. New York: Longman.

Rybakova, L., Moroz E. and Panova, E. (1993). 'Trudnosti uchitel'skoi professii' *Pedagogika*, no. 2, pp. 59–63.

Sarason, S. (1971). *The Culture of the School and the Problem of Change*. Boston: Allyn & Bacon.

Shchedrovitskii, P. (1994). 'Chto budet so shkoloi?' *Pervoe sentiabria*, no. 12, 1 February, p. 1.

Shturman, D. (1988). *The Soviet Secondary School*. London: Routledge.

Suddaby, A. (1989) 'An Evaluation of the Contribution of the Teacher-Innovators to Soviet Educational Reform' *Comparative Education*, vol. 25, no. 2, pp. 245–56.

Tumalev, V. (1997). 'The Teaching Profession in a Situation of Social and Political Change: Part 1 – The Teaching Profession as a Socio-Occupational Stratum' *Russian Education and Society*, vol. 39, no. 3, pp. 4–90 (translated from *Uchitel'stvo v situatsii sotsial'no-politicheskikh peremen* (1995) St Petersburg: Izdatel'stvo Sankt-Peterburgskogo universiteta ekonomiki i finansov.

Tumova, N. (1998). 'Za chto nam ne platiat' *Uchitel'skaia gazeta*, nos. 14–15, 14 April, p. 6.

Webber, S. (1996). 'Demand and Supply: Meeting the Need for Teachers in the "New" Russian School' *Journal of Education for Teaching*, vol. 22, no. 1, pp. 9–26.

Webber, S. (2000). *School, Reform and Society in the New Russia*. Basingstoke: Palgrave.

Webber, S. and Webber, T. (1994a). 'Issues in Teacher Education' in A. Jones (ed.) *Education and Society in the New Russia*. Armonk NY: M.E. Sharpe, pp. 231–59.

Webber, S. and Webber, T. (1994b). 'Restructuring Initial Teacher Education in Russia' *Education in Russia, the Independent States and Eastern Europe*, vol. 12, no. 1, pp. 4–9.

16
Pedagogy in Transition: from Labour Training to Humanistic Technology Education in Russia

James Pitt and Margarita Pavlova

Origins of the subject of 'Technology' in the Russian curriculum

The predecessors of Russian Technology education in the Soviet period were Labour Training and the 'polytechnic principle', subjects in which the scientific principles of manufacturing processes were taught in a cross-curricular approach, and which included training in practical skills, using different tools and equipment. In 1993, Technology education as a learning area was introduced into Russian schools' curriculum as part of the general process of educational reforms.[1] Having replaced Labour Training, it is now a compulsory subject from Class 1 to Class 11,[2] with 808 hours allocated over this period.

The Russian Technology curriculum has not been widely analysed in Western literature, so a brief historical overview is presented here. During the 1920s, Dewey's ideas became popular in Russia (Vulfson 1992), as teachers in all subject areas began to adopt the ideas of progressive education with a child-centred, 'project approach'. These experiments were, however, a failure. The economic situation in Russia was so dire that the main aim of education at that period was that of giving minimum skills and knowledge so that the students could start working as soon as possible.

For most of the Soviet period the subject of Labour Training (or Labour Preparation) was compulsory for all school students. However, for a period of ten years (just after the Second World War) it was omitted from the schools. The main aim then was to prepare engineers and scientists to win the competition with capitalist countries. As a result of this policy almost 100 per cent of school graduates entered universities, colleges and institutes, with the result that there were more engineers than workers (Tkhorzhevskii 1987).

With such technological achievement the Soviet Union was able to put Sputnik into space. The 'Sputnik syndrome' was significant, as Soviet education came to be considered to be among the best in the world, largely because of the excellent standard of science and mathematics education. Western governments, which had mistakenly considered Russian science and technology to be somewhat backward, were alarmed: the Americans published a report *A Nation at Risk*[3] in which they advocated improvement in maths and science education in the US as being essential for national security (National Commission on Excellence in Education 1983). Within the Soviet Union, however, there was concern that too many school leavers were insufficiently prepared for working in industry. Labour Training came back into Russian schools, and its content was closely connected to maths and science through the polytechnic principle. Many Russian Labour Training teachers began to think that their approach was also the best.

The main change to Labour Training within the 1984 reforms of the Soviet education system was to strengthen links between school and industry. Each factory had several schools appointed to it as partners. The school had to organise productive labour in school for students up to the age of 15, and in the factory from 15 till 17. Thus, in addition to the aim of helping the students to develop their future careers, policy-makers also had in mind the goal of cultivating a positive attitude towards labour from an ideological point of view. The educational value of this was debatable (de Moura Castro *et al.* 1997). Few children displayed any great desire to continue to work in a factory, and chose instead other career paths.

In the wood and metal workshops, students were taught industrial skills of the sort that might be needed in factories in any part of the world. Although linked to local manpower needs, there was nothing particularly Russian about such work from a cultural perspective. However, there was pressure from some educationalists to use the curriculum in part to transfer cultural traditions and values. Accordingly, in the Gorbachev period many schools received permission to teach Crafts, which meant making wooden artefacts painted with traditional designs, lace work and embroidery, wood carving (for example, chopping boards and decorative doors, shutters, window frames), wooden toys and traditional Russian clothes and meals. Thus the focus was very different from Labour Training. This interest in crafts was seen as a progressive movement that led towards further changes, and in some parts of Russia it became very strong.

Which way now for Russian Technology education?

At the turn of the twenty-first century, Russian Technology education is being pulled in two directions: child-centred, process-based *versus* content/module-based and knowledge-oriented. The former is informed by a design-based, British approach.[4] It aspires to the ideals of the Russian Educational Law of 1992, which called for the development of creative, proactive individuals. In Russian this is called 'the project approach' as the Russian word '*dizain*' has very different connotations from the English 'design'.

The essence of the project approach is that children design and make real products in response to an identified need. Not all teaching is done through projects: the children still learn particular areas of skill and knowledge through focused exercises, and they still learn the theory of materials and manufacturing processes. But they do this through analysing the designs of products rather than just listening to lectures from their teacher. Putting the child much more in charge of his or her own learning requires a revolution in teaching approaches. In contrast, the second direction for Russian Technology education, in which the current draft Federal Standard or curriculum order for Technology is rooted, is an extension of traditional Labour Training.

The experimental approach and the 'Technology & Enterprise Education in Russia' programme

Background[5]

This programme grew from action-research in the field of Technology education in Russia. From 1991 to 1994, Margarita Pavlova trained Technology teachers at Herzen University (the main initial teacher-training institute in St Petersburg) and St Petersburg State University for Pedagogical Arts (an in-service training centre for teachers). She based her work on the results of her research into the Design and Technology (D&T) curriculum in the UK (Pavlova 1991). This caught the imagination of many of her students, some of whom began to implement a project approach in their schools. They were supported by a two-week seminar given by James Pitt in October 1994. By 1996 Margarita Pavlova was able to visit a number of other Russian cities (Moscow, Briansk, Pskov and Nizhnii Novgorod) with two British teachers, and examples of pupils' work from St Petersburg and schools in England were shown. Again, there was huge interest, shown by the fact that there were requests for similar visits from fifteen other pedagogical universities where Technology teachers are trained. The Federal Ministry of Education and the Institute for General Secondary Education at the Russian Academy of Education supported the idea of a programme based on experiments in four pilot regions, and a programme titled 'Technology & Enterprise Education in Russia' came into being.

Programme structure and activities

The programme started with pilot projects to test the feasibility of teaching Technology through the project approach. There were ten official pilot schools in each of St Petersburg, Nizhnii Novgorod, Novgorod and Kaliningrad – 40 schools in total. By the end of February 1998, twenty training courses had been conducted. Teachers in all of these areas had tried the 'project approach' in their schools, and had also worked on developing new methods and teaching materials in Russian.

The pilot schools demonstrated the feasibility of the project approach as a central, integrative method of teaching Technology in Russian schools. By 1999, efforts were being concentrated in Nizhnii Novgorod and other cities in the Greater Volga region to:

- train a corps of teachers to teach according to the project approach;
- train them to develop locally appropriate teaching materials;
- train them as trainers;
- develop model programmes of study for Classes 5, 6 and 7, and Classes 8 and 9;
- link the project approach to Technology education in school (Classes 5 to 9) with the outcomes-based approach to vocational training for post-16 students. (This has been developed successfully in Omsk and Nizhnii Novgorod by the regional administrations in those cities in conjunction with the Scottish Qualifications Authority.)

The programme is managed by a Co-ordinating Committee consisting of representatives from the pilot projects, the Ministry of Professional and General Education of the Russian Federation, the Institute of General Secondary Education of the Russian Academy of Education, the Russian Association of Deans of Faculties of Technology and Enterprise (that is, the pedagogical universities), experts from the UK (Her Majesty's Inspectorate (HMI), The Qualifications and Curriculum Authority (QCA), Nuffield Design and Technology, the British Council and the authors). There are also advisory panels of experts in the UK and Russia.

Early problems

Although the teachers involved broadly welcomed the project approach, a number of problems had become apparent by the end of the first full year of the pilot projects.

(a)   Problems of teaching and learning for students and teachers

The 'normal' method of Labour Training in Russia was the frontal exposition of fact or skill. Teachers relied on the official programme and textbook: there was no tradition of teacher-generated curriculum development. The curriculum was developed by the central Soviet authorities and disseminated through the bureaucratic structure (Muckle 1988). The seminars we have presented have been based partly on lecture format (with extensive use of slides to show examples of pupils' work in the UK and, more recently, of Russian students' work), and partly through group-work, brainstorming and one-to-one peer teaching. These methods have caused as much interest as the content. However, many teachers have not found it so easy to use different teaching methods in the classroom. The pupils expect the teacher to know what is what and to explain it to them. For a teacher to reply to a student's question with the words, 'I don't know! How do you think you might find out?' is fairly shocking.

Secondly, some teachers expect to be told (in a prescriptive way) how to run their classes in an enabling rather than prescriptive manner. Since each person's teaching style is essentially personal, such advice is inappropriate. It is not clear whether general admonitions of 'do what comes naturally' are useful. Curiously, this expectation of being told what to do in the classroom is in marked contrast with Russians' flexibility in day-to-day living in which the unexpected is forever happening and people have excellent problem-solving skills for coping!

Thirdly, both teachers and pupils expect to see progression or results in answering questions correctly, and in making standard artefacts to an increasingly high quality. Designing has never been part of the curriculum, and the idea that one can progress in holistic skills of designing is not easy to grasp. The design sheets of 11 and 12-year-old Russian pupils tend to be very formal and beautifully laid out, reflecting a tradition of careful presentation. To demand quick concept sketches, with immediate annotation, is again asking pupils to set aside everything they have been taught up until now.

Finally, there is little tradition of product evaluation, which we call 'design analysis'. Children are not used to being asked for their own views (Karakovskii 1993).

(b) Problems of language

The word 'design' in Russia has had a chequered history. When the twentieth-century concept of design emerged in the West after the war, Stalin actually banned its use. By the end of the 1980s, the word *'dizain'* really meant 'styling' in the sense that a product could come in a number of different designs, but it was essentially the same product. You cannot easily talk of 'designing a product' as a purposeful response to human need. There are a number of Russian words in use. You can 'invent' a new product (*'razrabotat''*), or develop/modify an existing product (*'modifitsirovat''*). An engineer or architect might be engaged in 'projecting' a bridge or new building (*'sproektirovat''*). Whereas in English there is one word 'design' for 'Design (a) and Technology', the 'design (b) process', 'the design (c) of a control system', coming up with some original 'designs' (d), in Russian there are many different words: *'dizain'* (a), *'proektirovanie i izgotovlenie'* (b), *'razrabotka'* (c) and *'predlozhenie'* (d). The idea that 'design' is inseparable from 'technology', and that both should be construed as a purposeful response to human need are certainly novel to many Russians. A similar problem arises with trying to translate the word 'plan' or 'planning', which in Russian has connotations with an instructional chart or a five-year economic objective.

(c)   Problems of programme management and acceptability

Obtaining funding for the programme was a key problem. (Until June 1998 everyone concerned gave their time free of charge.) At the end of the 1980s Labour Training ranked as the third most important subject in the Russian Secondary school curriculum as measured by timetable allocation, after Russian and maths, and just in front of all the sciences put together (Muckle 1988: 5–6). It still remains a huge commitment in terms of time and resources, yet few people have been taking it seriously as an area for curriculum reform.[6] Both statutory and NGO Western agencies took the view that priorities in Russia should be education in the Humanities – in this they followed the lead of a previous Minister of Education[7] – and in the mechanics of transition to a market economy. It has been difficult to generate interest in a humanistic approach to Technology education: the impression of the authors is that funding agencies and grant-giving bodies like to generate their own programmes, rather than support local initiatives which have grown from the base. It is difficult to break into their charmed circle. However, since June 1998 the British Council has given financial support to the work in Nizhnii Novgorod, and have promised further funds for the project in Novgorod the Great. This support has made a huge difference.

A second problematic area concerns 'ownership' of the programme. Is it a Russian response to a new situation in Russia, or a British/Western import? Who will make money from it – Russian teachers and academics, or foreign experts on ex-patriot level 'allowances'? Within the Federal Ministry, however, the programme is seen as a home-grown initiative.[8]

(d)   Problems for participants

There have been difficulties concerning the role of the INSET training establishments. Many teachers had bad experiences of them in the past, partly because their perceived role was more to do with maintaining correct lines of thinking and instruction than professional development in new pedagogical approaches. An additional problem occurs because training is often based on residential courses: since most Russian teachers are women and most Russian women are expected both to have a full-time job and run the home, attendance is not easy (Graham and Moon 1992).

On a personal level, teachers are suffering hardship that is almost unimaginable to Western colleagues. Even when they are paid, salaries are in the region of \$45–\$75 per month. On top of this there is the uncertain political climate. The experience of the authors is that most of the participants of the programme, and probably most professionals in the public sector, have adopted a 'wait-and-see' stance towards macro-political and economic change. In the course of some fifteen visits to Russia over the period 1996–99, we have had many conversations with colleagues about the future. A common response is the raising of eyebrows, a shrug and the comment,

'Who knows? – but someone has to teach our children'. We have had similar responses from educational administrators, doctors and dentists. This makes working for change an act of faith, with little guarantee of success or personal reward.

(e) Problems of assessment

The aim of the programme is to establish a humanistic approach to Technology education in Russian schools. How should the impact of the programme be assessed? The traditional way of assessing innovations in Russia is to set up an experiment, acquire quantitative data and form a conclusion. When we operate with concepts such as 'creativity', 'proactivity' and 'problem-solving capability', it is difficult to assess them in quantitative terms. We have already provided two tests, in which control and experimental classes were involved. We wanted to assess the achievement of the students and analyse the difference. Certainly the 'experimental' students demonstrate more 'original' or 'creative' ideas as judged by the teachers, but it was difficult to measure the level of creativity in quantitative terms. We have also had difficulties in finding matching control groups because, in every pilot school, the classes of the same age students are streamed by achievement in the main subjects. So, if the teacher chooses one class as the experimental group the other class will not be matched. However, we have to continue to develop such tests in order to propose a rigorous way of assessing the programme. Within British universities, a qualitative approach to educational research is much more acceptable. From this perspective, more appropriate tools might be illuminative evaluations and case studies, generated through participant observation.

Huge interest in the programme

Despite this, the authors have received a very positive response to their seminars. Perhaps the most promising sign is the response from many teachers, heads and pupils. Not untypical are these comments from a Technology advisory teacher in St Petersburg:

> The training seminars have clarified the philosophy of the new subject 'Technology'. Together we developed a curriculum and projects. During the last term I tried these with my students. I saw the enthusiasm of the children, their desire to realise their projects, their activity. They proposed a lot of ideas and taught me how to make some things! In total, their behaviour was completely different compared to previous classes. I am not young, but I am very glad that at last I have found the approach that I had been looking for all my life. I felt that something existed in these methods that made my students happy. Now I know what it is.
>
> (From communication to the authors by
> V.A. Shmidova, St Petersburg, 1996)

The programme has generated huge interest from all over Russia. In June 1997 a group of thirty Russian educationalists visited schools, teacher-training universities and research centres in the UK to see how Design & Technology features in the national curriculum for England and Wales. Further introductory seminars on the project approach have been given as far away as Krasnoiarsk and Iakutiia. Over two thousand Russian teachers have attended courses given by the authors. Their accompanying book entitled *The Educational Area Technology – theoretical approaches and teaching methods* (Pavlova and Pitt 1997a) has been reprinted in two cities. Responding to widespread demand, a second book on how to teach designing skills within technology projects is currently being written by the authors. Most teachers and teacher-trainers who have tried this approach report higher levels of pupil motivation and teacher satisfaction.[9]

As mentioned above, the Steering Committee of Russian–British Educational Projects (composed mainly of representatives of the Russian Federal Ministry of Education and the British Council) decided in 1998 to support the development of Technology education and Professional Orientation in Nizhnii Novgorod and the Greater Volga Region, with funds over three years. The aim of this is to contribute to the development of a humanistic curriculum for Technology and professional orientation, appropriate for Russian schools in the early twenty-first century. A team of teachers there is developing classroom materials and in-service training methods, based on the project approach, and linking this with 'professional orientation' (in England this would be called 'careers education'). Significantly, the main push for funding came from the Russian side. Dr Viktor Bolotov, Deputy Minister of Education, described this initiative as an 'important development of significance to the whole of Russia, and one that has the full support of the ministry'. In September 1999 the Steering Committee decided to extend this financial support to a second project in Novgorod the Great and north-west Russia. In this project the focus will be more on using the project approach in initial vocational education, and the reform of initial teacher training of Technology teachers.

In both the Nizhnii Novgorod and Greater Novgorod projects, a new element is present. Many people at the Russian Federal Ministry of Education have been impressed by the outcomes-based, modular approach to post-16 vocational training that has been developed (with the help of consultants from the Scottish Qualifications Authority and support by the British Council) in Omsk and Nizhnii Novgorod. The focus of this dimension of the work is the creation of a new approach to vocational training, in which courses are assembled from discrete modules written in terms of *learning outcomes* rather than *teacher inputs*. These modules encourage the trainees to be proactive self-learners – hence the congruence of *aims* with the work being done by Technology & Enterprise Education in Russia in the area of school-based Technology education. The two projects hope to effect a 'seamless transition' between students' experience of Technology as part of the general curriculum, and vocational education.

There has been little interest, however, from industry in Russia. When one of the authors announced at an educational conference in 1999 that we were seeking to develop links with enterprises in Nizhnii Novgorod, there was a general look of puzzlement amongst many of the Russian delegates, who questioned whether industrialists knew anything about education! There was a similar response from teachers in Nizhnii Novgorod when the matter was first raised there. Interestingly, the push for greater collaboration between educational experiments and enterprise in Nizhnii Novgorod is coming from the Vice-Governor for International Relations, who has responsibility for inward investment, as well as the Vice-Governor responsible for education and science. Although Labour Training was linked with local manpower needs in the 1980s, it seems that this relationship has, along with many industrial plants, all but disappeared. The demand from the Steering Committee and senior members of the administration of the Nizhnii Novgorod region that we try to rebuild these links in the two projects referred to above demonstrates a concern at a central level, but one which is not reflected on the ground.

More recent problems

However, further problems were identified during the 1997–98 academic year.[10] Some teachers reported a resistance among pupils to commit their design ideas to paper. They might think creatively, investigate, and come up with original ideas, but have little incentive to spend time 'doing paperwork'. Their whole perception of Technology classes is that time should be spent on tools. Teachers do not have surplus cash to buy graphic materials needed for a more design-based approach.

There has also been considerable confusion among professional colleagues. The situation in Russian Technology education *is* very confusing because the philosophy and rationale of the new subject have not been thoroughly developed, let alone widely accepted. It is very difficult for many teachers to understand why they need to change their own practice. Traditionally, the main way of introducing something new in Russian education was the development of theory, and then its implementation. This contrasts with the approach in Britain, which has been a more pragmatic one of trying out something new in the classroom, and then, if it is successful, trying to figure out afterwards why it works! (Pavlova 1997a)

Questionnaires were presented at the end of introductory seminars on design-based, child-centred approach to Technology education. Analysis of the results demonstrates strong teacher support for the new ideas, but doubt about the possibilities of implementation. For example, all 40 respondents from the Nizhnii Novgorod seminars stated that the project or design-based approach could be used during the lessons. They emphasise the following positive effects:

- it helps the creative development of pupils;
- it increases the level of knowledge, and motivation for skills and knowledge acquisition;
- it widens children's interests;
- it helps them to think and plan independently.

In response to a query about their plans for implementing ideas in their schools following the seminar, five respondents out of 40 had no suggestions at the moment (some were unemployed and retraining as teachers). The other 35 stated that they were going to try the whole approach or some elements of it, such as introducing design-analysis, homework, resource tasks (exercises), changing the sequences of topics (with projects during the year), changing the assessment system for students' work, giving the opportunity to students to think by themselves, introducing elements of graphic communication in Class 5, introducing more mini-projects, or trying this approach with some students (not with a whole class). However, 15 respondents identified more serious problems, including the following:

- teachers and students were not ready for these innovations;
- it would be difficult to change the attitude of students to the subject;
- workshops need more equipment and other resources;
- a scheme of work based on design has not been developed;
- there are not enough teaching materials;
- changes should start in primary school and be phased in gradually;
- the officially recommended Khotunsev–Simonenko programme (see below) has too many topics, so there is not enough time for projects;
- if teachers start their own approach it could create problems with school administrators;
- inspectors do not understand what the teachers are trying to do: if teachers get poor ratings in inspections this can have an adverse effect on salaries.

The mainstream approach and the draft Federal Standard for Technology

The Federal Standard (one of a set of educational standards, developed for all subjects, intended to serve as a guideline to the content of courses) defines the content of Technology education as 'a body of knowledge regarding the transformative activities of man – especially the re-shaping of materials, energy and information – to serve the interests of man, society, environment'.[11] This understanding is conceptually different from the British approach, in which Technology education is defined as an activity. The difference can be explained from the perspective of educational traditions. In Russia *'pansofia'* – a general wisdom – was accepted as the main aim of education: educational tradition is 'encyclopaedist'. It started from the ideas of Comenius with a belief that all students should acquire as much knowledge as possible about all valid subjects appropriate to their age. The development of proactive, critical thinkers was not emphasised in school strategies. Ideology implied that there was one correct answer for a particular question, and that this answer was written in the textbook. There was little or no discussion in the classrooms. Scepticism with regard to the words of the teacher was not allowed (Pavlova 1997b).

Based on knowledge-based presuppositions, the aims of Technology education are defined as follows in the draft Federal Standard:[12]

- to develop students' polytechnical skills, to acquaint them with the fundamentals of *'tekhnika'*,[13] and modern and prospective technologies of processing materials, energy and information, with the application of knowledge in the areas of economics, ecology and enterprise;
- to acquire general working and life-skills and practices, including those in the area of organising work and behaviour;
- to study the world of professions, and the acquisition of work experience which could serve as a basis for career orientation;
- to develop a creative approach and an aesthetic attitude to reality in the process of learning and carrying out projects.

It should be noted that reference is made to a 'creative approach' and 'projects'. But these have been tacked on to the end and sit uncomfortably with the central thrust of the 14-page document.

Within these aims, the content of Technology Education is broken into the following areas:

1 *'tekhnika'* or engineering
2 The processing and transformation of materials, energy and information: this includes technical work, agricultural work, house-keeping / service work
3 The culture of work
4 Technical drawing
5 Classification of industries and career orientation
6 The culture of the home and social and domestic competence.

Teachers have to choose one of two forms for their courses: *either 'tekhnika'* and technical creativity (technical work), *or* the culture of the home and artistic/craft creativity (house-keeping and service work). In practice this means that there are different curricula for boys and girls. There are also urban and rural variants. There is no differentiation by age or stage of schooling. Content and skills are highly specified.

The only other place in which the word 'project' appears is at the end of the General Regulations: 'In the absence of the necessary computing and electronic equipment, the study of information technology can be replaced by instruction in the creative, artistic fashioning of material *or the execution of projects'* [our italics]. There is neither encouragement nor space for pupils to investigate, think for themselves, be creative in response to human need. Teachers can continue with the old content and methods, because projects are seen only as a *method* of teaching. The Standard describes only the content. Method of teaching and content are kept separate.

The Khotunsev–Simonenko approach: modernised Labour Training?

At present there are two main approaches in Russia to Technology teaching. We have already outlined the active learning approach being developed through Technology & Enterprise Education in Russia. The most widely accepted one, which conforms philosophically to the draft Federal Standard, is the concept of the subject as developed by E. Khotunsev and V. Simonenko, who propose the following content (Khotunsev and Simonenko 1995):

1 Mechanical sciences and technology of materials
2 Electrical engineering, radio-electronics, automatic machinery, computing
3 Information Technology
4 Graphics
5 The culture of the home, including food technology and textile technology
6 Building and maintenance works
7 Artistic development of materials, technical creativity
8 The branches of industry and career guidance
9 Industry and environment
10 Home economics and the basis of enterprise.

The Khotunsev–Simonenko scheme uses the old philosophy of Labour Training and old methods of teaching, and simply adds some new modules and one project of approximately 20 hours at the end of each academic year.

A new push from the centre

However, there is a thirst among many teacher-trainers and teachers at the grass-roots for a humanistic, project approach to Technology education which is Russian, but informed by developments in other parts of the world. The argument continues between those who wish to retain a knowledge-based approach, and the protagonists of the project approach. Dr M. Leontieva, the official in the Russian ministry of education with overall responsibility for the school curriculum, made a significant contribution to this debate towards the end of 1997 (Leontieva 1997). Addressing the nature of Technology education and the most effective methods of teaching it, she wrote:

> It is necessary to elaborate a system of teaching in which the project method is at the heart of the programme . . . Undertaking creative projects is considered one of the more effective means of labour training and technological education. Through realising projects, students develop and strengthen the habit of analysing situations relating to consumers, economics, ecology and technology. It is important [for students] to develop their ability to evaluate ideas, starting from real needs and material resources, to learn how to make technological and economic decisions appropriate to their designs, the needs of the school and the potential market.

According to Leontieva, it is essential to transfer gradually to teaching by the project method, taking into account concrete conditions in schools and vocational educational establishments, while maintaining continuity. She concludes:

> The Directorate of General Secondary Education is interested in listening to teaching experience and is ready to consider it and publish. We await your comments, concrete proposals and general conclusions from teaching the curriculum of the educational area of 'Technology'.

The project approach received a further boost early in 1998. The administrations of the City of Greater Novgorod and the surrounding region (*oblast'*), in conjunction with the University of Novgorod, organised a large conference called 'Technology '98'. The conference attracted delegates from all over Russia, many of whom had read Leontieva's article and wanted to know more about the 'project approach'. Some were frankly incredulous that school children were capable of designing as well as making: work shown by an English 'A' level student[14] who designed a gag for dogs undergoing dental surgery provoked one comment, 'This is not a pupil's work – you have copied it from the patent office'! But most participants were impressed by the testimonies of Russian teachers from other cities, who had tried the project approach, as well as inputs from Technology & Enterprise Education in Russia. Such was the interest generated by this event that the federal ministry issued a further circular to all regions of Russia, recommending active consideration of the project approach at all levels (Leontieva 1998).

Discussion and conclusions

Empirical evidence from questionnaires to teachers in pilot schools and interviews demonstrates that there is a strong desire among teachers to try and implement the project approach. They need a Federal Standard that does not prescribe each step of their teaching, but gives them the opportunity to create their own scheme of work.

In the authors' view, broader features remain significant in shaping Technology teaching and learning in Russian schools:[15]

- a strong teacher-centred educational tradition;
- a strong national craft tradition, which is different for different parts of the country;
- a high level of development of skills among the students in making things from wood, metal, textiles and so on, because of the training approach;
- a complete absence of any design tradition;
- a tension between the announcement of high educational principles and the process of their implementation;
- a lack of financial resources (which means that students have to make products in Technology lessons that will then be sold);
- a misplaced pride in the Russian system of Technology education as being 'the best' and little desire to use international experience (resulting from limited communication with the outside world);
- a different Technology curriculum for boys and girls.

Imagination is needed to recognise the British inspiration of Technology education in its Russian version. But it is there. This raises the question – is it an imposition from the West? As mentioned above, it is seen in Russia as a home-grown initiative which is informed by good practice from Britain. If Russian educators *choose* to 'import' ideas about good practice from outside the country, this is very different from Western educators choosing to export their pedagogical methods to unwilling subjects!

It might be useful to consider this work in the context of education for citizenship. Some Western educators have been promoting in Russia a concept of citizenship education which has evolved in the US and Western Europe. Many Russians have felt this is inappropriate in Russia. We would suggest tentatively that the sorts of skills and attitudes which are embedded in the project approach to Technology education might contribute towards educating children to be active and useful citizens. These would include:

- developing a generic, problem-solving capability;
- developing an ability to seek out, order and use information as and when required;

- encouraging children to explore different ways of tackling problems and evaluate them before opting for a solution;
- encouraging children constantly to evaluate their own activities;
- most importantly, encouraging students to take more responsibility for their own learning.

We do not claim that the project approach in Technology is the only way of achieving these results. We would suggest that it does provide a useful learning environment that can contribute towards active citizenship.

There has been confusion over the term 'project approach'. It is not to be confused with early experiments in Soviet education which were inspired by the writings of Dewey, although the same term has been used. We have chosen 'project approach' because of the difficulties in translating the more appropriate English term 'design-based approach'.

Further developments continue within the framework of Technology & Enterprise Education in Russia, as well as in an increasing number of independent initiatives. A synthesis of the old approach, which emphasises systematic knowledge and skills, with active, child-centred teaching methods, is being elaborated. However, progressive teachers are in a difficult situation. They fully support the design-based approach, but the environment is not propitious. They feel limited by the 'official' Khotunsev–Simonenko programme. They lack the knowledge they need to develop innovations by themselves, and are crying out for teaching materials. The Ministry of Education document on educational policy states that the project approach should lie at the 'heart of the programme'. But if this principle is not established firmly at local level, school administrations are likely to push the teachers into following the undemanding, 'official' Khotunsev–Simonenko programme. The experience of other countries, notably Britain (Kimbell 1997), is that change cannot easily be imposed from the centre. It really is too early to say whether or not the 'project approach' in Technology education will take root in Russia.

Notes

1 The Russian Education Law of 1992 provided the framework for the new curriculum. Technology became a compulsory part of the federal curriculum in 1993 – see Order No. 273 of the Ministry of Education on 7 June 1993.
2 Primary education in Russia begins with Class 1 (ages 6–7 years) and continues to Class 4 (9–10 years). Children usually remain in the same school for secondary education from Class 5 (11 years) through to Class 9 (16 years), 10 (17 years) or 11 (18 years), although some attend primary vocational institutes from Class 8 (15 years).
3 National Commission on Excellence in Education (1983).
4 The curricula for England and Wales, and Scotland, require that pupils both design and make products. Thus pupils do not simply make artefacts to a design or pattern

given by the teacher, rather they undertake a complex process which includes investigating and analysing an area of human activity to see what people need. Their tasks include writing design briefs and performance specifications, investigating other products to learn about materials, manufacturing methods, human factors (ergonomics) and environmental issues, generating a wide range of ideas for possible solutions to a problem, and evaluating, refining and developing these ideas to the point that the product can be made.

5   For more detail about the early years of the programme see Pitt and Pavlova (1997b).

6   Authors' conversations with representatives of the Federal Ministry of Education, the British Council, Ford and MacArthur Foundations, Open Society Institute, European Union.

7   For a better understanding of the terms 'humanisation' and 'humanitarisation' see Borisov (1994); Tkachenko (1996).

8   Letter from G.K. Shestakov (Head of Department of Educational Standards and Programmes at The Federal Ministry of Education) to Professor Irina Sasova (Director of the Programme 'Technology Education in Russia') 14 January 1997.

9   Evidence gathered during interviews with teachers in the pilot projects in June 1997.

10   Evidence from further interviews with teachers in January – February 1998.

11   Ministry of General and Professional Education (1998). *Federal'nyi komponent: Obrazovatel'naia oblast' Tekhnologiia. Prilozhenie No. 11 k federal'nomu zakonu 'O gosudarstvennom obrazovatel'nom standarte osnovnogo obshchego obrazovaniia* [Federal Component: Educational Area –Technology. Supplement 11. For the Federal Law About State Educational Standard of General Education]. Non-published draft.

12   *Ibid.*

13   There is no English word for this. Essentially it refers to hardware of technology – machines, how things work, the techniques needed to operate them. It could be translated loosely as 'engineering'. The Russian word 'tekhnologiia' includes 'tekhnika', but also has connotations of intention and process. On the philosophical level, traditions have developed differently in German and English-speaking countries. The former analyses 'Technic' (tools, equipment, machinery – the result of man's activity) as the main symbol of the non-natural reality. In the latter 'Technology' is the more generally understood phenomenon. In a broad understanding these two concepts are very close, but the difference still exists. Until now Russia has had the Technic approach, but recently there has been movement to the direction of Technology.

14   In England most post-16 children following an academic route at school, choose to study two or three subjects in depth prior to university entrance at 18. These courses lead to an exam after two years in each of the chosen subjects. If the students are successful they are awarded a qualification called 'General Certificate of Education – Advanced Level' or 'A' level for short.

15   Analysis of data collected in discussion with teachers, teacher-trainers, officials in the Ministry of General and Professional Education, and educational administrators in June 1997, January – February 1998, and March 1998.

References

Borisov, V. (1994). 'An Interview with E.V. Tkachenko' *Russian Education and Society*, vol. 36, no. 8, pp. 43–50.

Graham, P. and Moon, R. (1992). *A Feasibility Study Examining the Potential for Developing Distance Education Materials and Programmes in Planning for Retraining Social Sciences and Humanities Teachers in Russian Secondary and Higher Education*. Milton Keynes: Internal Paper for The Centre for Research in Teacher Education, Open University.

Karakovskii, V. (1993). 'The School in Russia Today and Tomorrow' *Compare*, vol. 23, no. 3, pp. 277–88.

Khotunsev, E. and Simonenko, V. (1995). *Programma srednikh obshcheobrazovatel'nykh uchrezdenii: Trudovoe obuchenie: Tekhnologiia (1–4 klassy, 5–11 klassy)*. Moscow: Prosveshchenie.

Kimbell, R. (1997). *Assessing Technology – International Trends in Curriculum Assessment*. Buckingham: Oxford University Press.

Leontieva, M. (1997). *Ob osobennostiiakh obucheniia po programmam obrazovatel'noi oblasti 'Tekhnologiia'*. Moscow: Ministerstvo obshchego i professional'nogo obrazovaniia.

Leontieva, M. (1998). *O reshenii konferentsii 'Tekhnologicheskoe obrazovanie – 98'*. Moscow: Ministerstvo obshchego i professional'nogo obrazovaniia.

Ministry of General and Professional Education (1998). *Federal'nyi komponent: Obrazovatel'naia oblast' Tekhnologiia. Prilozhenie No.11 k federal'nomu zakonu 'O gosudarstvennom obrazovatel'nom standarte osnovnogo obshchego obrazovaniia*. Moscow: Ministerstvo obshchego i professional'nogo obrazovaniia. Unpublished draft.

de Moura Castro, C., Feonova, M. and Litman, A. (1997). *Education and Production in the Russian Federation: What are the lessons?* Paris: International Institute for Educational Planning, UNESCO.

Muckle, J. (1988). *Guide to the Soviet Curriculum – What the Russian Child is Taught in School*. Beckenham: Croom Helm.

National Commission on Excellence in Education (1983). *A Nation at Risk*. Washington DC: US Department of Education.

Pavlova, M. (1991). *Socio-Pedagogical Foundations for the Preparation of British Youth for Adult Working Life at the Compulsory School*. Dissertation for Doctoral Degree. Moscow Academy of Pedagogical Sciences (in Russian).

Pavlova, M. (1997a). 'Educational Transfer: The Case of the Russian Adoption of the British Technology Education Model' in F. Williams (Compil.) *Education, Equity and Transformation in a Post-Colonial World. Conference Papers*. ANZCIES: University of Ballarat, pp. 149–61.

Pavlova, M. (1997b). 'Technology Education in Russia' *Technotes*, vol. 10, no.4, pp. 23–5.

Pavlova, M. and Pitt, J. (1997a). *Obrazovatel'naia oblast' Tekhnologiia: Teoreticheskie podkhody i metodicheskie rekomendatsii*. York: Tekhnologicheskoe i predprinimatel'skoe obrazovanie v Rossii and The University of York.

Pitt, J. and Pavlova, M. (1997b). 'Russia in Transition: The Concept and Practice of Technology Education in Schools – The Programme 'Technology and Enterprise Education in Russia' in J. Smith (ed.) *IDATER 97 International Conference in Design and Technology Education Research and Curriculum Development*. Department of Design and Technology, Loughborough University of Technology, pp. 99–105.

Tkachenko, E. (1996). 'The Humanisation of Russian Education' *Russian Education and Society*, vol. 38, no. 10, pp. 47–56.

Tkhorzhevskii, D. (ed.) (1987). *Metodika trudovogo obucheniia*. Moscow: Prosveshchenie.

Vulfson, B. (1992). 'John Dewey and Soviet Pedagogy' *Pedagogika*, pp. 9–10.

17

Political Aspects of Reforming the Higher Education System in Ukraine

Liubov Pivneva

Introduction

The Ukrainian higher education system clearly has a potentially important role to play in the processes of democratic transition and the development of a market economy. Indeed, the reform of the system began in the immediate aftermath of the declaration of independence in 1991, with the following principal goals: to develop a national system of education; to ensure that the higher education system be adapted to suit the demands of a market economy; to create the conditions for the emergence of a non-state higher education sector; to place emphasis on the development of the humanitarian aspect of higher education studies; to promote the broader introduction of computers in the process of study in higher education.

These aims were to be facilitated by the passing of the following legislation:

- the Law on Education (1991);
- The State National Programme on Education (Ukraine of the twenty-first century);
- the second edition of the Law on Education confirmed by the Supreme *Rada* (parliament) on 23 March 1996;
- the Law on Higher Education (under consideration in mid-1999).

These reforms reflected the political mentality that existed and developed in Ukraine following independence. They delineated the jurisdiction of the state and local branches of the administration of the higher education system, and were intended to outline the general trends for its reform based on democratic principles.

The changes were to be implemented against the backdrop of political, social and economic crises faced by Ukrainian society as a whole. The effects have been keenly felt in the higher education system, which has had to come to terms with the collapse of communist ideology, the decline in the nation's economic production, and the problem of graduate unemployment. As a result, by the late 1990s, Ukraine occupied one of the lowest positions in the Commonwealth of Independent States (CIS) with regard to the number of graduates per 10 000 population, and the rate of growth in the number of graduates is the lowest in Europe (*Scientific Notes of Kharkiv Humanitarian University* 1997: 39).

Nevertheless, despite the presence of a systemic crisis, the number of higher education establishments in Ukraine has risen considerably since independence. According to the data of the Interstate Statistical Committee of CIS, the figure has grown from 156 in 1991–92 to 232, 254, 274 in 1993–94, 1994–95 and 1995–96 respectively. In 1996–97 the number remained at 274 (*Commonwealth of Independent States* ... 1997: 582). This growth can be explained principally by the appearance of a private sector in higher education, and by the new demands of the market economy. The types and numbers of institutions now found in the system are shown in Table 17.1.

The growth of the higher education sector represents a response to a perceived and pressing need to bring the higher education establishments of Ukraine up to the level of world standards in education and integrate them into the international scientific-educational arena. In this chapter I will examine the extent to which such a transformation has proceeded to date, and highlight the ways in which the system has been influenced by the post-communist transformation in Ukraine.

Table 17.1 Types and Numbers of Institutions in the Ukraine Higher Education System

Type of institution	Number
Classical universities	12
Technical and technological higher educational establishments	61
Medical and pharmaceutical institutes	20
Teacher training institutes	36
Agricultural institutes	18
Economic and law institutes	80
Humanitarian institutes	12
Cultural institutes	12
Others	23
TOTAL	274

Note: Of the total, 83 are private licensed higher educational establishments.

Source: (*Higher Education Establishments of Ukraine* 1995: 284–7).

Higher education and the effects of independence

National identity and language policy

The population of Ukraine includes some 100 nationalities, with ethnic Ukrainians (including Russophones) and Russians the most numerous. As Shulman notes:

> Since independence in 1991 ethnic Ukrainians, who are concentrated in Western Ukraine, and ethnic Russians and Russified Ukrainians, who are concentrated in Eastern and Southern Ukraine, have been engaged in a struggle to define the national identity of their new country and to promote the advancement of their respective cultures. These communities tend to disagree on the extent to which Ukraine should integrate with Europe and North America or with Russia and the Commonwealth of Independent States.
>
> (Shulman 1998: 288)

This divergence in political and cultural ideas has been reflected in the sphere of higher education as well. One area in particular that has proved controversial is that of language policy. From the outset, following independence, the use of Ukrainian in the teaching process was promoted vigorously not only through national legislation, but also through directives and recommendations from the Ministry of Education, particularly in the period 1992–94. The most important came in Spring 1993, stipulating that entrance examinations to higher education establishments be taken in Ukrainian, and that first-year classes should be taught in Ukrainian (Arel 1995: 175). After initial slow progress, the number of students and lecturers using Ukrainian steadily increased: by 1993–94 some 37 per cent of academic courses were conducted in Ukrainian compared with 23 per cent in 1991; by 1997–1998 this figure had risen to 66 per cent (Pogribny 1999: 2). It is difficult to predict whether this figure will grow further, as the material hardships of everyday life act as an obstacle to university lecturers' own study of Ukrainian.

The need for structural amendments

Independence also brought with it the task of re-structuring the higher education system. The breaking of ties with other parts of the CIS caused the problem, for example, of the correlation of the number of institutions to the demands of the country. In the former USSR specialists could be sent to different regions apart from the Ukrainian Republic, but now Ukraine has to use the newly educated specialists inside its own borders. The higher education system of the former USSR was oriented to the preparation of narrow profile specialists in a wide range of specialities, a framework that did not correspond to the needs of independent Ukraine, and thus a great deal of

Table 17.2 Number of Establishments Offering Degrees in
Various Disciplines

Subject	Number of establishments offering courses
Law	53
History	43
Psychology	30
Ecology	29
Geography	24
Sociology	24
International relations	21
Political science	11
Philosophy	5
Religious studies	1

effort has been made to develop the range of courses on offer in the higher education system. In particular, there has been a trend towards increasing provision in the humanities, as shown in Table 17.2.

The most impressive figure, however, relates to the variety of degree programmes in economics – 238 – which means that practically all higher educational institutions in Ukraine have economic faculties (*Higher Educational Establishments of Ukraine* 1995: 288–300). This sharp increase in the study of business, management and marketing, as well as foreign languages, shows that higher educational establishments were eager to begin to adapt to the new demands of the market economy. For example, in Kharkiv, as a response to market demands and to the general tendency towards the 'humanisation' of education, new courses in marketing, commercial law, cultural studies, environmental protection, and journalism have been created. Also significant is the growth in provision for computer studies.

Such developments have been noted with concern by some, who point to the corresponding neglect of scientific and technical disciplines. With regard to postgraduate studies, for instance, in comparison with 1993, when 158 doctoral and 330 candidates' dissertations in physics and maths were defended in Ukraine, by 1996 the figures were only 47 and 148 respectively (Lasynsky 1997: 2). There is disquiet in society towards the state policy of promoting the study of popular courses, without taking into consideration the overall need for such skills. Courses in law, business, management and languages may be in demand today, but physicists, mathematicians and engineers will surely be in great demand in the years to come.

The re-ideologisation of the humanities

It was the humanities disciplines that were in most need, of course, of radical revision following the end of Soviet rule (indeed, the process of dealing with the communist legacy in educational curricula had already begun at the end of the Soviet period). Thus the new Ukrainian state was eager to see that the Marxist–Leninist bias be removed from the system of higher education, and saw the opportunity to replace it with an emphasis on a Ukrainian national idea. The rationale was that a strong future for the country could only be ensured through national and cultural unity, in which issues of state-building and Ukrainian patriotism would be key elements.

A strong adherence to Ukrainian national traditions and culture, with an orientation towards the West, became widespread in the teaching of social science and humanities subjects. New subjects emerged (for example, scientific communism was replaced by '*politologiia*'), and a greater number of hours was allocated to the humanities in the curriculum. In addition, a new core subject, compulsory for all students – the History of Ukraine – was introduced. For all subjects, a great deal of emphasis was placed on the development of new textbooks and new syllabi (overseen at the state level). Implementing such change has not proved easy, of course, particularly in the immediate post-independence period: university lecturers compiled the first textbooks and materials from scratch, very often learning the content of courses just ahead of teaching their students.

In 1993 all higher educational establishments in Ukraine received a letter from the Ministry of Education (document N1/9–64 of 19 May 1993), which set down the list of obligatory subjects in the social sciences and humanities. Among them were:

- the history of Ukraine;
- the basics of economic theory;
- political studies;
- sociology;
- law;
- the basics of social ecology;
- Ukrainian language.

Of these, the most notable – and controversial – subject is the History of Ukraine, in which the sphere of Ukrainian–Russian relations receives considerable emphasis, of course. Russia's role in Ukrainian history – and *vice versa* – are 'redefined', even to the extent of changing the chronological sequence of certain events. The treatment of some issues, such as the role of Ukraine in the Second World War, have given rise to considerable debate.

With regard to the organisation and delivery of the curricula, it should be mentioned that the Ministry of Education itself presented a number of programmes in the social sciences, but they were not obligatory, carrying only the status of recommendations. Overall, the Ministry of Education has given much greater freedom to universities to decide matters on curricular content and delivery than was the case in the USSR, thus stimulating a much freer approach to research and the dissemination of knowledge, promoting the creative potential of staff (even in the face of material hardship), and leading to a higher level of recognition for the lecturers' work by their students and colleagues.

However, certain attempts by the Ministry of Education to introduce new ideological frameworks have ended in failure. The most vivid example is provided by the case of a Letter of Instruction sent by the Ministry of Education, written by three professors from the Kiev Shevchenko University, in 1993, with the title 'The Conceptual Foundation of Ukrainian Political Science'. This Letter of Instruction proposed a syllabus of a new course, scientific nationalism, to be adopted by higher education establishments. The syllabus began by expanding upon the urgent need to restore to Ukraine its political history, the study of Ukrainian political life, history and political thought; but very soon this thesis took a somewhat different turn. The authors of the letter maintained that 'so-called general political science', which had been created 'largely by the West', lacks a clearly defined research object. Rather, it was seen only as a series of abstract theoretical claims (Bystrytsky 1995: 55). The majority of academics gave a negative reaction to these proposals, and they were not adopted.

The most acute problem in teaching social sciences has been the lack of up-to-date textbooks that would also fit in with the ideological standards of the young Ukrainian state (with its emphases on state-building, promoting cultural traditions, patriotism, and a Western orientation, and so on). This problem has started gradually to be solved, partly through the help of the Ukrainian diaspora (for example, the edition of the Ukrainian translation of the textbook *Ukraine, history* (Subtelny 1993), in Ukrainian, filled a gap at that time and, since then, it has been in wide use in Ukraine). Various foreign funds (for example, the Soros Foundation) have also provided much needed assistance, while a decision by President Kuchma to lessen the tax burden on publishing houses printing Ukrainian language textbooks served as a further boost (Sharov 1999: 3). Nevertheless, in 1999 the textbook problem remained acute.

Coping with funding crises

The severity of the funding crisis in Ukrainian higher education – the roots of which can be traced back deep into the Soviet period – led in the aftermath of independence to many institutions seeking solutions through commercial activities, such as leasing their premises and a widespread trend of charging fees for part or all of a student's education. Often the search for extra money led to controversy: for example, at Kharkiv State Pedagogical University, in a period during 1995, students were obliged to pay if they missed classes without a medical certificate. These and similar measures cannot solve the problems of financing, of course, but they have contributed to the undermining of student–staff relations in some cases.

The Ukrainian government developed measures for supporting the education system, but these were restricted because of the lack of funds available in the national budget. The dissatisfaction of academic staff was made clear to the government and parliament through petitions, yet such demands were only taken into account to a limited extent. Indeed, for 1999 the amount allocated was actually reduced: whereas in the 1998 budget 1.56 billion Gryvnias were allocated to education, with higher education given 967.5 million Gryvnias (Issues of Supreme Rada no. 21 1998: 335), in 1999 the total allocation for education was 341 million Gryvnias. Nevertheless, there were some positive trends, with measures to ensure that allocations of sums to the regions be returned to the state budget if they were not used for educational purposes; and the introduction of ring-fenced expenditure on certain items (e.g. the salaries of employees of state-run establishments) (Issues of Supreme Rada no. 8 1999: 137 and 139).

The development of the private higher education sector

Since independence, the private higher education sector has developed like an avalanche: by 1999, some 30 per cent of Ukrainian higher education establishments were private. Their number varies in different regions of Ukraine: in western Ukraine there are relatively few, with a small number of small establishments in Ternopol, L'viv and Rivno regions, and fewer still in Vinnytse and Kmelnytskyi regions, while such cities as Kiev, Kharkiv and Donetsk have a higher proportion. The Association of Private Higher Educational Establishments was formed in 1993.

In general, private establishments focus on teaching, commercial activities and international co-operation, and do not engage in research. Some, such as the International Science-Technological University, the International Solomon University, the Ukrainian–Finnish Institute of Management and Business, the Academy of Law and Social Relations in Kiev, and the Kharkiv Humanitarian Institute People's Ukrainian Academy have acquired a sound reputation. In other cases, however, the quality of the work of private establishments has been less impressive, and one can state that the rapid increase in the numbers of such institutions has contributed to the growing destabilisation of the system of higher education. In the course of the 1990s, for example, around 500 higher education establishments proclaimed themselves to be universities, colleges, international academies, and so on, without having received any authorisation. They claimed to be able to teach everything to anybody, as long as they received payment for it. Such behaviour has threatened to compromise the idea of non-state education (Medvedev 1996: 63). The sector received an increasing amount of criticism from the public and from the Ministry of Education with regard to the admission policies they employ, the approaches to teaching, the development of their infrastructure, the quality of the academic staff and the approaches to recruiting staff.

In order to deal with this issue, licensing measures were introduced and have been refined during the 1990s, with all private establishments required to apply for a licence from the Accreditation Commission organised by the Ministry of Education (local authorities cannot register newly formed establishments if they do not have a state licence). All higher educational establishments founded before 4 June 1994 had to acquire licences by 1 June 1995, otherwise they would be required to close. According to Article 4 of the Law on Education (1996), the private sector is supposed to operate according to state standards, and they are subordinated to the control of the Ukraine Ministry of Higher Education.

The problem of licensing has another dimension, a moral one, because it goes hand in hand not only with the preparation of the required set of documents, but also with the payment of considerable sums of money for it, a situation which, inevitably, can lead to abuse in the form of corruption.

Private higher education establishments have encountered severe funding problems: in line with inflation, tuition fees have risen considerably, with the student intake contracting as a result (private education is mostly oriented at the middle class, which is small and underdeveloped) (Korol'ev 1996: 18–19). Further, most establishments have experienced problems in ensuring that instruction is provided through the medium of Ukrainian.

Ukrainian youth and higher education

While the number of students has not risen as sharply as the number of higher education establishments since 1991, a notable increase has, nevertheless, occurred. In 1992–93 the number of students stood at 855 900; by 1997–98 it had grown to 976 900. Meanwhile, the number of students graduating annually rose from 137 000 in 1991 to 155 700 in 1996 (*Commonwealth of Independent States . . .* 1997: 582). This indicates that the youth of Ukraine still place value on receiving education, despite the problems associated with the transition period.

Graduate employment, however, is a difficult issue. According to data provided by the Minister of Education, in 1997 some 40 per cent of graduates could not find jobs that matched their specialisation, owing to the discrepancy between the skills and knowledge provided by the system of higher education, and the changed demands of society (Zgurovsky 1997: 3). In the transition to the market, the Soviet practice of 'distribution' of graduates to employment for a fixed period (three years) after completion of their studies was abandoned, leaving graduates free to find work on their own initiative – if they were able to do so.

A sociological poll conducted in the Kharkiv region showed a mixed reaction to this: 45.2 per cent of students considered that a highly qualified specialist will always be able to find employment, while 20.7 per cent considered that the university and the local education authorities should provide jobs for them after graduation, and 17.3 per cent categorically demanded the restoration of the practice of obligatory allocation of graduates to employment. According to the latter group, higher education establishments and the Ministry of Higher Education, that is, the state, must be committed to the preservation of the potential of graduates, in order to strengthen the position of Ukraine as a country (*Scientific Notes of Kharkiv Humanitarian University People's Ukrainian Academy...* 1997: 17).

With the introduction of the private sector, young people have increased freedom of choice with regard to higher education, in principle, although in practice, of course, the ability to pay fees dictates the extent to which this choice can be enjoyed. Children from well-to-do families, the so-called 'new Ukrainians', can afford to study at private establishments and even go abroad and pay for their education, while the majority of young people try to enter the state sector of higher education and avoid having to pay for their studies. Most young people combine work and study, performing unqualified work because of financial need: the stipends are very low, equivalent to the price of a monthly metro pass, and not paid regularly. In order to help their families to survive, they are forced to miss some classes, which has an adverse effect on their academic achievements.

As far as political activity is concerned, it should be mentioned that it had its peak in 1990, during the hunger strike in Kiev that contributed to the resignation of Prime Minister E. Masol. In general, though, the political activity of young people is very low, with students remaining mostly passive not only during mass political campaigns, but even during elections. The Young Communist League (Komsomol) was dissolved after independence, and a new organisation – the Union of Youth – was formed, with the aim of uniting young people regardless of their political views. The most active student demonstrations are concerned with the protection of their social rights, for example, in protests against the abolition of the 50 per cent subsidy on transport fares in some cities, and strikes against corruption in the universities.

Problems of academic staff

The transition period in Ukraine has had a dramatic effect on the higher education system with regard to the position of academic staff, as well as other professions with highly qualified personnel. Engineers, teachers, doctors and scientists have in considerable numbers left their positions to find jobs in the commercial sector, or even to take up manual jobs (Gorodia-nenko and Lipovskaia 1994: 39–44). There has also been a brain drain of specialists leaving Ukraine, including many academics.

Such factors have contributed to the problems associated with the quality of teaching and research in Ukrainian higher education establishments. The average age of staff has risen owing to the difficulty of recruiting and retaining younger lecturers, who are deterred from an academic career by the relatively poor salary and conditions. By way of an example, according to the Kharkiv newspaper *Gruny* in April 1998, academic staff salaries in the Kharkiv Military University had not been paid for January, February, November and December of 1997, nor had staff been paid compensation for not taking their holidays in 1997 (teachers sometimes have no opportunity to take leave, because of the peculiarities of the teaching process at the military university). The same problem occurred in 1998: at the same establishment, the salary for October 1997 still had not been paid by January 1998 (Tyrnov 1998: 3).

For those staff who remain, there is inadequate support for implementing change in the teaching process at the majority of establishments, and material problems hinder plans to introduce new textbooks. The decision of the Ministry of Education to increase the student–teacher ratio to the level of 1991, and to increase staff teaching and workloads by 25 per cent, has also had a detrimental effect on teaching quality. It reflects the fact that staff have become hostages of a political system that is unable to ensure the necessary working conditions because of the imposition of cuts in the budget allocation for higher education.

Such difficulties have led to protests by students and lecturers: on 5–6 February 1997, for example, on the initiative of the Trade Union of the Workers of Education and Science of Ukraine, an All-Ukrainian protest was held (Mochvan 1997: 2). In comparison with school teachers, miners and other groups, higher education staff are not that active. Some concessions have, however, been obtained from the government, for instance in the law 'On Scientific and Scientific-Technical Activity' (adopted by the Supreme Rada in 1998) that provided for increases in the pensions of teachers and lecturers in the state sector (although the implementation of such decisions gave rise to new problems in the universities).

Entering the international higher education arena

Despite the above-mentioned problems, a process of bringing the system up to world standards has continued throughout the 1990s. During the first years after independence new state standards for categories of qualifications were developed (Ligotzky 1995: 3). A system of bachelor's and master's degrees was also introduced to replace the Soviet five-year *diplom* model of higher education, while postgraduate education underwent additional rationalisation, new teaching methods were promoted, and computer systems were updated. Ukraine signed the Lisbon convention on the mutual recognition of qualifications in higher education in 1997, and is also a member of the International Accreditation Committee of the European Centre of National Cadres of UNESCO and the Council of Europe. Ukraine is also participating in the Euro-diploma project.

For the first time in Ukraine's history, one of its higher education establishments – the Higher School of Business in Alchevsk – has been given a certificate of the International Bureau of Accreditation of the USA, a sign of the growing degree of integration with the international education community. The active participation of the Ukrainian academy in various international programmes also serves to promote change in the approaches to teaching and research in the Ukrainian higher education system.

Concluding remarks

The system of higher education in Ukraine is in a state of flux. Large-scale structural and organisational changes are already taking place or planned, but are hampered, even threatened by funding shortages. Such problems will only be resolved, of course, when the country is finally able successfully to pull itself out of the crisis situation that it currently finds itself in. Only then will it be possible to deal with the weak material base of the institutions, to stop the decline in numbers of graduates in society, to provide institutions with the teaching and research material they need, to raise the salaries of the lecturing staff and increase the prestige of the teaching profession, and to attract students to a career as higher education lecturers. Given the importance of higher education as a guarantor of national security and sovereignty, solving the crisis of this system must become a priority of state policy.

References

Arel, D. (1995). 'Ukraine: The Temptation of the Nationalizing State' in V. Tismaneanu (ed.) *Political Culture and Civil Society in Russia and the New States of Eurasia.* Armonk NY: M.E. Sharpe. pp. 157–88.

Bystrytsky, E. (1995) (ed.). *The Political Analysis of Postcommunism. Understanding Post-communist Societies.* Kyiv: Political Thought.

Commonwealth of Independent States in 1996: Statistical Yearbook (1997). Moscow: Interstate Statistical Committee of the CIS.

Gorodianenko, V. and Lipovskaia, N. (1994). 'Will There Be Enough Intellect for Us?' *Contemporary Society* no. 3, pp. 39–44.

Higher Education Establishments of Ukraine, vol. 2 (1995). Kiev: K.I.C.

Iasynsky, V. (1997). 'Fried Cockerel has Already Pecked: How to Save Ukrainian Higher Education from a Crash' *Vremia,* 17 July, p. 2.

Issues of the Supreme Rada: Official edition (1998). no. 21.

Issues of the Supreme Rada: Official edition (1999). no. 8.

Korol'ev, B. (1996). 'Private Education – not Private Affairs' *Tribune*. nos. 5–6, pp. 18–20.

Ligotzky, A. (1995). *Standardisation of Higher Education: Methodical Recommendations*. Kiev.

Medvedev, V. (1996). 'Non-State Higher Education: First Steps' *Native School* no. 2, p. 63.

Movchan, V. (1997). '5 February: All-Ukrainian Advance Notification of Protest' *Osvita Ukraine*, nos. 2–3, p. 2.

Pogribny, A. (1999). 'State Language and Higher Education in Contemporary Ukraine' *Osvita*, 29 April–5 May, p. 2.

Sharov, I. (1999). 'We Need Different Establishments, but They Must Be of a High Standard' *Urayadovy Kurier*, no. 64, 7 April, p. 3

Shulman, S. (1998). 'Cultures in Competition: Ukrainian Foreign Policy and the "Cultural Threat" from Abroad' *Europe–Asia Studies* vol. 50, no. 2, pp. 287–303.

Scientific Notes of Kharkiv Humanitarian University Peoples' Ukrainian Academy (1997). Kharkiv: Oko.

Subtelny, O. (1991). *Ukraine: history* (translated from English by U. Schertchnk). Kiev: Lybel, p. 512.

Tyrnov, V. (1998). '"Hello, Professor". *Gruny*'s Correspondent Talked "About Life" with Kharkiv Scientists. Life Turned Out To Be Like a Dog's Life' *Gruny*, 24–30 April, p. 3.

Zgurovsky, M. (1997). 'Phenomena Caused by Economic Crises Shouldn't Darken Positive Work Results' *Osvita Ukraine*, nos. 4–5, p. 3.

18
Civic Education for Russia: an Outsider's View[1]

Janet G. Vaillant

The introduction of new types of civic education in Russia gives rise to an important question: how does civic education in a time of transition differ from civic education in a relatively stable society? International projects in civic education that have involved Western and Russian collaborations have taught many lessons about collaboration among educators from different cultures. It is time now to think about the particularities of civic education in times of change in connection with any future project of civic education in which experts from Western Europe or the United States, relatively stable societies, work with Russians or others from less stable ones.

Civic education is like an iceberg. The visible tip is made up of knowledge about laws and government institutions. All would agree that providing students with this knowledge is a task of civic education. What is sometimes less obvious is that the citizens in any society must also possess skills, both intellectual and personal ones, that prepare them for life in their own society. To be effective citizens in a democratic, pluralistic society, for example, students need to learn how to think critically, analyse points of view, develop their own position and speak clearly in its defence. They also need to develop certain attitudes and behaviour, the ability to listen and tolerate different points of view, work effectively in groups, obey the law, and value their country's achievements. Such attitudes and skills are the underwater part of the iceberg that supports effective citizenship. It is often difficult, therefore, in Russia as well as in the West, to define precisely the line between civic education and general schooling (Audigier and Lagalee 1993: 2; Center for Civic Education 1994: vi, 2–4).

Civic education in Russia and international collaboration: the first phase

Russian government officials and educators have learned a great deal about civic education over the last decade. The vocabulary for discussing it has evolved as well. It is worth looking briefly at the history of this first phase of educational reform and international projects in civic education in order to understand what remains to be done.

The initial push to reform civic education during the period of *perestroika* came in the form of a 1988 proposal from the chairman of the Soviet State Committee on Education that the entire social studies and history curriculum be revised in order to carry out what was then called the 'humanisation and democratisation' of education. The main new course for high school was to be an interdisciplinary social studies course for classes 8–11, the last four years of secondary school (ages 13–17) called 'Mankind and Society'. It was to include material from many disciplines, including history, economics, law, and political science as well as philosophy, individual psychology and ethics. It continued the Soviet tradition of linking teaching about values, now called 'universal human values', together with the social studies, but presumably now without indoctrination. How this would be accomplished was left unspecified. The course covered subjects that people in many countries consider to be part of civic education, but the ministry officials did not identify 'Mankind and Society' as a course in civics. Instead they called for civic education to take place in one of two courses for Class 9, between which schools could choose, 'Civics' (*grazhdanovedenie*) or 'Politics and the Law', sometimes called 'To Children About the Law' (Iagodin 1989: 3–5; Iagodin 1990: 3–6). It has since been proposed that both of these courses be introduced for younger children as well. These curricular innovations, proposed first by the Soviet ministry, were immediately confirmed and extended by the central education ministry of the Russian Federation after the breakup of the old USSR in the early 1990s. Yeltsin himself called on schools to teach about the constitution, and the Russian Ministry of Education sent out decrees requiring schools to offer courses on civics (*grazhdanovedenie*). Western funders and experts, notably from the United States but also from Holland and Great Britain, rushed in to provide advice and help to build democracy in Russia.

In this first phase, American experts on civic education offered Russian colleagues the benefit of their experience. Seminars and teaching materials were developed based on Western traditions of democratic, representative government. Few of the Americans involved had a deep knowledge or understanding of Russian history or culture and so were unable to connect their experience in the United States with Russia's quite different situation. None the less the projects were useful because they initiated contacts between Russian and American educators and introduced Russians to new teaching methods and educational developments in the West. They supported the development of informational courses that now exist in Russian schools. Such projects were only the first step, however, because they tended to be short term and tended to ignore the special needs of civic education in a time of social change.

Ten years later, by 1998, despite the enormous material difficulties that confront the education sector, despite debate about whether free education accessible to all should be available to grade 11, or only to grade 9, despite continuing political battles over what precisely new texts should contain, texts for all of the proposed civics courses now exist (Vaillant 1994: 141–68). International projects and Western support have played a small part in developing some of the pilot materials first used in these courses, for *grazhdanovedenie*. The education press, particularly newspapers such as the *Teachers' Gazette* (*Uchitel'skaia gazeta*), and the *First of September* (*Pervoe sentiabria*) and their specialised supplements on civics, as well as journals such as *Teaching History in School* (*Prepodavanie istorii v shkole*), and the relatively new *Social Studies in School* (*Obshchestvoznanie v shkole*) have played an important role in distributing new ideas and materials, compensating in part for a shortfall in textbook production and the schools' lack of money to buy books. There is at least one professional organisation devoted to civic education, the International Association for Citizen Education, that is closely connected to the newspaper *Teachers' Gazette*. Because regions, localities and schools have some choice about what to teach, and the central ministry has no funds to investigate what is actually going on in schools, it is impossible to know how many school children actually take these courses at present. It is likely that most schools have a course devoted to civic education. In this sense, great strides have been made under exceedingly difficult circumstances, both in creating materials and in making space for civics courses in schools.

Civic education in the late 1990s

Today teachers and civics educators believe that much yet remains to be done. Many are dissatisfied with the purely informational, course-oriented approach to civic education. The course, *grazhdanovedenie,* is under particular attack. Teachers in the elite gymnasia and lyceums question whether there is any value at all in teaching the course, and other urban teachers find the most widely used text, by I.V. Sokolov, too superficial for their students and refuse to use it (Lebedev 1994; Sokolov 1997a and 1997b). Others find it, as well as other materials available for *grazhdanovedenie*, too remote, abstract or difficult for their students. Outspoken teachers point out that the constitution is constantly changing and political institutions do not function properly so it makes little sense to teach children about them (numerous personal communications, 1995, 1997, 1998; Krasnikova 1998: 7).

There is, none the less, now a large and powerful constituency that favours more law-related education in schools. Polls carried out in 1996 and 1997 found that adults were concerned that they did not fully understand their rights and had little faith that laws would be enforced. Among students, those in class 10 identified law as one of the courses most likely to be useful to them in later life, after foreign languages, mathematics, and computers

(Iankelovich Partners International 1996). School courses were not satisfying this need. In fact the students who took part in the all-Russian law Olympiada, held in Samara in April 1997, reported that they learned more about the law from newspapers and books than from their teachers. A group of Moscow students said that newspapers and television were their main sources of legal information (Gainer 1997). Responding to this situation, both the Open Society Institute in Moscow and the Russian Foundation for Legal Reform have undertaken projects to create accurate and accessible teaching materials for schools. Other smaller groups have sprung up to work with young people on law-related education, such as the Moscow Public Center for Legal and Judicial Reform, an NGO that offers Saturday classes for school children. It is noteworthy that the initiative for these projects comes from a variety of governmental and non-governmental institutions, but not from the Ministry of Education. For the most part, these projects of law-related education aim to provide new informational courses, just as courses such as *grazhdanovedenie* provide information about political ideas and institutions.

What might be called the informational course continues to be the most widespread form of civic education in Russia today. In addition to 'Mankind and Society' and *grazhdanovedenie*, which are widely taught, there are materials available for a number of optional courses or modules for older students on such topics as economics, law, politics and law, psychology, ecology, political science (*politologiia*). New courses fit easily into the existing structure of the school and the expectations and skills of the schools' ageing teaching force. They can be taught by older teachers according to traditional methods. Facts and definitions presented in a text can be learned by students and easily tested.

There continues to be a gap, however, between the words and concepts learned by the students in these courses and what goes on in the society around them, as well as between the words and concepts the students are supposed to learn and their everyday vocabulary. Most of the new words and concepts that abound in the texts on law, democracy and political life developed their meaning in a social and political environment foreign to Russia. The fact that many of the authors of these texts were influenced by Western materials and practice has exacerbated the problem. Basic words such as power (*vlast'*), freedom (*svoboda, volia*), and law (*zakon, pravo*) and most significantly of all, government or state (*pravitel'stvo, gosudarstvo*) refer to ideas and institutions that have very different histories in the English-speaking, and Russian-speaking worlds. They have been applied to denote quite different specific goals and realities. As a result they carry very different connotations in the two languages. The meanings can be sufficiently different so that connections between words that seem logical in one language are strained or non-existent in the other. Ideas common in English, such as, that the government and state defend individual freedoms, or that rights and duties are opposite sides of a single coin, need considerable explanation if they are going to make sense to a Russian school child brought up on Russian and Soviet history and observant of the world around him. Literal, linguistic translation is inadequate, unless accompanied by what might be called cultural translation as well. None of the existing texts for civic education, inspired as they are by West European or American examples has, to my knowledge, attempted this cultural translation. Such texts float awkwardly above the present Russian world without making direct contact with it. Recognising that something is wrong, teachers report that civic education courses are difficult to teach, abstract, and are having little apparent effect on the students that take them. Sometimes teachers call them too ideological, which may express their sense that the concepts denoted by the Russian words are not placed in a logical relationship to one another (Krasnikova 1998). Creative teachers who introduce active methods of instruction to help students make connections between these abstract concepts and their own vocabulary and experience are taking a first step towards remedying the problem.

Civic education: the second stage

Many Russian civic educators have now begun to argue that informational courses are not enough. For them, as they now see it, the most important task is to provide students with new intellectual and personal skills that will enable them to take responsibility for themselves and function well in the new democratic, law-governed society. Teachers of all courses can and should play a part in teaching these personal and social skills. Russians call this the interdisciplinary (*mezhpredmetnyi*) approach. Accordingly, all teachers are, to an extent, civic educators.

Educators working in history took up this idea in the early 1990s. They began to write about the importance of discussing political concepts in various historical periods and developing the analytical skills to evaluate sources and choices available at different moments in the past. One text, for example, drew students' attention to concepts of democracy and leadership as they existed in classical Greece and Rome, and at the time of the French Revolution, thus alerting students to the fact that the meanings of these terms have changed over time and are connected to the particular conditions in which people use them (Khachaturian 1994: 55, 67–8). This is one kind of answer to the problem of the civic course that offers definitions of abstract terms as if their meanings were obvious and eternal. Recently published history materials provide teachers with primary sources and different interpretations of the same event, and include questions designed to provoke student analysis and discussion. These writers would like students to learn to compare sources, analyse bias and develop their own points of view. New materials focus on turning points in Russian history, urging students to consider what alternatives existed, why leaders chose as they did, and what they themselves might have done under similar circumstances. The writers who present these materials and discuss how they should be used are quite explicit about their objectives. They want to develop students' critical thinking and decision-making skills so that they can become effective citizens (Boitsev and Khromora 1998; Kirilov and Kulagina 1995; Ukolova and Katseva 1999).

Other educators have begun to bring up the question of moral education, touching on issues long buried as part of a general revulsion against the indoctrination of the Soviet era. Anatolii F. Nikitin, author of many of the first texts on politics and law, has written of his sudden realisation that, without ethical underpinning, government and the law are simply bandit games. It still remains difficult, however, for Russian educators to separate the idea of discussing moral issues from that of moralising or indoctrinating students (Nikitin 1995: 23–6). In one of our project's seminars about methods of leading discussion in history classes, all but one Russian teacher-trainer opposed discussing the morality of various policy options considered at the time of the liberation of the serfs in the nineteenth century. Another later conceded that you might consider the moral thinking of that time as part of your historical subject, but students should not be asked to express their own moral judgements. This hesitation seems to represent a lingering fear of forcing values on young people, an understandable legacy of the Soviet past. It may also reflect Russian teachers' lack of experience with discussion teaching and framing open-ended questions so that students are encouraged and able to express their own points of view without a teacher imposing judgement. Ultimately it is probably connected with the underlying assumption, still very widespread among even the most reform-minded Russian educators, that the teacher is the authority who conveys knowledge and values to students, and that there is one single right answer to every question.

Support for the idea that all teachers of all subjects should be conscious of their role in civic education is growing. This is not a new idea in Russian pedagogy. The idea that all teachers had a role in *vospitanie* was an assumption of the Soviet era. Every teacher was supposed to teach the skills and attitudes necessary for the good Soviet citizen. Recent efforts to rethink the teaching of all the humanities and social studies to promote democratic, humanitarian values, the so-called *mezhpredmetnyi* approach, is based on the recognition that all these subjects bear on the teaching of values and attitudes. Today many civic education reformers would like to convince every teacher to make an effort to teach attitudes of respect and tolerance for others. They would like to encourage students to develop their own individuality, and capacity for self-expression and critical thinking. They argue that this can be furthered in all courses from literature and history to psychology and ecology. While such a co-ordinated approach may sound like a return to Soviet-style *vospitanie*, it is more akin to a different strand in Russian pedagogy, marginalised in the Soviet period, that put the interests of the child first with the idea that individual development need not conflict with group membership or loyal citizenship. This current was kept flowing in Soviet times by such pedagogues as V.A. Sukhomlinskii (1918–70), a Ukrainian educator who emphasised the need to work with a child's individual personality and natural proclivities to develop intellectual, social and ethical capacities; and, to a lesser extent, L.S. Vygotskii (1896–1934), best known in the West for his theory of the zone of proximal development but important also for emphasising that learning takes place in the social interaction between teachers and child, and that both are embedded in a particular society and culture. Of particular importance in this regard was the communard movement, founded by I.P. Ivanov in Leningrad in the 1950s, which provided an important example of shaping an entire environment in keeping with a child's needs and teaching responsibility and other social qualities by giving children the opportunity to experience their results directly. The communard movement greatly influenced educators later prominent in education reform, such as S. Soloveichik (1930–96) and Oleg Gazman (1936–96) (Sidorkin 1995:148–58; Soloveichik 1989, 1997). Just before he died, the late Oleg Gazman bravely suggested that there was much that was good in the old Soviet school and that educators had been too quick to throw out the good with the bad. He argued that attention to the moral and personal development of children was a key obligation of the school (Gazman 1996). He and his colleagues have developed what they call the pedagogy of support that takes as its primary goal helping each child learn to understand his own talents and options, make choices and take responsibility for them. This is not necessarily in conflict with learning to be a responsible member of the community, as was clear in the work of Sukhomlinskii as well as the communard movement.

There is a somewhat larger group of research-minded educators, mostly psychologists such as Boris Elkonin, who build on the ideas of the late Vasilii Davydov and gather under the rubric of the pedagogy of development (*razvivaiushee obuchenie*). These educators focus on designing pedagogical techniques and an educational environment that will benefit the individual child. Their emphasis, however, is primarily on individual intellectual development, rather than on personal, moral or social skills. Russian civic educators can derive some theoretical support from these relatively small groups, but their immediate practical work focuses on teaching those skills that will help students become responsible, effective citizens.

The idea that teachers of all courses should be conscious of teaching skills, knowledge and attitudes that support effective citizenship has recently been extended to the idea of transforming the school as a whole. Recognising that abstract teaching about a democratic and law-abiding society is not enough, even if it were to lead to intellectual understanding, some reformers wish to create a new type of school environment. Their objective goes beyond the individual classroom where teachers may encourage discussion, respect for others and the development of individual points of view to the goal of creating in the school a small society where children can practise their new skills. They are introducing elected school councils, for example, and encouraging students to take the initiative in organising independent student groups and extra-curricular activities (Frumin 1998; author's observations 1995, 1996, 1998). The irony is that they are reintroducing student institutions that look remarkably similar in form to the Soviet ones thrown out by the first wave of school reform. This irony is not lost on proponents of this approach, but they insist that the dynamic and use of these new institutions is entirely different from those of the old Soviet school. Furthermore, as Gazman has pointed out, there were many positive ideas in Soviet pedagogy and practice that can be rethought and recast with great benefit.

The rightfully admired Tubel'skii School of Self-definition takes the whole-school approach as does the school 'Univers', in Krasnoiarsk, directed by Isak Frumin. The overarching objective of these school directors is to provide children with some understanding of the benefits of living in a society based on legal and democratic principles, as well as to develop habits and behaviour that reinforce such principles. Leaders of innovative schools have created an independent organisation that meets regularly and holds an annual contest for excellent practice. The winners present their school and its approach at an annual festival (Frumin 1997: 23–4). Such schools provide one example of the resources and potential for Russian school reform, reform that seems to overlap increasingly with attention to civic education. These whole-school projects, however, face a problem that haunts all educational reformers. How can effective practice be extended beyond the realm of its creator? The introduction of the festival and indeed the very existence of an organisation to support innovative practice is one attempt to address this issue. Reformers also hope that creating and publicising detailed teaching materials to be adapted by individual schools and teachers to their individual situation and needs will also help. It is important to remember, however, that such innovative schools represent only a tiny fraction of the total. New teaching methods are spreading only slowly, and the great majority of schools continue to consider their task to be transferring knowledge directly to students by means of lecture and memorisation.

Implications for future international projects

Russian educators have identified many of the differences between civic education in relatively stable societies and what is needed now in Russia. They have learned much from their international experience: now they are ready to move on to a second stage in their work. They want to build on the resources of their own tradition, an approach that is more likely to lead to sustainable practice than simply introducing fragments of successful international approaches. If their international supporters truly wish to help them they, too, must move on to a second stage in thinking about their role and focus. Russian reformers have recognised that civic education in a time of transition cannot ignore the underwater part of the iceberg. Many of the Western educators who worked on first-phase projects did not understand that many of the skills and habits that are taken for granted in their Western societies did not exist in Russia. Socialisation that takes place as a matter of course in stable societies, in the family, in the schools and in society as a whole must be undertaken explicitly in Russian schools. What does this imply for international projects?

The most important prerequisite for successful international collaboration is that participants on each side must truly listen to the views of the other side, and spend time and energy trying to understand different assumptions, starting points and goals. Let me describe some lessons we learned from a joint project on civic education carried out in 1997 by Russian and US educators who had had considerable earlier experience with such projects. We developed a model that is not perfect but, for us at least, represented a step forward and may include features that will be useful to others.

The civic education project of MARIOS (Moscow) and ACTR/ACCELS (Washington, DC) began with discussion among project directors who had considerable knowledge and experience gained from working in each other's countries. The US leaders put a question to their Russian colleagues: what are your most important needs in civic education today and which of these needs might be met by working with us? There are two parts to this question. What do you need? What are we able to provide? Our Russian colleagues identified a need for highly skilled teacher-trainers who would be able to work with other trainers and teachers on the following issues: critical thinking, conflict resolution, co-operative learning, moral education and democratic school management. The project director on the American side suggested other topics as well, such as discussion teaching and multicultural education, but the final decision lay with the Russian side. Having identified these areas, the US director of the project arranged a six-week academic programme in the US. There two teams of four Russian teacher-trainers, one group from Krasnoiarsk and one from Moscow, studied with US experts at the Indiana University School of Education under the overall direction of Howard Mehlinger, former dean of that school. There they developed modules for training workshops. After their return to Russia, each team offered two workshops at each of the two sites, Krasnoiarsk and Moscow, using evaluations from the first to refine the second. A representative of the US side attended each workshop as an observer. The project had its difficult moments, most of which had to do with problems of cultural translation. A simple example will suffice to indicate how quickly a discussion can be blunted by such misunderstandings. Russian participants were listening carefully to a discussion of critical thinking led by a university-based US expert in this field. Towards the end, one Russian timidly asked, 'what is the difference between critical thinking and higher order thinking?' The lecturer simply could not answer this question. Later, in the period of reflection on the day, it occurred to the US leader present at this that 'critical thinking' was a term coined and brought into wide use by teacher-activists in the 1960s interested in teaching their students to question authority and giving them the tools to do so. 'Critical thinking' is, in a sense, a slogan, a bit of jargon, a term that is now so widely used in American education that few stop to question its meaning. This moment served as a reminder of how many basic terms and assumptions, on both sides, need to be examined in order for good work to take place. It often takes knowledge of education in both cultures, as well as trust among colleagues, to ask these apparently simple questions and attend to their answers.

The project as a whole, despite its short duration, proved relatively successful in that the Russians involved have continued to work together after the project and its funding concluded and to offer professional development seminars in this area. They remain in contact with the US project leaders. We believe that the following conditions contributed in important ways to the project's success:

- Russian and US co-directors worked together to define and plan, as well as carry out the project. Each selected members of his team in consultation with the other side.
- Responsibility was shared: Americans organised training in the US, Russians organised the follow-up seminars.
- Russian and US co-directors understood the educational culture of each other's country.
- All Russian participants were English-speakers, four participants including the group leaders had significant US experience, and other participants were young.
- US leaders were attentive to cultural translation and set aside ample time for daily reflection and to discuss implicit assumptions of American educators.
- Seminar modules were written in Russian by participants while in the US so that they were virtually complete when Russians returned home to their busy schedules.
- Follow-up, the seminars in Russia, was an integral part of the project and carried out totally by Russians, with Americans present as inconspicuous observers or minor participants.
- Both Russian and American participants had sufficient experience with the culture and language of the other to be able to spend their energies on the professional work of the project rather than overcoming basic cultural misunderstandings.

- Russian and US co-directors knew each other by reputation and in person and so were able to work on the basis of trust and mutual respect from the beginning of the project. This is essential for short-term projects such as this one.
- One goal of the project was to free Russian trainers to work independently after the project was completed. The project therefore emphasised the importance of the Moscow and Krasnoiarsk seminars; that is, the trans-formation of what was learned in the US into a useful form in Russia.

Conclusion

It is ironic that it has taken almost a decade, during which support for international projects in education was quite abundant, to discover appro-priate colleagues and methods for Russian and US educators to work together effectively. Now that we have more knowledge, financial support for our joint work is becoming scarcer. It was Hegel who reminded us that the owl of Minerva takes flight at dusk. Let us hope that the owl none the less has happy hunting. Owls often do. International collaboration con-tinues to be important for all of us working in education because new perspectives force us to re-examine our assumptions and think more deeply about what we do. It is also important for us to remember the importance of continuity and follow-up. Long-term projects, three or four years, are far more cost effective than short ones. If the project must be short because of funding constraints, it must be carefully planned if it is to have any con-tinuing impact. This is particularly true now because the education sector in Russia possesses so few financial resources that it is difficult for our Russian colleagues to carry on independently once the first phase of a project is completed. It is important now to support nascent teacher-training centres in Russia, to develop the capacity of Russians who do participate in inter-national projects to share their experience with others (in conferences such as this one, for example), and work together and with other educators in their regions. We believe that training Russians to train other Russians will prove the most cost-effective approach to supporting this second stage of civic education in Russia. The tasks of this stage are difficult and will require great sensitivity to cultural differences.

Russia, like other CIS states, is undergoing such sweeping change that civic education cannot be limited to conveying new information. Let us listen to Russian innovators in education and take our lead from them. Under the present conditions in Russia, civic education requires explicit attention to creating the skills and habits necessary for effective citizenship, that is, the bottom part of the iceberg. At a time when migration of large numbers of people and swift cultural change is transforming many Western countries, a similar task, albeit with less urgency, presses upon us as well. It is in area in which international educators can learn from their work together.

Note

1   An earlier version of this chapter appeared in the Newsletter of the Institute for the Study of Russian Education (ISRE), a publication of Indiana University, and was also published in Russian in Frumin (1999).

References

In addition to the following published sources, this article is based on numerous personal communications with Russian educators and teachers and school visits between 1991 and 1999, and confirmed by many conversations and presentations at the conference 'Za grazhdanskoe obrazovanie,' Moscow, 16–20 May, 1999.

Audigier, F. and Lagelee, G. (1993). *Fifty-seventh European Teachers' Seminar on Civic Education*. Paris: Council of Europe.
Boitsev, M. and Khromova, I. (1998). *Poslevoennoe desiatiletie 1945–1955*. Moscow: Enrochio.
Center for Civic Education (1994). *National Standards for Civics and Government*. Calabasas CA
Frumin I. (1997). 'The Festival of the Russian Association of Innovative Schools' *ISRE Newsletter on East European, Eurasian and Russian Education*, vol. 6, no. 1, pp. 23–4.
Frumin, I. (1998). *Vvedenie v teoriiu i praktiku demokraticheskogo obrazovaniia*. Krasnoiarsk: ZNANIE.
Frumin, I. (1999). *Grazhdanskoe obrazovanie v informatsionnyi vek: Sbornik materialov mezhdunarodnoi konferentsii*. Conference proceedings – Krasnoiarsk, Russia, 18–20 June 1998.
Gainer, M. (1997). *Starsheklassniki o prave*. Moscow: Open Society Institute.
Gazman, O. (1996). 'Poteri i obreteniia v vospitanii posle 10 let perestroiki' *Vospitanie i pedagogicheskaia podderzhka detei v obrazovanii: materialy vserossiiskoi konferentsii*. Moscow: pp. 4–5.
Iagodin, G. (1989) 'Ob ekzamenakh po istorii SSSR i drugim obshchestvennym distsiplinam v srednikh uchebnykh zavedeniiakh' Gosudarstvennyi komitet SSSR po narodnomu obrazovaniiu, Prikaz 571 (30 December, 1988). *Prepodavanie istorii v shkole*, no.2, pp. 3–5.
Iagodin, G. (1990). Prikaz: 'O perestroike prepodavaniia obshchestvennykh distsiplin v srednikh uchebnykh zavedeniiakh' *Prepodavanie istorii v shkole*, no. 4, pp. 3–6.
Iankelovich Partners International – Validata (1996). 'Report on Research: Legal Situation in Russia'. Unpublished report. Moscow.
Khachaturian, V. (1994). 'Fragment from *History of World Civilisations*', *Preopodavanie istorii v shkole*, no. 7, pp. 55, 67–8.
Kirilov V. and Kulagina, G. (1995). *Istoriia* (Supplement to *Pervoe sentiabria*, nos. 34 and 35.
Krasnikova, E. (1998). 'Modeli grazhdanskogo obrazovaniia' *Upravlenie shkoloi*, no. 14, pp.1–8.
Lebedev V. (1994). 'O diletanstve i demokratii' *Uchitel'skaia gazeta* no. 11, 22 March, p. 7.
Nikitin, A. (1995). 'O grazhdanskom obrazovanii' *Preopodavanie istorii v shkole*, no. 1, pp. 23–6.
Sidorkin, A. (1995) 'The Communard Movement in Russia, the View of a Participant' *East–West Education*, vol. 16, no. 2. pp. 148–58.

Sokolov, I. (1997a) *Grazhdanovedenie. 6 Klass.* Moscow: IVTs Grazhdanin.
Sokolov, I. (1997b) *Grazhdanovedenie.* 5 Klass. Moscow: IVTs Grazhdanin.
Soloveichik, S. (1989) *Vospitanie po ivanovu*, Moscow: Pedagogika.
Soloveichik, S. (1997) 'Chelovek svobodnyi' *Pervoe sentiabria*, no. 75, 19 July, p. 1.
Ukolova, I. and Katseva, L. (1999). *Perestroika 1985–1991.* Moscow.
Vaillant, J. (1994) 'History and Social Studies Education' in A. Jones (ed.) *Education and Society in the New Russia.* Armonk NY: M.E. Sharpe, pp. 141–68.

Index